ARAB AND AMERICAN CULTURES

A Conference Sponsored by the
American Enterprise Institute for Public Policy Research

DATE DUE			

ARAB AND
AMERICAN CULTURES

Edited by George N. Atiyeh

American Enterprise Institute for Public Policy Research
Washington, D.C.

The publisher wishes to thank Alfred A. Knopf, Inc.,
for permission to use excerpts from
John Updike's story, "I am Dying, Egypt, Dying.",
Copyright © 1969 by John Updike. Reprinted from
Museums and Women and Other Stories, by John Updike,
by permission of Alfred A. Knopf, Inc.

ISBN 0-8447-2115-8 (Paper)
ISBN 0-8447-2116-6 (Cloth)

Library of Congress Catalog Card No. 77-94069

Printed in the United States of America

CONTRIBUTORS

Aziz Suryal Atiya
Professor Emeritus, University of Utah

Dorothy Brown
Chairman, Department of History, Georgetown University

Sahair el-Calamawy
Professor of Literature, University of Cairo

Paul Conkin
Professor of History, University of Wisconsin, Madison

Wilton S. Dillon
Director of Seminars and Symposia, Smithsonian Institution

Boutros Boutros-Ghali
Editor of Arabic quarterly, *International Affairs,*
and Acting Foreign Minister of Egypt

Samuel P. Huntington
Professor of Government, Harvard University

Salma Jayyusi
Professor of Literature, University of Algiers

Mansour Khalid
Minister of Foreign Affairs, The Republic of Sudan

Stanley J. Kunitz
Poet, Former Consultant in Poetry,
Library of Congress

Abdallah Laroui
Professor of History, Muhammad V. University, Rabat, Morocco

CONTENTS

PART FOUR
Politics

PART FIVE
Can Cultures Communicate?

APPENDIXES

PREFACE

The Conference on Arab and American Cultures, sponsored by the American Enterprise Institute, was held in Washington, D.C., from September 22 to 23, 1976. Two public lectures were given at the Library of Congress, and the other activities took place at the Madison Hotel. The basic purpose of the conference was to bring together leading Arab and American intellectuals, in an atmosphere of live and frank dialogue, to examine and explain the visions that Americans and Arabs hold of their own cultures. Although economic and political relations between the United States and the Arab world are rapidly expanding, an understanding and appreciation of the vast human diversity in American and Arab cultures has not received the serious consideration it deserves. This conference is merely a first step toward a human understanding between the two peoples.

The participants in the panels were invited from among eminent representatives of the disciplines of the humanities and the social sciences. An attempt was made, with some success, to have a regional representation from the various parts of the Arab world. The selection of topics was left to each participant. We requested only that they be germane to the purpose of the conference, and, in response, the participants dealt with subjects that brought out the uniqueness of each culture and some of the problems that face the peoples of the Arab world and the United States.

Abdallah Laroui considered the approaches, goals, and points of convergence of Arab ideologies as they relate to the Arab political condition. He pointed out that there is an Arab System, that it is operational, but that it is difficult to explain in a logical manner. William Leuchtenburg took a look at the place of Americans of Arab descent in the historical consciousness of America, but he found little or no awareness of their presence. Aziz Suryal Atiya summed up the contributions of Arab-Muslim civilization to its Western counterpart. Paul K. Conkin considered American historical development and found characteristics distinct from the rest of the West: liberty based on productive property;

popular government; and the institution of black slavery, which was pregnant with great historical significance.

The precarious and difficult position of writers, both Arab and American, were considered by John Updike and Sahair el-Calamawy. John Updike focused on the cultural situation of the American writer. The American writer enjoys the advantages of freedom of speech, a vast audience, affluence, and the Protestant ethic, all of which, however, disguise certain disadvantages that hamper him from going about his business of writing and illuminating truth and reality. Arab writers, according to Dr. el-Calamawy, find themselves in a bind. Tradition, which is more a model to imitate than a shackle to be released from, has taxed them heavily. They are torn between the modern and the old. Their aspirations extend beyond the use of the classical Arabic form to the absorption and acceptance of the content of the new civilization. Tradition as a value and as a model should not be abandoned, according to Dr. el-Calamawy, but reconstructed and renewed.

Nizar Qabbani's comments centered on the universal nature of poetry and on its place in Arab culture. The Arab poet in modern times has had to struggle against a conservative society, against a conservative set of moral codes, and against inherited poetical forms. Stanley Kunitz's comments on the place of poets in American society brought out their financial difficulties, but he added that the function of the poet is to preserve the purity and energy of the language, to record the sensibility of the age, and to serve as the conscience of the "tribe."

On the subject of culture, Zaki Naguib Mahmoud singled out those rational aspects of Arab culture that manifest themselves in language, jurisprudence, philosophy, science, and theology. The Arab mind was more attuned to Greek rationalism than the Indian mind was, and that is why the Arabs tried, and were able, to absorb and to improve upon Greek philosophical and scientific thought. Robert Nisbet, probing the idea of community as an important element in American culture, saw it as a quest conspicuous throughout American history. He surveyed American literature dealing with the community and its ethics and with American utopian endeavors, concluding that the idea of community is not dead, though it has receded in recent years.

Dr. Mustafa Safwan commented on the characteristics of Arab culture as they are manifested in the centrality of the book (the Koran), in the translation of the Greek scientific heritage, and in the "non-Arabism" of its greatest contributors. After considering different levels of rationality, he concluded that Arab culture has remained "Eastern" in spite of its rationalistic aspects. Laura Nader focused on the need to look at the concept of the community comparatively. She considered what has been happening to the communities in America in the context of the family structure and urban life.

In politics, Mansour Khalid dealt with the sociocultural setting of Arab diplomacy and considered the relation of the culture to Arab personality, to Arab values, and to the role of Islam and Western influences in the determination and formulation of foreign policy. Samuel P. Huntington discussed the "anti-government" character of the American creed and the dilemma posed for the conduct of foreign affairs as prevailing norms of American democracy and traditional American values impose moral and political restraints on government behavior. The United States faces the problem of wanting to keep its ideals and values in a world that increasingly sees these ideals as irrevelant to foreign policy formulation. Boutros Boutros-Ghali commented on the modern history of Arab diplomacy and pointed out the areas of its failures and successes. Helen Thomas commented on what Americans of Arab descent feel towards the United States. Her experience as a White House correspondent has corroborated the view that, as the power of the White House grows, so does the mistrust of the people, perhaps because Americans mistrust authority and not necessarily their government.

A televised round table discussion, "Can Cultures Communicate?," financed through a grant from the National Endowment for the Humanities, concludes the proceedings of the conference. The appendixes contain the texts of the lectures at the Library of Congress and the paper of Professor Boutros Boutros-Ghali.

The conference was directed by George N. Atiyeh, head of the Near East Section of the Library of Congress, who also edited the proceedings. Robert J. Pranger, director of Foreign Policy Studies of the American Enterprise Institute coordinated the various facets of the conference, and Dennis F. Verhoff, also of the American Enterprise Institute, coordinated the program.

PART ONE

HISTORY

SANDS AND DREAMS

Abdallah Laroui

General de Gaulle, receiving the credentials of a new ambassador from Syria to France after a long break in diplomatic relations between the two countries, said (in a phrase worthy of André Malraux), "I know your sands and your dreams." That could as appropriately be addressed to the representative of any other Arab country, referring not only to the tangible sands of the desert, but also to the shifting sands of policies that have neither center nor boundaries— reveries in the middle of an undominated space. In certain regions, the dunes, if we are to believe Saint-John Perse, are "snatches of centuries on the move." [1]

Memories and aspirations are at the same time the strength and the weakness of millions of Arabs—united and divided, rich and poor, illiterate and cultured. They are masters of a region which, because of its contrasts, is the one spot of the planet where the equilibrium of the world is the most fragile and the peace the most threatened.

Has any of these countries ever successfully defined *an* Arab policy? On the other hand, has any of these countries not found such a policy necessary each day? No sooner do relations with Iraq improve than a crisis emerges with Egypt or Tunisia, and a nation that becomes an ally of Morocco thereby also becomes suspect to Algeria or Libya. How can there be *one* Arab policy if regimes, economic interests, and diplomatic choices are so diverse? Why develop such a policy if the notion of the Arab world is merely geographic? A warm welcome given to an Egyptian chief of state imperils commercial relations with Syria or Libya. Economic and strategic ties can easily be planned with each Arab country, and they can just as easily be invalidated by an "Arab dream" that defies definition.

Politics is rational in relation to a goal explicitly affirmed by the actors or reconstructed *a posteriori* by the observer. Only such a goal

I would like to draw the reader's attention to the collection of papers presented by a group of Arab intellectuals at a conference organized by the Catholic University of Louvain in October 1970 and published under the title *Renaissance du monde arabe*, edited by Abdel Aziz Belal (Belgium: Editions Duculot, 1972).
[1] Saint-John Perse, *Anabase*, VII.

permits a judgment to be made on the choice of means and an evaluation to be made of the results. The goal itself, however, cannot be judged because it is the result of a collective life, determined by values inherited from the past, by particular visions, by group interests. Can any tactical or strategic goals, explicit or implicit, be discerned today in the political activity of Arab states, parties, and professional and cultural associations? Can we rationalize this activity by linking it to an aim rather than to its inadequate means or to its frequently unsatisfactory results?

Beyond the immediate ends pursued from day to day by each state, we must attempt to unveil the long-term goals defined in the important speeches of men like Nasser, Qaddafi, and Bourguiba; in the platforms of parties like the Syrian Baath, the Iraqi Communist Party, the Algerian FLN (National Liberation Front), and the Moroccan USFP (Socialist Union of Popular Forces); and in the manifestoes of the intellectuals. In what order are we to analyze them? According to the influence of the leaders who developed them as slogans, the impact they seem to have had on the Arab masses, or the real or apparent depth of the analyses accompanying them? Choosing any of these orders risks giving it undue importance in the eyes of the reader when, as will be shown later, regimes and parties distinguish themselves in hierarchies entirely apart from the goals pursued. Let us content ourselves at the present stage with a vaguely chronological order, taking into consideration the moment when this or that slogan dominated the Arab scene.

(1) Unity. Who has not heard of the unionist ideology formulated by the Baath, popularized by Nasser, and faithfully guarded by Qaddafi? Foreign observers consider it for the most part a myth, which has caused much harm both to the Arabs and to the non-Arabs. They applaud those who have tirelessly fostered division. And yet nearly three years ago, in the aftermath of the October War of 1973 and the petroleum crisis that resulted from it, the heads of several countries were wondering if it was not time to take this myth seriously.

What escapes the foreign observer is that the frequency of inter-Arab crisis—the inability of different regimes to achieve true coexistence by accepting the principle of nonintervention in a neighbor's affairs—proves the existence of a real inter-Arab system, even if it is not institutionalized. This system objectively limits the sovereignty of each state, so that each domestic crisis rapidly becomes an inter-Arab crisis and vice versa.[2] No Arab chief of state, even when he really acts in the

---

[2] The justification for Arab interference in each other's affairs was clearly expressed in the public exchange which took place in March 1976 between President Qaddafi of Libya and King Hassan II of Morocco concerning the decolonization of the western Sahara.

4

interest of those he governs and with their assent, is totally free in his movements. He must assure for himself the good will of his counterparts, and he must not offend pan-Arab opinion, seemingly silent but in the long run exerting a sure influence.

A *united Arab republic* obviously does not exist, but neither is there a mere aggregation of sovereign and independent Arab states. We must deal with a system sui generis, with original ideas. It must be analyzed as such, and not be hastily assimilated with others that are superficially similar. Certainly the simplistic realist may deny its existence but, in our opinion, he will stumble sooner or later over a fact difficult to deny, that is, the distrust of even those Arabs he would wish to deal with and to favor. To say this is simply to draw attention to a reality that is too often neglected.

(2) Nonalignment. It would seem obvious that after so many years of foreign domination—centuries in some cases—Arab peoples, states, parties, and leaders would be anxious to safeguard a liberty so dearly acquired and still so fragile. No Arab country, entering into a bilateral or multilateral alliance, can hope to have its point of view prevail and still less to oblige its partners to take its individual interests into consideration. In spite of the Arabs' commendable goal of preserving their liberty, the reality of Arab dependence on foreigners is inescapable. One state is the ally, declared or not, of a great power; another depends on a second great power for its armament, its financing, and even its food supply; all appeal to the outside world for their economic or technological development. How can we, under these conditions, speak of nonalignment and of neutrality?

Westerners have long asked how much confidence their Arab clients merit; the countries of the East are beginning to ask similar questions. Where does this mistrust come from? It is a fact that the Arabs are comfortable neither in Africa nor in Asia, neither in the East nor in the West. It is with Western Europe, in spite of—or because of—a long series of conflicts, that they seem to find a common language most easily.[3] The Koran describes the Arab-Islamic community as an intermediary nation[4]—Is the desire to remain apart from blocs a distant recollection of this description, which can be interpreted as a prescription? The Arab states exhibit their divergences in all international forums, but up to the present none of them has dared to integrate itself into a family other than its own, regardless of its momentary interests or

---

[3] Thus, projects of Euro-Arab-African collaboration are eloquently defended in France, in Tunisia, and in Senegal.
[4] "Thus We have made of you an equitable nation in order that you will be witnesses to all Men." *Koran*, 2:143.

5

ideological preferences. Any alliance outside the Arab area remains a more apparent than real possibility.

(3) Socialism. Modern socialism was conceived as a dictatorship of the industrial proletariat, aiming to construct the material and human foundations of a classless society. From outside, it is seen as the monolithic power of a modernizing intelligentsia, organized in the image of an armed detachment. From this double point of view, Arab socialism scarcely merits its name. No Arab regime pretends to represent a proletariat, which is nonexistent or numerically weak in Arab nations. Most of the Arab leaders, far from being militarized intellectuals, are career military, whose comprehension of modernism is at best selective. Everywhere one observes the predominance of the social over the economic, of consumption over production, of enjoyment over the production of riches—thus reversing the logical process for the establishment of socialism. It follows that egalitarian socialism has the best chance of being achieved in the Arab countries that have populations with the smallest social differences and that enjoy important petroleum revenues.[5]

Of what sort will Arab socialism be? All evidence indicates it will not be—and need not be—proletarian in the foreseeable future. Neither will it be liberal like that of Western Europe. It can be petit bourgeois, or feudal, as Marx himself conceived.[6] What should be emphasized above everything else, in our opinion, is that the ideological alignment of any Arab regime is no less circumstantial than its diplomatic alignment. In the end, it is industrial alienation itself, whether capitalist or socialist, that the Arab nations have difficulty acknowledging.

(4) Democracy. During brief periods, some Arab countries have known institutions comparable to those of the West. Other Arab nations declare they are paving the way for such institutions, and still others claim to have moved beyond them, by setting up local assemblies where producers decide freely on projects to fill individual and collective needs. Nevertheless, voices are being raised almost everywhere to complain that liberties are flouted and social or "national" rights are ignored. Even in so-called democracy *à la base,* collective interests are never defined in terms of classes of ethnolinguistic groups (Lebanon being the exception

---

[5] The word *ta'aduliyya* (egalitarianism) had been coined by Tawfiq al-Hakim before the 1952 Egyptian revolution. The egalitarian ideology inspires the social projects of most of the Arab countries which are termed modern; it is the official doctrine of the Istiqlal party of Morocco; it recaptures or reinvents the principal elements of nineteenth century liberal democracy.

[6] "Thus, federal socialism was born: half lamentation and half lampoon, an echo of the past and a menace of the future: at times, by its bitter, witty and incisive criticism, striking at the bourgeoisie to the very heart's core." Karl Marx, *Le manifesto communiste* (Paris: Editions Gallimard, 1963), p. 183.

that proves the rule). Compared with the regimes of black Africa, Latin America, and Southeast Asia, however, Arab governments are striking because of their relative stability, in spite of the lack of institutionalized authority and the occasional bloody outbreaks.[7]

The fact is that apparently dissimilar Arab regimes share a political system, with appreciably the same deep structure, which guarantees a durable sociopolitical equilibrium. Whether the country is a constitutional monarchy or a republic, whether it has a national assembly or not, whether it ignores parties or lets one or several function, it must resolve a problem that concerns, not individuals or clearly defined social classes, but rather multifunctional groups, with significant geographic, social, and cultural differences. By means of tacit accords, regimes cope with the problems raised by the changing relations between these groups, which never coincide precisely with parties, professional associations, unions, or clans. The democratic demand most often heard in the Arab world concerns the promulgation of a national charter of a constitution to regularize these unwritten pacts. Ideologically, neither a pluralist parliamentary democracy nor a one-party popular democracy has the favor of the majority of the Arab political elite. It seems that the effectively functioning Arab system is difficult to institutionalize because it is not in accord with the broad categories—individuals, classes, corporations, local collectivities—recognized by the various regimes.[8]

We have tried to describe an Arab reality, which is not evident to everyone, without justifying it in the rhetorical manner of Arab leaders and without judging it solely by its results as foreign observers habitually do. Arab leaders and ideologues speak of unity, of nonalignment, of socialism, of democracy. Their criticisms, from inside and outside, underline disunity, economic lag, dependency, and autocracy. Reality seems to invalidate their judgments since the policies emerging from them fail in most cases. Truth appears to be on the side of those who accept the existence of an inter-Arab system, which is effective even if not supported by a unitary state. This system embodies an egalitarianism not yet realized but desired by all, a political system which is not a liberal or popular democracy but which guarantees a certain sociopolitical equilibrium, and a diplomatic independence, of necessity taking the

---

[7] Even countries characterized as unstable, such as Syria, Iraq, and Sudan, are less so than the unstable countries of Latin America or Africa. The autocracy of these Arab governments does not account for the relative stability since such autocracy is also found elsewhere.

[8] This problematical proposal must, in principle, eliminate all normative value from the ideas of legitimacy, social structure, and equilibrium or, better, dispense with them completely, because they have until now encouraged researchers to concentrate their attention on certain, perhaps minor, facts and made them blind to other, perhaps more decisive, facts.

form of evasiveness and unpredictability. Because of a lack of conceptual imagination, this unique system is rarely analyzed, but it alone seems able to explain apparently misleading acts and words.

Our first concern here has been to establish this uniqueness before determining its consequences for Arabs and non-Arabs. Certain current analyses, at first sight objective and reasonable, seem to supply historical, sociological, and political causes for it; in reality they succeed only in obscuring it. We must thus say a few words about it.

The Arab peoples, it is pointed out, share a historical heritage combining an egalitarian tribal ethic, an Islamic theocentricity, and an anticolonial humanism.[9] In each Arab social structure are juxtaposed, in varying degrees, the separation of the Bedouins, the corporatism of the Islamic city, and the class stratification of capitalism. Enormous petroleum revenues permit harvesting the fruits of science and technology without having to master them beforehand. These economic, social, cultural conditions cause the Arab countries to be analogous and different at the same time, opposed and complementary, close and distant, unified and competitive. Everywhere culture and society contain the same elements; the proportion alone changes and gives a country a particular aspect. The distribution of population does not coincide with resources, any more than wealth coincides with progress.

These observations are incontestably correct, but we cannot draw from them any conclusions concerning the problem that preoccupies us here. Starting with these premises, we can just as well conclude that Arab unity is a necessity dictated by economic exigencies rather than a consequence of a social and mental structure, now on the verge of disappearing. The opposition and complementarity are either an abstract game, applicable to any group of countries and irrelevant to Arab reality, or else they exercise a decisive influence on Arab life, acting as a scarcely articulated *ensemble* by its presence alone. Certain Western European and Latin American countries share as many similarities as the Arab countries do, but we cannot identify any comparable regional system in them, either actual or potential. Attributing inter-Arab relations to a residue of common cultural traditions or to temporary interests is to take them for the result of chance (of concomitant stages of development); it is to deny that they can be an independent factor in the policy of each Arab state.

A similar lack of understanding can be found among those who believe they have discovered the primordial motive of Arab activism in either sociopolitical or technoeconomic factors. All interpret the slogans

---

[9] This humanism springs from the liberal, anticolonial European tradition, that of the nineteenth century English radicals and French socialists.

of unity and nonalignment as ideological alibis, serving to promote either social revolution or economic development. A large sector of leftist opinion maintains that the masses are transformed primarily by the will to end inequalities and privileges. Street demonstrations, *coups d'etat,* and wars are episodes in one and the same revolution. According to circumstances, slogans of unity and nonalignment are adopted by some to advance that revolution, and by others to frustrate it; but the driving force of Arab political activity cannot be stayed. Explicit aims are nothing but tools in the hands of one group or another.

Economists and bureaucrats think that internal quarrels, social contradictions, and opposition among leaders can be explained by economic and technological lag and by disagreement on the best means of catching up. Socialism is a technique for mobilizing energies to build a modern economy; unity is a means of facilitating transfers of capital and labor; nonalignment is a way of obtaining from all sides aid for development at the best price. Let us also recall that for Marxists this explanation in itself reflects an ideology serving the interests of a bureaucratic bourgeoisie, which dominates and exploits unorganized masses.[10]

These analyses are on the whole pertinent on their level; they take at least partial account of the policy of certain Arab countries, particularly Egypt. But in our opinion they leave the essential question unexplained. If the real motive of Arab activism is the elimination of social inequalities, why does it not express itself directly; why must it hide behind the myth of unity and nondependence? If the driving force is development, for which the unity myth is but an instrument to obtain subsidies and get rid of surplus population, why should a petitioning Arab state expect a more favorable response from inside the Arab area than from outside? The deep and general influence of Arab-Islamic culture bears on the first question, just as an affirmation of a preestablished concordance of interests bears on the second, and both presuppose the existence of a system functioning as a determining factor, and not merely as the result of a fortuitous set of circumstances.

Although there are cultural, historic, and social similarities among the Arab countries, they do not cover all of the reality. The interests of opposing groups probably underlie declared objectives but the inter-Arab system should not therefore be judged deceitful or transitory. The objective elements cited above do help in understanding certain aspects of the day-to-day policy of each state, but the principle most deserving

---

[10] See Abdel Aziz Belal, ed., *Renaissance du monde arabe,* pp. 17-37; Nathan Weinstock, *Le movement révolutionnaire arabe* (Paris: 1970); Maxime Rodinson, *Marxisme et monde musulman* (Paris: 1972), pp. 453-526; Fred Halliday, *Arabia without Sultans* (London: Hammondsworth, 1974), pp. 24, 30.

of serious and unprejudiced analysis is a certain common will of the Arab masses. The preceding analyses, however pertinent on their own level, unfortunately say nothing of this.

Let us continue then with the four explicit aims—unity, nonalignment, socialism, and democracy—not preoccupying ourselves with their degree of realization, their proximate or remote causes, or the motives they express and hide at the same time. Let us ask this question: Are the four goals all desired at the same time and with the same intensity? In other words, can we develop a significant typology of Arab regimes and parties by identifying different orders of priority? Let us take four among the possible combinations: (1) nonalignment, unity, socialism, democracy; (2) unity, socialism, nonalignment, democracy; (3) socialism, nonalignment, democracy, unity; and (4) democracy, nonalignment, socialism, unity. Order 1 can readily be linked with Nasser's Egypt, order 2 with Baathist Syria, order 3 with Boumedienne's Algeria, and order 4 with present-day Tunisia. The same criteria can be used to distinguish political parties.

The inter-Arab system reveals itself in the consequences of non-concordance with the orders of priority established at a given time by Arab leaders. If short or moderate-term concordance could be assured, it would be the harbinger of an imminent unified state. If every isolated state could dissociate itself from the choices of others, the hypothesis of an inter-Arab system would have no more reason for being. In fact, each order of priorities is presented by its proponents not as a strategic choice but as the shortest path to realize all goals at once. It follows that each chief of state, in defining his policy and thus his hierarchy of objectives, is condemned to have detractors at home and supporters abroad, and, if he tries to exchange the former for the latter by changing the order of priorities, the same situation will persist with different groups. For these reasons, the intervention of an Arab leader in the affairs of another country is nowhere really condemned, and the idea of state sovereignty is largely ignored.

Such considerations also explain the particular place of the Palestinians on the Arab scene. Aided by all regimes, applauded by public opinion, claiming extraterritorial status, they nevertheless cannot avoid creating a situation difficult to accept in a modern state. It is not enough to observe that sometimes they are applauded and sometimes they are allowed to be massacred; the remarkable fact is that no one ever criticizes their action politically. To neutralize them militarily here or there is to admit implicitly an inability to discredit them politically. No chief of state has expressly placed his own tactics in opposition to theirs by questioning the results of their action. The fact is that they incarnate the Arabs' inability to choose a single objective and relegate the others to an indeterminate future.

The universal ideas of socialism, democracy, unity, and national independence evidently undergo profound modifications in the Arab area. Must these modifications be linked to the internal structure of each state, as is generally maintained, or do they become more intelligible, as we believe, when seen under the influence exerted by the ensemble of an inter-Arab system? If this is the case, what is the long-term significance of this influence?

It is not enough to say that certain traits inherited from the past must alter democracy in all Arab regimes, that technological lag reduces socialism to a means of mobilizing the masses, that the linguistic and cultural unity sustained by the mass media accounts for the emergence of the unity myth despite the continuous reinforcement of the newly established national states, that economic weakness explains the mistrust towards the great powers. Neither is it enough to suggest that a cultural and political lag veils the reality of class struggles, which leaders find it expedient to obscure with an illusory unanimity. None of these explanations applies when the Arabs display their undeniable specificity.

Beyond what the chiefs of state, party leaders, and intellectuals say and do, and beyond what can be explained by historical facts or sociological motivations, there remains what the Arabs desire, which is irreducible to either history or sociology.

What they desire is manifested more clearly in what they refuse than in what they tolerate. They do not resign themselves to the nation-state in the Western sense, to industrial alienation under a capitalist or socialist-bureaucratic regime, to partisan parliamentarianism, or to an abstract universalism that equalizes all historical communities.

If we allow our vision to be clouded by historical precedents, we can make a superficial comparison to pan-Americanism or pan-Slavism and see in this attitude the momentary consequence of a romantic rejection of modernism.[11] But when we contemplate the failure of all policies founded on such hasty judgments, we must content ourselves merely to enumerate the aspects of a complex reality, without claiming to foresee the future.

I have sometimes criticized an illusion propagated by certain ideologues who believe that the inter-Arab system is presently stabilized, in full bloom and complete, already offering a concrete alternative to the two ideologies that divide the world. I doubt that there is room for a

---

[11] This is not to say that any comparison between these movements is impossible but rather to emphasize that the destiny of the one is not necessarily the future of the other. Edouard Bénés, Où vont les Slaves (Paris: 1947) is very enriching for an Arab reader.

third ideology for the simple reason that liberalism and Marxism are founded on the same premises, which cannot be rejected except by consciously choosing an historical "death." [12] But there is room for another way of living under one or the other of these two ideologies. In my criticism, I attacked the lack of lucidity, the unjustified satisfaction, and the bad choice of means of the inter-Arab ideologue—not the actuality or validity of an Arab will to difference, which is but another facet of community liberty.

Beyond that, one can perceive a political strategy whose principal elements we have singled out, an historical plan expressed by authenticity, fidelity, and specificity, which aims at preserving for the Arab community—by one means or another and at one level or another—its distinctive traits. It is a great ambition to be by oneself an *umma* (nation); powerful states have not done so. Is it reasonable? Is it still possible? Mundane spirits cannot keep from asking such questions, which only the future will answer. Instead, one should ask, Can the Arabs choose another attitude?

Arab specificity is not just the result of a different history and social structure, of an unfavorable international position, and of great regional disparities. It is desired. It represents a strategic aim. Under these circumstances, it cannot be judged on the level of visible differences because the Arabs cannot be anything but different. Rather, Arab specificity must be considered in reference to a renewal of an Arab sociopolitical organization. At present, this consideration is almost negligible, but the ambition itself is not therefore hopeless, because the future is always open.

The Arabs cannot escape the concurrent influence of liberalism and Marxism any more than they can eliminate from their bosom group struggles and the contradictions of regimes. They may lean to one side or the other, just as they can divide themselves into two subwheels, separated geographically and ideologically. But in any eventuality, they will remain apart: *salafism* (a reform movement) will be a liberalism that Westerners will have a hard time recognizing, and local socialism will be unassimilable by that practiced in the East or West.

Most foreigners base their Arab policy on visible facts: armed confrontations, propaganda warfare, competition on world markets. Gaullist France decided, despite the skepticism of its allies and part of its domestic opinion, to take seriously the hypothesis of the strategic

---

[12] Abdallah Laroui, *La crise des intellectuels arabes* (Paris: 1974), pp. 192-197. Compare with Hachem Djait, *La personalité et le devenir arabo-islamique* (Paris: 1974); Mary Matossian, "Ideologies of Delayed Industrialization: Some Tensions and Ambiguities," in John Kautsky, ed., *Political Change in Underdeveloped Countries* (New York: John Wiley & Sons, Inc., 1967), pp. 252-264.

aim we have discussed. The future will tell who has made the most rewarding judgment for his own future interests. In the meantime, to the extent there is a pan-Arab opinion limiting the maneuverability of chiefs of state, it seems to us that the Arabs will give their lasting friendship only to those who, while following their own objectives, will assist materially or morally in the realization of the supreme Arab ambition, that is, to those who will know how to perceive the Arabs' dream in the sand.

THE AMERICAN PERCEPTION
OF THE ARAB WORLD

William E. Leuchtenburg

From the perspective of the American historian, the most striking aspect of the relationship between Arab and American cultures is that, to Americans, the Arabs are a people who have lived outside of history. On the face of it, this statement seems absurd. Arabs had, after all, developed a sophisticated civilization some 2,500 years before Columbus sailed to the New World. Nearly a millennium before the first Pilgrim set foot on Plymouth Rock, Arabs had built the Great Mosque in Tunisia, evolved a well-articulated jurisprudence, and founded a school of medicine in Baghdad. Nonetheless, the generalization stands. For one may read any standard account of the history of America, until the most recent times, and derive from it the impression either that the Arabs have had no history or that it was only of the most inconsequential sort.

Even when American historians engage in writing comparative history, something they have been notoriously reluctant to do, this same conclusion emerges. Some ten years ago the Voice of America asked the Sterling Professor of American History at Yale, C. Vann Woodward, to invite twenty-two historians to prepare scripts which were subsequently broadcast, in a great many different languages and dialects throughout the world and then published in a volume entitled *The Comparative Approach to American History*.[1] During this entire collective enterprise, not one of the twenty-two historians saw fit to make any reference to the Arab experience. In my own essay on the Great Depression, I found useful parallels in New Zealand and in Sweden, in Ireland and in Mexico, in Australia and in Brazil, but at no time did it occur to me to ask how the Great Depression affected the Arab world, or how Arabs responded to it.[2] In the other essays, some of America's

---

[1] C. Vann Woodward, *The Comparative Approach to American History* (New York: Basic Books, 1968).

[2] In fact, my essay was the only one that mentioned any Arab land, but the reference was insignificant. "From countries as distant as Russia and Arabia, foreign visitors flocked to the United States to study such innovations as shelterbelts and the Tennessee Valley Authority." William E. Leuchtenburg, "The Great Depression," in Woodward, *The Comparative Approach to American History*, p. 307.

most distinguished historians ranged over subjects like revolution, immigration, mobility, civil war, urbanization, socialism, political parties, and social democracy without once ever mentioning Arabs.

Far from being an exception, the Woodward volume is characteristic of the attitude of American historians toward the subject of Arabs, both abroad and at home. When the prestigious *Harvard Guide to American History* appeared in 1954 with nearly seven hundred pages of fine print on the writings in the field, not a single reference to Arabs appeared in the index, and the section on immigration, which finds room for monographs on Russian Mennonites, Czecho-Slovaks, Norwegians, and Chinese, lists not one book on any Arabic group.[3] *Foreign Influences in American Life* might seem to be a promising title, but this collection of essays and critical bibliographies, too, ignores Arabs altogether.[4] If we turn to the very best works on immigration to America, we will look in vain for awareness of an Arab presence. Marcus Lee Hansen's classic account, *The Immigrant in American History,* says nothing about Arabs and makes but one glancing allusion to Syrians, while such first-rate studies as John Higham's *Strangers in the Land* and Oscar Handlin's *The Uprooted* do not even do that.[5] When Louis Adamic, himself an immigrant, decided to challenge the view that the United States was an Anglo-Saxon country, he wrote *A Nation of Nations,* a book that aimed to show that American culture was woven from the strands of many diverse ethnic groups, but in developing this theme over some four hundred pages, he never once finds an occasion to cite any Arab contribution.[6]

How does one account for this absence of Arabs in histories of America? There are at least three possibilities.

One is that there has been so little contact between the United States and the Arab world that there is no reason for American historians to devote much attention to this subject.

A second possibility is that the Arab experience has been so different from that of Americans that the history of Arabs cannot serve even as a measuring rod.

And there is still a third possibility—that American historians do not write about Arab-American relations because they are so densely

---

[3] Oscar Handlin et al., *Harvard Guide to American History* (Cambridge, Mass.: Belknap Press of Harvard University Press, 1954).

[4] David F. Bowers, *Foreign Influences in American Life* (Princeton: Princeton University Press, 1944).

[5] Marcus Lee Hansen, *The Immigrant in American History* (Cambridge: Harvard University Press, 1948), p. 173; John Higham, *Strangers in the Land* (New Brunswick: Rutgers University Press, 1955); Oscar Handlin, *The Uprooted* (Boston: Little Brown, 1952).

[6] Louis Adamic, *A Nation of Nations* (New York: Harper, 1945).

ignorant of Arab history and of the Arab presence in the United States.

In varying degrees, all three of these explanations seem to me to be true.

Any consideration of this question must begin with the fact that, to a very large degree, the American nation has lived in isolation from the Arab world. It is quite possible for an American historian to write about the settlement of the North American continent, the theological disputes in Puritan New England, the revolution against the British, the Mexican War, the conflict over slavery, industrialization, the Age of Reform—in short, most of the major episodes of American history, without any reference to Arabs whatsoever. This is not to say that there have been no contacts at all between the two worlds, for there have, in fact, been a few events—such as the Barbary War—which get a line or a paragraph in the history books.[7] Similarly, there have been, well before the present day, some influences of America on the Arab world—as in the impact of evangelical missionaries engaged in propagating the gospel in the Levant, of the American universities at Beirut and Cairo, and of relief agencies in the Near East. But, for the most part, the historian of the United States has found only rarely a need to talk about Arabs, and, conversely, the historian of the Arab world has had little reason to speak of America.[8]

Not only has there been little relationship of the United States to the Arab lands, but the Arab presence in the United States has been inconspicuous also. In his pathbreaking work, *The Syrians in America,* Philip Hitti wrote that the first Syrian immigrant did not come to the United States until the middle of the nineteenth century; and *Syrian* is a term loosely used to embrace people not only from Syria but also from Lebanon and other Arabic-speaking lands.[9] Although Adele Younis has indicated that Arabic-speaking settlements in the United States came earlier and were more numerous, it is clear that they were insignificant

---

[7] Only in more specialized studies will one learn that in the eighteenth century American colonists built up a flourishing trade with North Africa in grain and dried fish; that in the first half of the nineteenth century American vessels sailed the Red Sea and the east coast of Africa from Mocha to Zanzibar; or that after the Civil War American officers went to Egypt to serve in the Khedive's army.

[8] Save for a passing reference to "the American Protestant mission," Bernard Lewis, in discussing "The Impact of the West" on the Arab world, does not mention the United States. Bernard Lewis, *The Arabs in History,* revised edition (New York: Harper and Row, 1966), p. 172. There is, however, some discussion of the interaction of the United States and Arab lands in Bernard Lewis, *The Middle East and the West* (Bloomington, Ind.: Indiana University Press, 1964). Lewis notes, in fact, that the term "Middle East" was coined by an American, Alfred Thayer Mahan. Ibid., p. 9. But even this book leaves the impression that before 1945 the American influence in the Arab world was negligible.

[9] Philip K. Hitti, *The Syrians in America* (New York: George H. Doran, 1924), p. 89.

before the Civil War era.[10] Of the million Syrians who fled the Ottoman Empire between 1870 and 1900, most wound up not in the United States but in Egypt, South America, and India.[11] Even during the "big wave" of immigration in the early twentieth century, the annual total in the peak year of 1914 was only 9,000. In the period since World War II, this situation has changed markedly, but for most of the time span of the United States, Abdo Elkholy is on firm ground in describing Arab-Americans as "the latest and smallest minority group in this nation-of-nations." [12]

Still, granted that there has been relatively little direct contact between the United States and the Arab world, and that, until recently, there has been no large influx of Arabs to this country, would it not be useful to make comparisons of the experiences of the American and Arab peoples? I think so. Yet one can understand why so little has been done. It is not merely the obstacle of language which requires a formidable commitment for American historians to do serious research in Arabic sources. Even more important is the fact that the experience of the United States has been so unlike that of Arab lands. There is, for example, no equivalent in the two centuries of the American republic for the mortification of living under foreign rule—of Turks, of French, or others. Nor is it possible to contrast American statecraft with that of Arab peoples *before* they had achieved statehood; that is, one cannot compare the diplomatic history of the United States to the diplomatic history of Iraq during the long period before there was an Iraq.[13] Even in more recent times American polity and American society has been quite dissimilar from that of nations like the Sudan. Often, the

---

[10] Adele L. Younis, "The Growth of Arabic-Speaking Settlements in the United States," in Elaine C. Hagopian and Ann Paden, eds., *The Arab-Americans* (Wilmette, Ill.: Medina University Press International, 1969); Younis, "Salem and the Early Syrian Adventure," *Essex Institute Historical Collections*, vol. 102 (1966), pp. 303-310.

[11] Maldwyn Jones, *American Immigration* (Chicago: University of Chicago Press, 1960), p. 203.

[12] Abdo Elkholy, "The Arab-Americans: Nationalism and Traditional Preservations," in Hagopian and Paden, *The Arab-Americans*, p. 3. See, too, Elkholy, *The Arab Moslems in the United States* (New Haven: College and University Press, 1966).

[13] A seasoned foreign service officer and historian has commented: "Affairs relating to Arab territories presented themselves to American officials as issues between the United States and the European powers or (until World War I) Turkey, not usually as United States-Arab matters. Only after World War II was the principle established that the United States had distinct geopolitical and economic interests of its own in the—now fully independent—Arab states. American policy toward the Arab countries, strictly speaking, thus has a relatively brief history." Robert W. Stookey, *America and the Arab States: An Uneasy Encounter* (New York: Wiley, 1975), p. xiii.

most that can be said, and without any judgment necessarily being implied, is, as Professor Laroui remarks, that "during *brief* periods, *some* Arab countries have known institutions comparable to those of the West." [14]

Nonetheless, the third consideration remains—that American writers have given so little attention to Arabs because of their ignorance of, and indifference to, Arab history and culture. Not all American writers, to be sure. Washington Irving wrote works like *The Alhambra* and *Mahomet and his Successors,* and there have long been scholars in the United States with an intense interest in Arab affairs—historians of the British empire, for example, or, even more directly, those engaged in Islamic studies. But these exceptions do not invalidate the observation that chroniclers of the history of the United States have paid little heed to Arabs. This is the result in part—though only in small part—of the fact that American historians have been Eurocentric, have been absorbed with the sources of American society in Europe, especially Western Europe, with the literary heritage not of the world but of England, with the religious traditions not of Islam and the other great creeds but almost solely of Christianity.

The assertion that writers on the history of the United States make little mention of Arabs does not, of course, hold for the period since 1945. No general history of the postwar era, certainly no diplomatic history, could fail to note the involvement of the United States in such episodes as the Suez crisis of 1956 or the conflicts between Israel and the Arab states. But the fact that historians now felt obligated to give at least some attention to Arab developments did not change the basic situation fundamentally. There seemed no more interest in pursuing Arab influences in the United States than there had ever been, and little more curiosity about intellectual or other developments in the Arab world. Furthermore, American historians, and American intellectuals generally, were overwhelmingly sympathetic to Israel, and perceived the Arab states as the enemies of the aspirations of the appallingly small remnant of Jews who had survived the Holocaust. The Middle East caused concern, too, because it was frequently seen as the likely place to offer a Sarajevo that would plunge the world into a war of nuclear devastation.

Even in this period when the Arab states were accorded front-page attention in the press and the tempo of Arab migration to the United States was accelerating, American historians showed no awareness of Arabic settlements in the United States—in large part because Arab-

---

[14] Abdallah Laroui, "Sands and Dreams," see page 6 of this volume. The emphasis has been added.

Americans were politically quiescent. Virtually every commentator on groups of Arabic origin in America has felt called upon to account for the low level of political participation. As early as 1924, the illustrious Professor Hitti noted: "Syrians cut no figure in the political life of this nation. Very few of them interest themselves in politics or aspire to office." [15] And as late as 1969 Ibrahim Abu-Lughod observed:

> It is significant that neither at the level of political behavior nor at an organizational level have the earlier Arab immigrants made their presence felt at critical times when the entire community has been subjected to serious political and social pressures. It has been widely known that the Arab-American community has exhibited a persistent tendency to refrain from the legitimate exercise of its privilege of utilizing the normal processes of politics.[16]

The relatively small size of the Arabic migration and the dispersion of the migrants in America also helps explain why historians and political scientists have not been disposed to speak of an "Arab vote" in the United States in the same way that they have about the balloting of other ethnic groups. When in 1957 an Ohio congressman was accused of being pro-Israel because it was to his political advantage, he replied that he was, in fact, "probably . . . the only member of Congress who has more Arabs in his district than he has Jews." [17] The congressman in question was Wayne Hays. And if he was accurate in what he said, history will have a *second* reason for remembering him.

Yet another element contributed to the virtual invisibility of Arab-Americans: the fact that only a very small percentage was Muslim. In the nineteenth century virtually all migrants from the Arab world to the United States were Christian; not until 1919 was the first mosque built

---

[15] Hitti, *The Syrians in America,* p. 89. For the role of Syrian-Americans on the League of Nations issue, see J. Joseph Huthmacher, *Massachusetts People and Politics, 1919-1933* (New York: Atheneum, 1969), pp. 22-23. I am indebted to James L. Baughman for memoranda on Arab-American relations.

[16] Hagopian and Paden, *The Arab-Americans,* p. vi. It is, however, unclear what Abu-Lughod means by "critical times when the entire community has been subjected to serious political and social pressures."

[17] Morroe Berger, "Americans from the Arab World," in James Kritzeck and R. Bayly Winder, eds., *The World of Islam: Studies in Honour of Philip K. Hitti* (London: Macmillan, 1960), p. 360. One study found that a crucial distinction was that those who spent their childhood and adolescence in Arab lands identified much more with the cause of Arab nationalism than did those who were raised in the United States. Atif A. Wasfi, *An Islamic-Lebanese Community in U.S.A.* (Beirut: Beirut Arab University, 1971), p. 49. For a regional kaleidoscope that makes reference to some of the basic literature on the subject, see C. Umhau Wolf, "Muslims in the American Mid-West," *Muslim World,* vol. 1 (January 1960), pp. 39-48.

here—in Highland Park, Michigan—and in 1959 it was estimated that only one Arab-American in eighteen was Muslim. In part as a consequence of this, Arab-Americans have, until recently, been slow to manifest support for the Arab cause abroad. In his 1952 University of Chicago dissertation on "The Arab Community in the Chicago Area," Abdul Jalil Ali al-Tahir commented:

> There are no amicable relations between the Christian Syrians and the Moslem Palestinians in the Chicago area. The Moslem Palestinians criticize the Christian Syrians because they neglect their Arabic traditions and do not have nationalistic aspirations. During the Palestinian war the Christian Syrians were not sympathetic and did not raise money for the Arab cause.[18]

This was the situation, then, up until a short time ago. So far as the American perception went, the Arabs were outside of history. Even when large numbers of Americans fought on Arab soil, the experience had no noticeable effect. North Africa in 1942 and Lebanon in 1958 merely provided the terrain on which the United States and European powers struggled for dominance; the Arab perspective was no more the primary concern than it was when Theodore Roosevelt helped persuade the British and French to confer at Algeciras. Nor was the Arab element in America any more visible. When the once-small Arab-American community in the United States passed the half-million mark in the 1960s, historians seemed unaware of it. It is not that Americans did not have some notion, from literature and the mass media, of Arabs, but their impressions had a curiously magical quality, as in Aladdin's lamp, which, in a vulgarized form, provided the basis for a "situation comedy" on American television.[19] In the movies, where Arabs always seemed to be Bedouins, they were gifted with remarkable powers as warriors who could corporealize out of nowhere from beyond the next sand dune (even if they were doomed to defeat in the final reel) or had such fantastic sexual prowess that in Hollywood melodramas there was no end to the number of flaxen-haired actresses waiting to be ravished. But as for any realistic conception of, or consciousness of, the Arab world, Americans seemed not unlike school

---

[18] Berger, "Americans from the Arab World," pp. 360-361.

[19] In his conceptualization of the Arab world, Malcolm X, it has been observed, was abstracting a pastoral ideal rather than describing the actuality of Arabia and Cairo, for "the Arab world is not exactly the paradise Malcolm saw." Abdelwahab M. Elmessiri, "Islam as a Pastoral in the Life of Malcolm X," in John Henrik Clarke, *Malcolm X: The Man and His Times* (Toronto: Collier, 1969), p. 69. The essay goes on to claim, however, that Malcolm X grasped as no other Westerner had "the essence of the Islamic God." Ibid., p. 74.

children doing an algebra assignment without a thought to where algebra came from.

The fall of 1973 brought an abrupt change. When Arab states cut back oil production, or embargoed shipments to the United States àltogether, at the same time that the Organization of Petroleum Exporting Countries raised oil prices sharply, the leading industrial nation in the world was made to feel keenly its dependence on the resources, and good will, of countries it had been accustomed to dismiss as underdeveloped.[20] For the first time, the average American had reason to think directly about the Arab world, as motorists queued up at gas pumps and homeowners watched their fuel bills soar. The panic had a drastic effect on a variety of institutions. It was estimated, for example, that the increase in the fuel bill of the University of Chicago was greater than the entire initial bequest by John D. Rockefeller to the university.

The oil crisis changed perceptibly the way in which the Arab states were portrayed in the media. King Faisal was accorded the greatest distinction that can come to any mortal—he was chosen *Time* magazine's man of the year.[21] More instructive is the fact that one American periodical published a commentary on the oil embargo under the title, "Arabs Reenter History." It observed, "One year ago, prior to the Yom Kippur war and the oil boycott, the Arabs did not exist as far as Western and especially American perception was concerned. . . . But, now, in the wake of the oil boycott, all has been transformed." Newspapers and magazines ran feature articles on Arab society, printed long interviews with Arab leaders, and treated the Arab states, for the first time, as "a major world power." One article concluded, "The last six months have witnessed a world historical event. The Arab world has reentered history, after a sleep of 500 years."[22] The truth, of course, was not that the Arabs had reentered history, where they had been all along, but that they had entered the American orbit of awareness.

Yet, ironically, Americans came finally to acknowledge the existence of Arabs at precisely the point when they were going through an agony of self-doubt which the rising prominence of the Arab states served to accentuate. America had long believed that it was, in Hegel's phrase, "the land of the future," but in the 1970s books were appearing

---

[20] "The Arab decision to embargo oil sales precipitated worldwide panic. Americans sought explanations for the horrible fact that their mighty economy was in danger of being brought to its knees by 'mere' Arabs." Richard B. Mancke, "The Genesis of the U.S. Oil Crisis," in Joseph S. Szyliowicz and Bard E. O'Neill, eds., *The Energy Crisis and U.S. Foreign Policy* (New York: Praeger, 1975), p. 63.
[21] *Time,* vol. 105 (January 6, 1975).
[22] "Arabs Reenter History," *National Review,* vol. 26 (April 12, 1974), p. 410.

with titles like *The End of the American Future*.[23] The violent up-heavals of the 1960s, the feckless war in Vietnam, and the Watergate scandals all fed speculation that the United States was, like ancient Rome, an empire in decline. In the last scene of one of John Updike's novels, the protagonist, having been savaged by the 1960s, finds he can no longer return to the garments of the 1950s, while in another Updike novel the narrator observes ruefully that "the androgynous homogenizing liberals of the world are in charge, and our American empire obligingly subsides to demonstrate how right they are." [24] At just this historic moment, when Americans were being told that they must lower their expectations and curb their aspirations, they saw Arabs, who had brought home to them their dependency, behaving like prototypical Americans. This summer, London estimated that Middle Eastern tour-ists were spending, per person, two and a half times as much as the average American visitor, and one magazine reported that there was a sheikdom with a per capita income more than seven times that of the United States.[25] For those agitated by the fear that the United States was on the decline, the rising Arab states seemed both a proximate cause, and a vexing reminder, of America's difficulties.

There are other impediments to improved relationships too. If intellectuals in America and in the Arab lands are to be drawn more closely together, the effort will have to be reciprocal. Yet serious Arab scholarship on the history of the United States can hardly be said to exist. Writers on the history of the United States take part in American Studies programs in Britain, in Russia, in Germany, and in Israel, but not in the Arab states.

For their part, American historians have only begun to show awareness of the Arab world. True enough, since 1960 historians in the West have published several important monographs on the United States and the Arab world.[26] However, these studies have yet to percolate

---

[23] Peter Schrag, *The End of the American Future* (New York: Simon and Schuster, 1973).

[24] John Updike, *Rabbit Redux* (New York: Knopf, 1971), p. 393; *A Month of Sundays* (Greenwich, Conn.: Fawcett Crest, 1976), pp. 240-241.

[25] "How To Talk Business With Arabs," *Forbes*, vol. 114 (September 15, 1974), p. 106.

[26] William B. Hesseltine and Hazel C. Wolf, *The Blue and Gray on the Nile* (Chicago: University of Chicago Press, 1961); John A. De Novo, *American Interests and Policies in the Middle East, 1900-1939* (Minneapolis: University of Minnesota Press, 1963); Laurence Evans, *United States Policy and the Partition of Turkey, 1914-1924* (Baltimore: Johns Hopkins, 1963); David H. Finnie, *Pioneers East: The Early American Experience in the Middle East* (Cambridge, Mass.: Harvard University Press, 1967); James A. Field, Jr., *America and the Mediterranean World, 1776-1882* (Princeton, N.J.: Princeton University Press, 1969); L. C. Wright, *United States Policy Toward Egypt, 1830-1914* (New York:

through the general histories or affect the perceptions of the American public. As late as 1975, William R. Polk still found it necessary to address the question, "Why should the United States be interested in the Middle East at all?" [27] and as recently as September 1976, a reviewer in the *New York Times* commented, "It is safe to say that most Americans know next to nothing about the Arab world." [28]

Furthermore, fantasies still persist. Whereas previously one was left with the impression that all Arabs are penniless nomads looking for the next waterhole, today one is given to understand that whenever any Arab wants a room for the night he buys a British castle out of his pocket money.

Finally, political outlooks diverge sharply. Arab intellectuals find it incomprehensible that American men of letters are so indifferent to the plight of Palestinian refugees, while American historians are dismayed to come upon works by writers on Arab affairs that refuse even to mention the name of the state of Israel and that refer only to "an international Zionist conspiracy."

Nonetheless, there has been a change, however glacial. For the first time in any significant way Americans, including American intellectuals, are aware of the Arab world. If Americans still appear to be only dimly conscious of an Arab presence in the United States, the immigration of some 100,000 Arabs in the decade after 1957 and the more active political disposition of the younger generation have made Arab-Americans more visible.[29] In 1958, in fact, the first American of Arabian descent was elected to Congress. Interest in Islam has been fostered by the attention generated by the Black Muslims and by the circumstance that the recent arrivals from the Arab world have been predominantly Muslim. To be sure, greater visibility has not always meant increased acceptance. In particular, efforts by Arab-American publicists to exculpate actions like the Olympic Village

---

Exposition Press, 1969); Robert L. Daniel, *American Philanthropy in the Near East, 1820-1960* (Athens, Ohio: Ohio University Press, 1970); Joseph L. Grabill, *Protestant Diplomacy and the Near East: Missionary Influence on American Policy, 1810-1927* (Minneapolis: University of Minnesota Press, 1971).

[27] William R. Polk, *The United States and the Arab World* (Cambridge, Mass.: Harvard University Press, 1975), p. 413.

[28] Alden Whitman, Review of Bernard Lewis, ed., *Islam and the Arab World* (New York: American Heritage, 1976), in *New York Times*, September 18, 1976, p. 17.

[29] For the identification of one group of Christian Arabs in the United States with the Palestinian cause, see the comments on the people of Ramallah in Detroit in Charles Swan and Leila B. Saba, "The Migration of a Minority," in Barbara C. Aswad, ed., *Arabic Speaking Communities in American Cities* (New York: The Center for Migration Studies of New York, Inc. and the Association of Arab-American University Graduates, Inc., 1974), pp. 104-105.

massacre have been distressing. Moreover, large numbers of citizens of Arabic lineage continue to prefer to think of themselves as Americans with no Old World allegiances, even if this means that in the arena of ethnic politics they are nonparticipants. Still, things are not what they were. There are large numbers of Arab-American scholars on university campuses; the size of the Arab-American settlement in the United States approaches a critical mass; and the American public has a vivid appreciation of how policies of the Arab states may affect its well-being. Americans and Arabs now seem part of the same world, sharing, to some degree, a common history, and given that circumstance, there is at least a possibility now of an interchange between the two cultures.

COMMENTARIES

Aziz Suryal Atiya

I listened attentively to both speakers and have great admiration for the profundity of their thinking and for the illuminating facts which they set forth. As a discussant I am bound to mention some disappointments. This does not take away from the magnificence of both accomplishments. But it was my personal expectation—within the framework of the Institute and this conference on Arab and American cultures—to hear more about culture. I listened with interest to the profound statements about the politics of the Arab states and the prophecies regarding their destiny. I am no prophet myself; I am a very antiquated historian and perhaps by nature and upbringing I am bound to remain a medievalist, even at a meeting like this.

And I must ask your indulgence in putting before you a footnote derived from my personal experience and my life work. Initially, we are here to build bridges, bridges of culture, which are permanent edifices. Political matters come and go, they are ambivalent, they depend on circumstances, but culture is a permanent thing. To highlight the bridges between our peoples, the first thing that should be stressed is the parallelism between the structure of the American nation and the structure of the Arab nation. I must go back to the early centuries of Islam. We know that when the Arabs came out of the desert, they had nothing to offer but their language and their religion. They conquered adjacent civilizations, but in their conquests they did not do what the Huns did in Europe or what Attila did in Rome; they did not barbarize existing civilizations. On the contrary, the Arabs lifted the barriers between two struggling cultures, the Sassanid or Persian theocracy and the Byzantine culture, between Oriental despotism and the miracle of the Greek pursuit of freedom. In this way, they pooled the advances of those civilizations, and even incorporated other cultures, such as the Coptic culture of Egypt and the Syrian culture of Palestine. Thus they laid the foundation for a new and united empire. This parallels the American effort to establish a world citizenry. America has been the crucible where people of all ethnic origins came together from different backgrounds to constitute the hundred-percent American. This parallelism of national structures is the first bridge which should bring the original Arab culture and the novel American culture closer together.

When I first came here in 1951, I felt as Professor Leuchtenburg does, that America was a desert as far as Arab culture was concerned. Then I came here to found a program of Middle Eastern studies. My most successful course was one on Islamic culture and civilization. It took root and spread to many other institutions of higher learning. This desert began to bloom. At the University of Utah at least two thousand students a year attend courses of that type. Clearly America is awakening to the place of Arab culture. I must also mention the influx of thousands of Arab students into America. They have necessarily transferred certain aspects of American culture back to their homelands. Surely these are bridges that are being built between our cultures.

To be a little bit more specific, America would not be living today in the space age, Americans would not have walked on the moon or reached Mars, if it had not been for Arab contributions to the exact sciences. Take Arab mathematics, for example, and its impact on European science. Remember that when speaking of Europe, we mean the achievement of the Greek mind in Europe that has reached its full efflorescence in America. Europeans in the Dark Ages used Roman numerals. In the beginning of the second millennium of our era Pope Sylvester II issued a bull introducing the Arabic numerals. This was a major revolution in our cultural history, equal to the invention of fire or the wheel. We should never minimize the importance of the simple beginnings. In the same way, the use of the Arabic numerals was a tremendous event in the history of the world. Add to this the use of the word *cipher,* itself an Arabic word. It is true that the Arabs were not the inventors of these developments, but they had a willingness to learn from older masters, in this case from India. Arabs introduced the decimal in our computation. The science of algebra was created by an Arab, al-Khwarizmi, who lived in the nineth century. His name persists in our language in a corrupt way in the words *logarithm* and *algorithm.* Without these accomplishments, Americans of today would not be living in the space age.

If the Arabs had not introduced these advances into our culture, we might still be straggling in the eighteenth century. Other examples are legion. Paul Kunitzsch's *Arabische Sternennamen in Europa* shows that most stars have names derived from Arabic. The same applies to the experimental sciences, such as chemistry and technology. Jābir ibn Hayyān of Kūfa in the tenth century used the alembic for infiltration and produced oxidation by employing certain chemical reagents. *Alcohol, alkali,* and *alembic* are all Arabic words. Even the word *chemistry* comes from the Arabic word *alchemy.*

In technology we may be surprised to know that the pendulum was invented by Ibn Yūnus, an Egyptian, in 1009. This was about 650 years before Galileo discovered it.

The mariner's compass was introduced to Europe by Ibn Mājid, who took the Portuguese round the Cape of Good Hope to India in the fifteenth century. The astrolabe, which was essential in medieval astronomy and nautical science, was perfected by al-Zarkali in Spain around 1050. The Arabs even played a part in the history of aviation. Abbās ibn Firnās in the tenth century observed the flight of kites and birds in the sky in preparation for his flying experiment. He tried to apply those principles and flew from a mountain and of course broke his neck.

Perhaps the most important Arab contribution to civilization was the introduction of paper. While conquering central Asia in 751, the first Abbasid Caliph al-Saffāh stumbled on three Chinese paper makers. He took them to Baghdad and started the first paper mill. The project flourished under the famous Caliph Haroun al-Rashīd around 794. By the ninth century, there were more mills in Egypt and by the tenth the industry spread to Spain. This changed the world of culture beyond recognition. Scribes could copy books or write new ones by the thousand, perhaps even by the million. Paper replaced parchment, which was scarce and costly, and papyrus, which was expensive and brittle. This must be regarded as one of the greatest developments in world history, and Americans and all Western peoples must recognize their debt to the Arab in this field.

Let us take a glance at Arab agriculture, banking, and medicine. In agriculture, the Arabs revolutionized the primitive way in which Europeans cultivated their lands. They introduced systems of irrigation and drainage. They introduced grafting and fertilizing. As a matter of fact, there is a twelfth century work entitled *Kitāb al-Filāha* (Book of Farming) by a Spanish Arab named Ibn al-'Awwām. That book dealt with 585 plants. The European names of certain plants are Arabic words. *Spinach,* for example, is an Arabic word. *Ginger, coffee, sugar, syrup, sherbet, cotton, sesame,* and *carob* are all Arabic words. *Pastèque,* the French word for watermelon, is a French corruption of the Arabic *Battīkh. Jasmine, saffron, lemon,* and *orange* are directly derived from Arabic. Actually the study of philology might give

29

us the key to an understanding of the influence of one culture on another. The late Professor Arnold Steigner of Zurich, an old friend, compiled a dictionary of Arabic words in the Romance languages. We can understand the Arabic influences by means of the classification of words borrowed from Arabic. Take nautical terminology. The word *admiral* is the Arabic *Amir-al-Bahr, traffic* is *tafriq, tariff* is *ta'rif, cable* is *habl,* and *arsenal* is *Dar-al-Sina'a.* I have already mentioned some of the terms in agriculture. In fact, the Arabic philological contribution to the Romance languages extends to dozens of disciplines: to music, industry, architecture, flora and fauna, clothing, war machines, and even to banking. The work *check* is the Arabic *Sakk* and *wechsel* (bill) is *wasl.* Like the Americans, the Arabs knew, if they did not invent, banking, corporations, and capitalism. [Laughter.]

I could spend hours on the economy or on the review of wealthy organizations which date from the tenth century. The Karimiya corporation in medieval times lent millions of dinars to various governments to save them from bankruptcy.

In the realm of medicine, the Arabs dominated the medieval scene. You may be surprised to know that the two standard works of reference in European universities up to the eighteenth century were *Kitāb al Hāwi* (Liber Continens, 24 vols.) by al-Rāzi (865-925) and *al-Qanūn fi al-Tibb* (Canon in Medicine) by Avicenna (980-1037). The first is known to have had forty editions in England before 1866 and the second had fifteen editions in Latin and twenty in Hebrew in the Middle Ages. The Arabs performed the Caesarian operation and the cataract operation, knew anesthesia and disinfecting, and practiced vaccination against smallpox. They had hospitals (*Bimaristans*) and a materia medica of 1,500 simples in the thirteenth century work on Ibn al-Bitar.

I am afraid I have taken more time than I should, but I wanted to give you some concrete examples illustrating the great contribution of Arab culture to American culture through Europe. At the root of Western (or for that matter, American) civilization, is the miracle of the Greek mind. But we must remember that its immediate successor was the miracle of the Arab mind, when the Arabs translated the monuments of Greek culture. The Caliphs sometimes stipulated the cession of a Greek manuscript in their peace treaties with a Byzantine adversary. The first phase in the genesis of this new heritage was one of interpretation, but soon it developed original and creative works. In this way, the efflorescence of the Arab genius became instrumental in generating the Renaissance and the birth of modern civilization.

Paul Conkin

I work under an obvious assumption—that our conference should promote understanding in both directions between Arabs and Americans. Our immediate task is to find some of the historical secrets of both cultures, if the word *culture* really fits. If I had enough time, I would give a paper fully parallel to the fascinating, but often mystifying, essay by Professor Laroui. I would call my brief abstract of such a paper "Forest and Dreams."

Professor Laroui sees four conjoined and inherently inseparable values or goals as a common Arab inheritance, or what he calls a system. The four goals may be awkwardly separated into the following: (1) a desired unity which overrides endless divisions and crises and in a sense defines them as Arab crises; (2) an essential Arab autonomy that makes all external alliances tentative and merely tactical; (3) a commitment to a form of socialism, or to a humane economy, which fits into no Marxist categories and entails none of the industrial discipline and alienation of the West; and (4) the search for various forms of government that can harmonize complex social groups but without the liberal features of Western democracies. Thus, Professor Laroui identifies an elusive covenant which never fully conforms to the artificial categories of Western political and economic analysis. He makes clear that a common will, or distinctive Arab attitude, lies behind these goals, and that the essence of this will is never properly expressed as one or other of the goals, or even in any interim and strategic ranking of all four, but rather in all of them conjoined in a holistic or organic unity. This must remain a distinctive cultural asset of Arabs. It fits none of the various forms of Western liberal or socialist understanding.

Can I make such an analysis for America? Not as easily. Apart from the area of language, I suspect that the richness and diversity of Arab cultures could best be compared with all of Western European civilization, rather than with the American subset. Or, at the very least, it should be compared with such larger, more inclusive subsets as Protestant culture or even British culture. In any case, the United States is part of Western Christian civilization, and it also shares in the many Protestant and British particularities of that civilization. I shall assume these commonalities, and engage the old issue of American distinctiveness. My question is, What, beyond the wide area of shared beliefs, attitudes, and even institutions, has distinguished American historical development from that of Western Europe? I am not speaking of some elusive American character, but of distinctive conditions or common modes of behavior. And in trying to search these out, I do sense a

31

tension between America and Europe—a sense of our differences, of our uniqueness—that in certain significant areas does point to a possible overlap with the distinctiveness that Professor Laroui referred to in the Arab world.

By independence, in 1776, America was distinct from any country of Western Europe in three critical respects: (1) all white men enjoyed a degree of liberty or personal independence, based on easy access to unentailed and unrestricted productive property. This independence was realized by only a small minority of Europeans. (2) In part as a result of such proprietary openness, Americans for the first time fully realized the old idea of popular government—that is, a nonsovereign government established by a constitutional process and strictly limited in its power by such a process. (3) America was distinct from Europe because of the institution of black slavery, a slavery pregnant with historical significance not only because of its magnitude but also because of its regional concentration.

My friends keep insisting upon other equally significant and distinctive characteristics. So far, I have successfully finessed their claims, or showed how my three characteristics variously included their own. The one I find most persuasive, but ultimately reject, is the theme of cultural pluralism, or the melting pot image, and with it the forms of tolerance and expressive freedom that Americans later had to accept. I am willing to concede that this became a distinctive aspect of American society by 1900 and that it was already distinctive in a few cosmopolitan areas even in 1800. But overall I believe that the most basic American institutions developed in the time of cultural homogeneity, and with it much less leeway for personal expression—in religion, speech, press, life style—than we enjoy (or is it suffer?) today. Now I will explore these three features.

First, there is personal independence or liberty. In 1800 white American men proudly claimed the status of freemen. In 1800 approximately 80 percent of them were also either freeholders or owners of other forms of productive property. Nature was fecund and open in America, and, because land was so abundant and cheap, proprietary status long seemed open to almost any white man. It was at least an option. Those who did not choose it—craftsmen or mechanics, or even wage employees—still enjoyed its economic and social benefits. They were also freemen because they could bargain their labor and skills as social equals, that is, without any sense of deference or servility. They gained the franchise, and they fought successfully for public schools. Although we had various levels of ability and of wealth in America, of education and social attainment, we would have no demeaning dependence or servility, and at least in theory no alienating labor. We had no economic class system, no remnants of feudalism. We had escaped the monopolistic land system of Europe, where the tillers of the soil were almost never free entrepreneurs, but were dependent tenants or peasants, without open access to land, or without full control over its management, or without full rights to what it produced. Similarly, we had no privileged owners of capital, no trading companies, no politically secured monopolies. Thus, we had no landless and dependent wage employees who had no alternative but to bargain their labor for whatever the market could pay—which is to say, no real alternative, no real freedom.

This American self-conception—largely justified in 1800 but so quickly to become illusory in some of its basic assumptions—has shaped not only much of American history but also many historical interpretations of American history. It supports a frontier hypothesis. At the very least, an abundance of cheap natural resources was a precondition of a proprietary society, of a nation of entrepreneurs, and thus of the independence this allows. But, personally, I do not see the existence of abundant resources, or the basic geographical distinctiveness of America, as the sufficient cause of a proprietary society, for it had to join with cultural predispositions, with the peculiar aspirations of those who first came to America, and with the entrepreneurial possibilities inherent in lax British colonial policies.

Free land, conjoined with American tenure policies, also supports the more harsh frontier theory of a William Appleman Williams. The development of new frontiers, the exploitation of the accrued capital of raw nature or the exploitation of other people, first at home and then abroad, became the favorite American response to all manner of social inequities. Since we allowed unlimited and unqualified acquisition of land, even glorified unearned increments and capital gains, and later politically abetted and then protected large accumulations of capital, we could only keep a semblance of open opportunity through continuous expansion, thus postponing the full accounting of our greed and our waste of resources.

Since in early America, the announced norm, and often the reality, was ownership of productive property and almost unlimited managerial freedom, our very conditions belied the assumptions behind most European economic analyses. Perhaps it fit us no better than it fits Arab countries today. Both Adam Smith, who believed that no more than one man in twenty in Europe combined ownership and labor, and Karl Marx, who took class exploitation as his point of departure, assumed economic dependence as the common lot of most of mankind. Landlords and tenants, capitalists and employees—who could understand a civilized society without reference to these distinct and separate classes?

33

The future alternatives also seemed clear—some form of corporate capitalism, or some form of socialism or communism. Only in primitive, undeveloped, and thus classless societies did the various economic functions combine in single individuals. Yet, America was not primitive. From the beginning it was highly productive and very commercial. Thus, it was an anomaly, but surely a temporary one, tied not to superior institutions but to the enormous and equalizing natural windfall reaped by early settlers. Perceptive Americans, such as John Adams and James Madison, feared that this was all too true, that with increasing population, the enclosure of all land, and the accumulated wealth and political clout of capable and unscrupulous Americans, the country would tend to converge with Europe in its institutions. Then classical or Marxist analysis would fit even American realities. Thus, they sought, sometimes with a sense of almost certain failure, to erect political institutions sufficient to preserve freedom—that is, in Adams's terms, to preserve the property and thus the independence of the mass of simple people, who faced ever greater threats from men of wealth and power.

We now live in an economy very similar to those of Western Europe. The proprietor is all but gone. Few Americans own productive property or enjoy managerial roles. Our economy, even in agriculture, is increasingly dominated by large centralized collectivities, with a managerial elite and wage-dependent employees. Individual property and free enterprise are haunting memories. Neither ownership nor managerial prerogatives compete with consumption and living standards as gauges of well-being. Yet, most forms of freedom have expanded in America since 1776. Many more groups now lay claim to freedom and equality. But interdependence, hierarchical systems, and subordinated roles are the norm, and liberty or independence in the eighteenth-century sense only a memory.

Yet, the proprietary ideal lives on, and it has vastly influenced both the course of economic development and, perhaps even more, the popular reactions to it. Look at the record. First, the intense opposition to special privileges for corporations, for banks, and for manufacturing. The determined efforts by mechanics to resist a wage system, to preserve open access to the land, to restrict corporate privileges for manufacturing interests, all led to dominant motifs of the early nineteenth-century workingman's organizations. Look at the attacks on the opportunity-destroying effects of absentee ownership, of land speculation, and of unearned increments, all of which culminated in the work of Henry George. More important, look at the long antipathy of Americans to large business enterprise, an antipathy that began to dissipate only in the 1920s. Equally important were American suspicions of the two necessary correlates of corporate collectivism—labor organization and government paternalism. Native Americans long resisted any self-image consistent with permanent employment status or wage dependence, and thus refused to think in class terms. Unions gained a degree of public acceptance only in the 1930s. A government oriented not so much to universal entrepreneurial opportunity but to a range of redistributive services on socialization of product, gained only grudging acceptance and its present orthodox status after World War II. In each case, these developments faced more resistance than they did in Europe, for in each case they violated self-conceptions and treasured ideals. In other words, corporations, large labor unions, and the welfare state (the polar opposites of property and free enterprise) long seemed un-American.

The second distinctive feature, constitutional government, will be traced only briefly here because I have written recently and extensively on the subject. The theory that government authority rests on the covenanted people of a community has ancient roots, and by the seventeenth century had a full theoretical development. But Europeans never found a way fully to implement the theory. Governments, whether monarchical or republican in form, remained sovereign, and citizens remained to some extent subject. By such innovations as the Constitutional Conventions, popular ratification, easy amendment devices, and a system of constitutional review in the court, Americans finally institutionalized the concept. We attained popular, not democratic, government. Not only did we establish the principle of constitutionalism, but we artfully devised constitutions that supported rigid limits on government power. A balanced separation of functions in each government, and a federal division of government jurisdictions abetted this goal. Generally we have preserved popular government, even in the midst of some of the most severe challenges to it—party politics, majoritarian sentiments, massed interest groups, sophisticated techniques of propaganda and opinion control, and even cults of personality or the mystique of leadership.

The third distinctive feature also requires little comment. Negro slavery was the festering cancer that accompanied American independence. The lingering tentacles of this cancer still eat away at our social organism, still offer the severest challenge to our political institutions. Ironies abound. Southern slave owners were often the most eloquent defenders of a free and proprietary society, the most avid supporters of the moral principles that underlie the right of universal access to a share of nature (that is, to property). Yet, Southerners developed a completely dependent and servile labor force, our first form of economic collectivism, in their factories of the field. Given the proprietary opportunities for white men in America, and high competitive wages, any profitable, large-scale investment in commodity agriculture required a dependent labor system. And, given the proprietary opportunities, such dependence had to rest on political disabilities of one type or another.

Some Southerners came to defend slavery not only on racial grounds but also on paternalistic grounds. Their arguments then joined with some of the most persuasive justifications of feudalism, or even with contemporary vindications of a welfare state, and thus with the perennial arguments for an interdependent, hierarchical, and paternalistic form of communalism. And that is the only realizable form of communalism if one despairs of the dream of complete equality and of communism. Conversely, Southern apologists of slavery offered some of the most perceptive early indictments of a Northern wage system, although they often did not fully understand the nuances of such a system. They believed wage dependence rested on coercive economic necessities faced by workers, hard necessities that were tied to political privileges and protections provided elite owners of pooled capital. Marx never probed the evils of the factory system, and of monopolies of capital, with greater zeal than Southerners. At the same time, Northern moralists probed all the evils of slavery, often without understanding its nuances. You know the outcome.

Within the framework of enduring constitutional forms, we have certainly alleviated some of the worst abuses of dependent labor—whether that of slaves, share croppers, or wage laborers. Today, we have neither the abject dependency that characterized the slave, nor do many people have the degree of independence, the effective liberty, and self-control, of earlier craftsmen and farmers. We have leveled down the extremes using governments to that end, but without making governments our masters. Who would deny, however, that a larger dependence on more and more government agencies threatens this dire consequence?

Two ideals symbolize the American Revolution: popular government and a free people. After many thorny challenges, popular government survives. But freedom, in the sense of independence, of being one's own boss, of eschewing all forms of deferential preference, is now an anachronistic value, seemingly at odds with economic realities. But no matter what the path we have traveled, the past still haunts us. Both slavery, at the one extreme, and open entrepreneurial opportunity, at the other, focus our sense of identity as Americans. We are what we are—Americans and thus quite distinct from Europeans—because we once were free, and abundantly so, or we once were slaves, and abjectly so.

36

DISCUSSION

PROFESSOR BROWN: Professor George Atiyeh of the Library of Congress, who was instrumental with the American Enterprise Institute in bringing us together, noted that many of you are distinguished historians, commentators, and journalists in your own right. As we look at our interaction and dialogue so far, we seem to have the deep roots of our birth and many of our scientific roots in the Arab world. There seems to be a dreadful lack of appreciation and perception of this and a lack of any interaction, as Professor Leuchtenburg pointed out. Our cultures are rooted in extremely different environments. Professor Atiyeh asked that we address ourselves as far as possible to the interaction of these diverse, but increasingly complementary cultures and the problems of getting our two cultures together. Would anyone like to raise a question or make a statement in an attempt, as Professor Atiya said, to build the bridge?

DONALD TANNENBAUM: I would be interested in hearing from the panel about those areas in which they see interaction between the cultures or perhaps common values, common institutions, or common outlooks, and the mechanisms or devices for bringing greater interaction between the cultures.

PROFESSOR CONKIN: There may be an area of common purpose between what Professor Laroui calls an Arab desire to resist the alienating and subordinating aspects of modern industrial society and what I trace in Arab proprietary origins and ideals. Perhaps there should be an effort by Americans within the context of Western industrial society to resist as long as possible the more alienating forms of labor within industrial society. Such an effort might give us sympathy for those people we call underdeveloped or nonindustrialized. It might give us some sympathy and some degree of communication with such people.

PROFESSOR LEUCHTENBURG: A few years ago, as Harmsworth professor at Oxford, I spent the year lecturing on American history, not only at Oxford but at various places in Scotland and Wales, where there were thriving programs of American study. There is a lively interest in American studies in Scandinavia, in Germany, in Israel, and in the U.S.S.R. In preparing a paper for this conference, I realized that neither I nor my colleagues had the same kind of familiarity with Arab universities. I know of no American studies programs there, or of works by Arab scholars on American history. And I wonder if that is because of my ignorance or because in fact those programs have not developed and that literature does not exist.

I was recently at Duke University, where someone told me that there is talk of an American studies program in Sudan. This is the most obvious kind of a mechanism for interchange. I wonder if there is more of it than I know of.

PROFESSOR ATIYA: The Franklin Book Programs has devoted a considerable budget to the rendering of American classics into Arabic. And I think that the project has been assigned to one of our speakers, Dr. Sahair el-Calamawy. This organization has published translations of four or five hundred American classics, which are widely circulated in the Arab world. Also, Public Law 480 authorizes the Library of Congress to have delegations in countries with blocked funds that might be used to import books from those countries into the United States. Egypt is one of those countries, and every book, pamphlet, and journal published in Egypt is exported to authorized American universities. We were among the founders of that flourishing program. While Egypt profits from the Arabization of American classics, America receives Arabic classics.

GEORGE ATIYEH: Although American books are being translated into Arabic in large numbers, the teaching of American history in the Arab World is limited to general notions found in universal history textbooks. The same may be said of the teaching of Arab history in American schools.

As far as I know only one book on American history has been written in this century by an Arab. It was by Professor Farhat Ziyadah and was published in 1947.

Certainly there are bridges being built, but the process is proceeding very slowly and precariously. The purpose of this conference is not simply to bring Arab and American intellectuals together, but to help in the building of stronger and more permanent bridges, the bridges of culture and mutual understanding. Once this is achieved, more histories are bound to be forthcoming.

PROFESSOR BROWN: I wonder if I might follow up on the original question. Professor Laroui did use the word *dreams*. He spoke of hopes and aspirations. He seems to see underneath the diversity and complexity a certain Arab specificity and certain unifying factors. American historians also speak of dreams. They also are aware of the difficulty of articulating these dreams. I wonder if Professor Laroui would address himself to the very difficult issue of the shared values and the basic humanness that comes out of these common goals and aspirations.

PROFESSOR LAROUI: I will try to clarify my position, which is very complex as you know. I did not speak about common values and common dreams because it seems to me that ideals like liberty—personal liberty, communal liberty, state liberty—mean independence, state independence, social justice, and humanism in the sense of giving man the power to master nature. These goals are values proposed by all the great civilizations, particularly those of India and China. All historical development is a kind of progressive realization of these goals. Even the two ideologies which divide the world today, Marxism and liberalism, share the same values—liberty, justice, humanism. Since we have these common values, the real problem is one of understanding. For example, everybody in the West feels he understands the Greeks because they are the common denominator of all Western civilization. People may understand Greek philosophers, but what about understanding the Greeks of today? Are they really understood by the Westerners? I am not sure.

The point is that it is not enough to understand what the Arabs did in the past. People in the universities probably understand the great Arab philosophers such as Ibn Khaldun, but that is not enough to permit an understanding of present-day Arabs. It is even possible that understanding the past may hinder an understanding of the present. After all, it is not difficult for an American to know or to accept Arab accomplishments in science or literature. But what is very difficult to understand and to accept is that the Arabs of today are different. Not different in racial terms, but in their political view of the future. The great difficulty is that people usually understand things by their relation to what they know from their own experience. There is the problem of Arab unity. Even great professors try to understand this fact by reference to Pan-Germanism, Pan-Slavism, and Pan-Americanism. Understanding something by reference to something we think we understand is, in my opinion, the great obstacle to understanding others as they are, as they want to be, and as they view their own future.

Explaining what the Arabs are is very difficult. Maybe fifty years from now we will still be discussing why the Arabs do not accept the idea of being in different states. They do not accept the idea that

Egyptians are only Egyptians and the Iraqis only Iraqis. But the fact is that they do not accept it. We cannot explain it completely, but it is a fact nonetheless.

We do not know why the Arab regimes are relatively stable, although as Arabs they have no institutions. Political scientists find this incomprehensible. How could states be stable and have no established constitutional organization? The African states, Latin American states, and even the states of Southeast Asia are not stable. The fact is that there are corrective social processes which are not institutionalized.

Therefore, it is important first of all to describe the Arabic situation as it is, without trying to explain it by reference to the past, even to the Arabic past, or to similar experiences in other countries. This is the first thing to do and the next is to accept the implications of the differences in culture, politics, social organization, and ideological affiliation. This will come in the future. Since the differences exist, the results will be different. We do not know what the result will be, but we are sure that it will be different. We have to accept this now. It is not necessary to see the Arab future in terms of Pan-Slavism. The Arab future is not the Slav present and not the Latin American present. It will be an Arab future. And, therefore, the important point is not the common values, because the values are human and are not reversible. But their realization, their apprehension, will be different but will have the same content.

KHALIL SEMAAN, professor of Arabic, State University of New York, Binghamton: I would like to return to the important question that was raised by Professor Leuchtenburg, namely, whether American history is taught in Arab universities.

I would like to add a couple of footnotes to what Professor Aziz Atiya and Professor George Atiyeh have said. In particular, I would like to stress the fact that the history of the United States is taught as a part of modern history. The contemporary history of the United States is dealt with extensively by Arab writers in relation to the Palestine Question. These political writers discuss aspects of American history and American foreign policy vis-à-vis the present state and the future of the Arab world. The work of Kāmil Abū Jābir, dean of the faculty of social sciences at the University of Jordan in Amman, is particularly notable. There have also been important works produced at the Institute of Palestine Studies.

This on the one hand; on the other, American history is usually presented to educated Arabs and students as the history of neocolonialism. This aspect of American history is stressed, especially by writers with socialistic tendencies. Therefore, American history in general and American diplomacy in particular are presented to Arab audiences from only one point of view, that of the antagonist.

What I think is interesting and important is that American literature is popular in the Arab world. As Professor Atiya has suggested, this actually was the reason the Franklin Book Programs undertook translations from English into Arabic. Translations from American letters, for example, the poetic translations by Yūsuf al-Khāl and others, were made much earlier than the Franklin Book Programs publications.

American influences on Arabic literature are many and certainly not of recent vintage. The works of Edgar Allan Poe, thanks to the French, were introduced to Arab audiences, and they exerted some influence. In our own day, T.S. Eliot (if we can call T.S. Eliot an American) has had a healthy influence on Arabic poetry and theater. I myself recently translated into English Salāh Abd al-Sabūr's *Ma'sat al-Hallāj*, which was inspired by Eliot. I transformed the title into English as "Murder in Baghdad."

America has a tremendous reservoir of good will, not only among the literate Arab masses but also in Arab universities. However, the situation is precarious. The teaching of American history in Arab universities is not on firm ground. Unless it is cultivated, the United States could lose its good will in Arab universities. This could result from the strong attacks being leveled at American foreign policy, which are reflected in the teaching of modern American history.

PROFESSOR ATIYA: I think we have to remember that there are two very important American universities in the Arab world: the American University of Beirut, and the American University in Cairo. These institutions render tremendous services to the field of American history and to Americans. In addition, we have a stream of Fulbright fellows through whom the Arab world becomes acquainted with America.

The University of Utah has an annual summer program in Tunisia. Under the auspices of the American Research Center in Egypt, of which I am one of the governors, at least thirty fellows every year do research in Egypt. They become acquainted with Egypt, and Egypt becomes acquainted with Americans.

These are minor bridges, and our duty is to widen the bridges and to multiply them whenever we can. America is not unknown in the Arab world. When I was a student, when we studied the French Revolution we also studied the American Revolution. That was many years ago, and progress has continued.

FAWZI NAJJAR, Michigan State University: I have one minor comment and then a question. The comment is in response to Professor Leuchtenburg's question concerning the interest in American programs in the Middle East. What has been said about translations and courses in universities is basically true. I even took a course on American history in my high school in Tripoli, Lebanon. I do not think we find quite the same thing taking place in the United States. Certain institutions are, however, seriously concerned with studies, sometimes original, of Arab culture and Arab institutions. So I do not think Americans need to be overly apologetic about their failure to understand the Arabs.

Americans are really doing a great deal to remedy the situation and this conference is evidence of this. Many other things are also taking place. If we look around, we find that in the last two or three decades a large number of Arabs, or Arab-Americans of Arab background, have entered academia. In earlier years there were only a few, mainly Jews who were interested in the history of the Middle East and Islam for obvious reasons. They controlled, and in many ways still control the programs in many universities. But at the same time we find the Arab element increasing where the Arabs have had the opportunity to interpret their cultures, their ideologies, and their aspirations. So I repeat, I do not think that the Americans need to be terribly apologetic. They are doing a great deal, and yet a great deal still needs to be done.

My question is addressed to Professor Laroui. You have not commented on the reason for the stability you observe in the Arab world. Since it is not essentially a political stability, or a constitutional stability, or an ideological stability, what is it then? Is religion really the basis for this form of stability, which assures a gradual adaptation to change while maintaining a unique Arabic or Islamic content?

PROFESSOR LAROUI: If we take such countries as Egypt, Lebanon, Algeria, and Morocco and compare them with the Black African states, or the Latin American states, or Indonesia, we find more political stability in the Arab world than in the others. We have only to look at Egypt. In a period of twenty years, Egypt has had only two heads, whereas many Latin American countries have had fourteen or fifteen. The same applies to Black Africa. It is a fact that there is more political stability in the Arab world than in other parts of the Third World. The reason may be that there is a specific political system behind the institutions. Take Algeria and Morocco. To journalists, the two appear to be very different states. One is ideologically aligned with the Eastern bloc, and the other is monarchical. But if we look at the real mechanism of politics in Morocco and Algeria, we see the same complex of political actions. My own conclusion is that we must go beyond the journalistic generalizations and try to see the true nature of the political system of the Arab states. It is not enough to say this state is socialistic or this other monarchical, elitist, or whatever. The reality is something deeper. Naturally I am suggesting that the political scientists try to go beyond what is apparent in the Arab political system.

PART TWO
LITERATURE

THE IMPACT OF TRADITION ON THE DEVELOPMENT OF MODERN ARABIC LITERATURE

Sahair el-Calamawy

Before beginning my paper, I would like to say why I chose this subject and how I feel it will contribute to the purpose of this conference —making bridges or bringing the two cultures together.

It is not only through drawing parallels or similarities that we build bridges between cultures. It is also by trying to see differences, in the spirit not of accepting them but rather of penetrating into their secrets in order to feel them as they are felt by the people of the other culture. Then we can see how some difficulty may paralyze those people.

My choice of a subject at the beginning was the contribution of the school of Syrian poets in New York—we call them the New School or the Immigrant School—and how much they suffered from the differences between their own culture, their own life, and the life of New York. But I would only have been able to discuss familiar aspects of Arab and American cultures. That is why I shifted to the difficulties authors in the Arab language are now suffering. So my subject became the impact of tradition on the development of the modern Arabic literature.

Tradition has an impact upon all culture but this impact differs greatly in age, intensity, and extent. A tradition may be a century old, as in some Western cultures, or it may be over a millennium as in Arab culture. It may be preserved in dead language, as European cultures are in Greek and Latin, or it may survive in a living language, as in Arab culture. Tradition may be felt chiefly in the realm of art, or it may have an impact on all aspects of human activity, as it does in Western and Arab cultures respectively.

Tradition in Arab/Muslim art and life differs somewhat from tradition in the West. In Arab cultures, tradition represents the highest qualities of excellence. *Traditional* in Arab culture means *genuine* and *excellent*. The language of a traditional poem today is the same language used by the Arab poets sixteen centuries ago. We still use the same language, more or less, with all that it implies as a way of thinking and a manner of living.

But tradition in literature has become a problem aggravated more and more by the great changes that Arab societies have been subjected to in the past century. In literature, the old poems of the pre-Islamic poets are still learned and recited by every cultured writer. These poems, said to have been written in gold and hung in the Holy House of Abraham in Mecca, are still fresh in the memory of all literature students. Moreover, the roles of rhetoric that governed their composition are still followed by many living poets of our day.

These literary rules of excellence were discovered, discussed, and then ossified for centuries. They were very binding. In the introduction to his well-known book *Poetry and the Poets,* the critic Ibn Qutaybah says he will evaluate the poets justly, regardless of their being ancient or modern, and he attacks the learned of his age for preferring the old just because it is old, even if the poetry is "stupid." Nevertheless, we are not surprised to hear the same critic affirm that there must be no deviation from the old methods in poetry: "It is forbidden for a contemporary poet to depart from the ancient forms and then stand by a newly built house and mourn the happy days that went by, because the ancient poets stood by the ruins and mourned their fleeting happiness, nor may he describe a donkey he rides because they described the camel." The new must adhere to the old model.

Many factors through the long, long years have cemented this attitude toward the classics. The most prominent is the concept of the sacredness of the Arabic language. The Sacred Book (Koran) is a miracle of language. Arabic was the tongue chosen by the Almighty to express his purpose through the angel to the Prophet. The sacred book's words were explained through usage by the pre-Islamic poets in their excellent poetry. Around the sacred book, all of the Arab cultural heritage had its roots, and the ancient poems provided the only accepted method of explaining the test of the holy Koran in any field of knowledge.

Whenever the Arabs entered a new country or were attacked by an enemy in their own, they cherished their language as an integral part of their personality. What binds the Arab world together—more than history, race, ambition, or future destiny—is the common language and the heritage of this language, especially in literature.

The Koranic text, which represents this language in its supreme excellence, is always present in the memory of all Arabs, Christians or Muslims. This text, now being chanted daily in radio and television in magnificent voices, becomes a more integral part of everyday life. People learn excellent ways of expressing themselves, and they feel that their ideas bind them together as long as the expression of these ideas is so similar. The old expressions form and shape the conception of the most modern ideas.

It is a challenge to express new feelings and ideas in an old language. For many centuries, however, the development of this language nearly stopped. After the Abbassids' golden days—that is, since the thirteenth century A.D.—lexicography and other studies of the language stopped. Repetitions, condensations, and explanations—with no new contributions at all—followed and continued until this century.

During the Ottoman period, the rulers (who in all parts of their empire were the patrons of art and artists) neither spoke nor understood Arabic. The poets were encouraged only by minor rulers, who were scarcely able to play the role of patron. When the Arabs mixed with other civilizations in the Levant, Persia, and Spain, they, being conquerors, assimilated these civilizations and propagated their own. With the Ottomans, they had no such choice. The Ottomans had no civilization, as such, and were terribly blinded by their belief in their own superiority and excellence.

In recent times, it was only natural that the parts of the Ottoman Empire that could free themselves from its yoke headed towards modernization. Egypt was the first and most prominent example. When Western or French civilization knocked on their doors, the Egyptians had many reasons not to respond, but they did respond, and the nineteenth century in Egypt witnessed a variety of ideas, creeds, and civilizations creeping into this ancient melting pot.

It took some time for literature to stir and move towards modernization, and the neoclassical era began towards the end of the century. Arabic poetry during its long life has witnessed only two attempts at innovative revolution. The first occurred soon after its golden age in the ninth century, when the famous Iraqi poet Abu Nuwas ridiculed the introduction of Arabic poetry. This was an abortive revolution, which died almost immediately. The second attempt was in Spain, and it dealt with the meter and music of the poem. Many innovations in rhyme, meter, and form developed, but the main metric system remained intact.

In modern times, there was a need to renew both form and content. The call to change the content was easier and met with little opposition. The world was already changing rapidly all around the Arab facts. There were no rulers to praise whose patronage could support the poet. The people were assuming the role of the patron. They wanted not only subjects that concerned them, but also a language they could understand.

Journalism and reformist writings opened new horizons of interest and concern, and the language tended to become simpler and nearer to the spoken dialect. Since then, concern over preserving the *Fuṣḥa* or pure language of the ancestors, has heightened significantly. The change in the poem was, after all, still limited.

With the translation of French and English poetry, new realms of thought and new images and situations became available. A translated poem proved that poetic emotions could be expressed in a simple, almost prosaic language. New music was heard and new forms of literary expression were introduced. Still, the Arabic poem remained under the influence of tradition. A school of critics in Egypt and a group of Arab poets in New York worked simultaneously to free the Arabic poem from the yoke of tradition. A romantic movement arose which was in harmony with the lyrical features of the traditional poem but moved a step forward. Some developments in rhyme were distinguishable, but the real harvest, after more than a half century, was the romantic trend, which won general approval and acceptance.

It was not until World War II that a really new type of poetry began to be firmly established. In almost all its stages since the first Islamic era, Arabic poetry has had distinguished female poets, but especially in the neoclassical, the romantic, and the new era. One of them claims to have pioneered this new movement in Iraq. Another one is our chairperson today.

This new movement, arising amid conflicting ideologies, had to change the rhyme and meter of the traditional poem, but after a quarter of a century the new forms are still not accepted in many Arab countries. The most prominent poets of this new form are condemned and have a very limited public. They are of interest to critics and literary historians only. The traditional poem is still more widely accepted, and on some occasions new poets write in the traditional form—not to prove that they can do so, as they did at the start of their career, but because a situation calls for a wide audience. Qabbani wrote in the new form but after the disaster of 1967 he wrote in the old form. Even the fervent innovator, Adonis (Ali Ahmad Said), whose works are quite eccentric, wrote a classical poem in 1975 (an elegy to an eminent dead religion scholar from Latakiya).

The new rhyme remains to be studied in great detail, but the first studies prove that it is new in only a few poems; the rest, printed differently, could easily conform to the Andalusian innovations of some centuries ago in Spain.

The constraints of the language are a great obstacle to new expressions and hence to a genuinely new poetry. Deviation from the meaning of a word in the more than seven-hundred-year-old dictionary is still regarded as a great mistake. Critics of the neoclassical era, in this century as in earlier centuries, forbade any deviation from the old poem in either subject matter or vocabulary. Change in rhyme and meter was beyond their imagination.

The question of how new a poem should be in modern Arabic literature is highly debatable. How far have the new poetic image and the extensive use of myth, legend, and symbol succeeded in overcoming the language problem?

The new forms of drama and the novel also encountered difficulties. They were rejected and condemned at first, and their pioneers had a great challenge, which most of them were unable to meet. The language problem in these forms differs from those in poetry, where a poet has seventy names for a lion and a hundred for a camel to choose from. The novelist and dramatist do not address the intelligentsia; they speak instead to a simple public that needs its anxieties and its pains expressed clearly and beautifully. The language must be understood easily by a semi-educated public. The colloquial is vivid, realistic, and nearer to the audience. But by using it not only is the prestige of a serious author lost but also there is a risk of losing the public in the Arab world.

To lose the public of the Arab world involves little economic loss (for no writer, however famous and prodigious, could live even today by his pen in the Arab world), but it does involve a loss of prestige and esteem in his own country. And thus the novelist sometimes has to sacrifice vivacity and realism. With the new media—film, radio, and television—this language problem has been further aggravated, and the heated debates around this problem often reflect political and religious feuds. Some poets like Rashid Ayoub in New York went as far as to use English words (*subway, car, submarine,* and so on) in their Arabic texts, but most writers, and especially poets, stuck to traditional or literary Arabic with very slight innovations.

Not only did the language problem confront writers in the new forms of literature, but also the subject matter proved to be a tremendous stumbling block. The struggle between man and fate is a totally alien concept to Arab culture (how much this factor has influenced the development of drama remains to be studied). The existence or necessity of such a struggle is being questioned anew because of the rise of conflicting new ideologies and social problems.

In both the drama and the novel, love themes have created another major problem. The poet could sing of his love, call his beloved, and make her talk and act lovingly; but a novelist or dramatist at the beginning could not. Folklore (*The Thousand and One Nights*)

51

abounds with love scenes and with women who act as they do in real life. But these women were slaves: free women pictured in love would be bereaved of respect. On the stage, women singers and dancers were common, but women acting in a play were not accepted. Singers and dancers were despised by the acting profession. No respectable family would tolerate a daughter becoming a singer or dancer. Until the 1920s, it was young boys who took the female roles in plays. Later female roles were played by Christian foreigners, Greeks, Armenians, Lebanese, et cetera. Only in the 1940s did Egyptian women step onto the stage, and only in the past decade has acting become an acceptable profession for women in the big cities and in some other places.

Tradition created an even greater hindrance in the action of women in the novel or in the play. Manfaluti, an eminent prose writer, both invented and translated some beautiful love stories. Mutran, an eminent poet, also wrote stories in poetry of women in love. Their favorite theme was the woman who dies in love—the young girl (rather, a child) wedded to an old man and dying in her misery, or the poor villager raped by her boss or by the son of the landowner. The theme of a woman sacrificing her love—in the manner of *La Dame Aux Camélias*—to preserve the prestige of her lover's family was repeated in many different versions. Most of the prostitutes in the works of Naguib Mahfouz (our most renowned novelist) are of this type, and they abound in his fiction. At the beginning of this century love was the subject of about 90 percent of Arab novels, and invariably the woman had to be a foreigner. A Lebanese Christian, for example, appears in al-Aqqad in the 1930s. The woman in such novels might be a poor village girl but not a member of a respectable urban family. It is interesting to follow the development and treatment of women characters in the Arabic novel. How much are local female characters based on the writer's recollections of his girl friend, especially in Paris, during his student days abroad? The woman's emancipation movement was far ahead of the women in our modern novel and theater. Women even wrote novels themselves, but unluckily some (especially in Beirut, where the whole atmosphere is freer than anywhere else in the Arab world) stuffed their writing with sex or obscenity, believing it would make them appear more emancipated. I emphatically say that I have not yet read about a truly emancipated woman in any novel by an Arab author.

The figure of the combatant woman has only recently begun to shine in our cloudy literary sky as she actually shines in our daily life. Of thirty or more novels written after the disaster of 1967, only a few omit a glorious picture of a woman who goes to fight honestly and bravely for her beleaguered country.

If life changes around us, literature is bound to change. Even if tradition is old and its impact intensive and extensive, literature must undergo the process of reconstruction. The goal is not to abolish tradition—it cannot be abolished, and in any case we cherish it and want to preserve it. The real goal is to move freely within it, as if in a framework. It has to be studied, revised, and renewed. Its old brown leaves must fall so that new green ones may grow, but the tree remains the same, always giving us its own rich fruit.

I AM DYING,
EGYPT, DYING

John Updike

I found Professor el-Calamawy's talk very suggestive and informative, and, in this matter of cultural bridges, I have been led to think about the religious importance Arab culture assigns to its language. We in English take our language rather for granted. We treat it rather roughly and shabbily. There is a kind of English called pidgin English which is spoken by most Americans now as well as by foreigners who do not know the language very well. One wonders how much the general tenor of prose, both in political speeches and in fiction and poetry has degenerated in the last two generations as people grow up without much knowledge of the King James version of the Bible and without studying Latin in school. In some curious way the study of this dead and intricate language enabled English writers, especially, to write a beautiful, clear, idiomatic English.

Evelyn Waugh, when asked about the major influence upon his very lucid style, said it was the Latin he studied in school. We have here a tradition in English that is in abeyance (though not quite faded away), and I think the general tenor of English prose has suffered accordingly.

In a paper I delivered at the Library of Congress as part of this conference,* I said that the special American experience has been the rapid taming and exploitation of an immense virgin territory discovered by Europeans at the historical moment when the Middle Ages were yielding to the centuries of technology, capitalism, and industrialism. The scope of available riches made a new sort of individualism possible.

In distinction from Latin America, the United States was settled by Protestants, and its expansion has continued right up to the moon shots in the ethos of Protestantism. I am, of course, speaking of English Protestantism and the Puritan offshoot of the Anglican church, but also to some degree the Calvinist or neo-Calvinist bias in Ameri-

---

* Editor's note: Mr. Updike's remarks repeat some he made in his paper, "The Cultural Situation of the American Writer," reproduced in full in Appendix B of this volume.

can culture. It was strengthened by the infusion of large numbers of German Calvinists and to some extent by the Irish Catholics who came later. They were more Calvinist than Calvin himself.

The communal theocracy of the Puritan settlements and the solidarity of the pioneers in the face of danger are makeshift fabrics compared with the ecclesiastical and feudal interdependencies of the Old World. By rejecting the mediating institutions of Catholicism, Luther and Calvin freed men to be independent, competitive, and lonely, and so Americans are. Also, by giving to the individual conscience full responsibility for relations with God, Protestantism in its Puritan shading conjures up a new virtue—that of *sincerity*. The abhorrence of the phony and the half-felt underlay the radical renovations of English prose and prosody by Ezra Pound and Ernest Hemingway. The same passion for sincerity, however, tends to bind the writer to a confessional honesty and to an intensity which cannot be consistently willed. Hence the American writer's erratic lapses from common sense, his frequent stridency and self-indulgence, his uncertain sense of proportion, his inability to make artistic capital out of mature experiences and social perceptions.

My characterization of American writers really describes, more or less, American professionals of any sort. Certainly the American writer does share in his general cultural situation the wish to make a "killing." A killing, in the highest sense, is certainly a pervasive American hope.

Among American novelists, Henry James is all but unique in continuing and extending his mastery through middle age and in ending strong. His career compares to that of George Bernard Shaw or William Butler Yeats or any number of European writers who improved right to the edge of the grave. And of course, James emigrated to England and became an English citizen at the end.

The American surge of agricultural settlement and industrial development created small space for the artist. Sermons and brothels were what the new land cried for. The wilderness, as it was destroyed, became in memory a paradise, and the ousted Indians its heroes. As soon as American literature found, in mid-nineteenth century, its mature voice, it scorned the enveloping creed of boosterism and expansion. "What's the railroad to me?" Thoreau asked in a poem.†

Thoreau's famous retreat to Walden Pond epitomizes a national type, the writer as hermit, as a dreamer of counter-reality. Poe and Hawthorne also epitomize this type, as does Emily Dickinson, whose shy life and exquisitely willful quatrains give us the closest we have

---

† See Appendix B.

to a literary saint. The alternative to the dreamer is perhaps the celebrant, the Whitmanesque embrace of American energy, of the splendid monism of the universe as expressed in American democracy. Yet the celebrant's posture, as later manifested in Carl Sandburg and Thomas Wolfe and Jack Kerouac, abandons tension—tension with the notions of selection and order that, whatever their position in a philosophical theory of art, seem to me essential to interesting reading.

One does not have to write very much or read very much American writing to feel this tension within one's self as well as in the authors that are read. This tension is felt between the Mandarin escapist from the circumambient reality on the one hand, and, on the other, the embracer, the lover of the American scene in its full, unselected, unsifted richness. Kerouac wrote some marvelous passages showing how he enjoys (*digs,* as they say now) the people who pick him up as he hitchhikes. These people include farmers, all of the people—the hidden people of America that Eastern establishment writers do not generally see. This wish to "dig," and dig everything, is our inheritance, I suppose, from Walt Whitman.

We read to confront reality as mediated to us by another human mind. Though Herman Melville spoke of American writers as ironic points of light, our literature contains, oddly, little light of the sort that intelligently and compassionately illumines the mundane world. The American writer, surprising to say, is rather typically baffled and disgusted by what would seem his prime subject, the daily life of his society. Instead he flees to the woods, to abroad. His wish is not so much to amuse or instruct, in Horace's famous formula, but to rape his audience, to shock it, to save it, to transform it.

Reading somebody like Norman Mailer, we feel his rage that what we hold in our hands is only a book and not a bomb, or something that could physically tear us from our easychairs and our cherished way of life.

In my youth, novels were the chief staple of the book industry. The bestsellers in those days were primarily fiction, and the writers of fiction were the heroes of the literary world. Now, I feel—and statistics bear me out—so-called nonfiction dominates, and the dominant mass medium is television. The characteristic form of television is not the play, not the made thing, not the designed fiction, but the event— the sports event, the panel discussion, the talk show, the quiz show. It seems to me that television functions in the American home as a kind of squat child of medium intelligence. Unlike the other children, this one can be turned off and on, but it is usually on. This sense of television as an electronic pet is quite strong.

I live in a small town, and walking to the store I am struck that the only house with its lights on at nine o'clock in the evening is the house I live in. All the others are dark, and, in a sense, America in general is darkening down, battening down with the television set. Television is certainly not a purveyor of art, but rather an extension of one's own family—a way to have a slightly larger family without going out the front door.

Television events are not made under conditions of high control. They happen. The language of happening and confrontation is common currency. The notion of art as an item, however exquisite of manufacture, is replaced by a sense of art as a detachable moment of the continuous dynamic medley and flow of forces that make up our immensely interconnected and self-conscious society.

Looking back, one can see the 1950s as a turning point when abstract expressionism proclaimed that painting was paint. Paint hardened in the course of the adventure of painting. When Norman Mailer was unable to write the novel his artistic superego demanded he write, he published instead a large book of fragments and self-interviews called *Advertisements for Myself.* In some insidious way, those of us with aspirations to be "serious" writers are driven to advertise ourselves. Kurt Vonnegut's new book, as it looks in the bookstore, seems to be saying, "It is me, another Vonnegut," and the cover merely echoes the back of the book, which shows Vonnegut's increasingly photogenic image.

Nor does the tide of cultural re-emphasis fail to reach the writing desk in the most intimate recesses of the creative process. When I sit down to draw a character or set a scene or devise a plot in the manner of my mighty predecessors in the art of fiction, strange forces drag at my pen. The itch to parody, a sure sign of decadence and impending revolution, takes over. The plot seems absurd, and character traits dissolve or manifest themselves as mechanical. Artlessness becomes a new art. The act of writing has become incorrigibly visible.

However determinedly one wears a veil of invention, one's own person seeps through like some overripe cheese pushing through the cheesecloth. Madison Avenue tells us that the way to sell books is to put the author's photo on the front of the jacket, not the back inside flap. Perhaps, we are reverting to some ancient bardic tradition, the harpist in the center of the mead hall. Yet, something vital goes out of fiction when the author cannot achieve self forgetfulness. An ancient magic, perhaps, comes into play with the donning of a mask. The American author, at the moment, has taken off his mask, revealing a rather vacant and embarrassed face.

On the matter of magic, it has always seemed to me that artistic endeavor, writing or not, in some way partakes of childhood magic, of the magical act of making something out of nothing, as a child would bring us a piece of paper with a drawing on it and say, "This is a man," or "This is a bear." Also there is something curiously and profoundly satisfying in making a set of something, of collecting like things. Marcel Proust somewhere says that the highest moment of art is the simile, but really the *only* literary art is the art of a simile. Proust's own breathtaking comparisons, of course, span his novel from one end to the other, but he is unique, I think, in actually defining art in terms of putting two things side by side.

At any rate, this kind of playing with the *word* and in some way making another world, I think, does belong to the world of art as distinct from the world of pronouncement, of propaganda, or even of building cultural bridges. There is something profoundly selfish and infantile about the artistic endeavor, and it is hard to harness to worthy projects, though writers, like other people, are members of society and have social consciences. I wouldn't want to take the vote from them, but I don't think the book should be asked to vote also.

I happen to have written a short story which has a little interaction in it between an American tourist and a set of Egyptians and English tourists that he encounters on a trip down the Nile. It is a fairly long story, called, after a line in Shakespeare which Antony says to his beloved Cleopatra, "I am dying, Egypt, dying."

Clem, the hero of the story, is in a way dead or dying. He is a handsome, but stiff and vacant, American, unmarried, childless, virtually parentless, but with money. He travels a great deal to relieve his loneliness, as if to find something to put into the highly polished, albeit stiff, shell of himself. The stiffness shows, and it is very appropriate to Egypt, because in the course of visiting the temples, he sees a lot of stiff-looking Pharaohs and comes to identify that stiffness as his own posture. But he cannot dance, and this, I think, emerges from these few pages of dialogue. My reading here may well be a mistake, a mistake made, however, in the name of Arab-American friendship.

Clem is boarding the boat that is going to take him down the Nile, or as you would say, up the Nile, south on the Nile.

> The boat was still tied up at the Luxor dock, a flight of stone steps; a few yards away, across a gulf of water and paved banking, a traffic of peddlers and cart drivers stared across. Clem liked that gulf and liked it when the boat cast loose and began gliding between the fields, the villages, the

59

desert. He liked the first temples: gargantuan Karnak, its pillars upholding the bright blank sky; gentler Luxor, with its built-in mosque and its little naked queen touching her king's giant calf; Hollywoodish Dendera—its restored roofs had brought in darkness and dampness and bats that moved on the walls like intelligent black gloves.

Clem even, at first, liked the peddlers. Tourist-starved, they touched him in their hunger, thrusting scarabs and old coins and clay mummy dolls at him, moaning and grunting English: "How much? How much you give me? Very fine. Fifty. Both. Take both. Both for thirty-five." Clem peeked down, caught his eye on a turquoise glint and wavered; his mother liked keepsakes and he had friends in Buffalo who would be amused. Into this flaw, this tentative crack of interest, they stuffed more things, strange sullied objects salvaged from the desert, alabaster vases, necklaces of mummy heads. Their brown hands probed and rubbed; their faces looked stunned, unblinking, as if, under the glaring sun, they were conducting business in the dark. Indeed, some did have eyes whitened by trachoma. Hoping to placate them with a purchase, Clem bargained for the smallest thing he could see, a lapis-lazuli bug the size of a fingernail. "Ten, then," the old peddler said, irritably making the "give me" gesture with his palm. Holding his wallet high, away from their hands, Clem leafed through the big notes for the absurdly small five-piaster bills, tattered and silky with use. The purchase, amounting to little more than a dime, excited the peddlers; ignoring the other tourists, they multiplied and crowded against him. Something warm and hard was inserted into his hand, his other sleeve was plucked, his pockets were patted and he wheeled, his tongue pinched between his teeth flirtatiously, trapped. It was a nightmare; the dream thought crossed his mind that he might be scratched.

He broke away and rejoined the other tourists in the sanctum of a temple courtyard. One of the Egyptian women came up to him and said, "I do not mean to remonstrate, but you are torturing them by letting them see all those fifties and hundreds in your wallet."

"I'm sorry." He blushed like a scolded schoolboy. "I just didn't want to be rude."

"You must be. There is no question of hurt feelings.

You are the man in the moon to them. They have no comprehension of your charm."

The strange phrasing of her last sentence, expressing not quite what she meant, restored his edge and dulled her rebuke. She was the shorter and the older of the two Egyptian women; her eyes were green and there was an earnest mischief, a slight pressure, in her upward glance. Clem relaxed, almost slouching. "The sad part is, some of their things, I'd rather like to buy."

"Then do," she said, and walked away, her hips swinging. So a move had been made. He had expected it to come from the Scandinavian girl.

That evening the Egyptian trio invited him to their table in the bar. The green-eyed woman said, "I hope I was not scolding. I did not mean to remonstrate, merely to inform."

"Of course," Clem said. "Listen. I was being plucked to death. I needed rescuing."

"Those men," the Egyptian man said, "are in a bad way. They say that around the hotels the shoeshine boys are starving." His face was triangular, pock-marked, saturnine. A heavy weary courtesy slowed his speech.

"What did you buy?" the other woman asked. She was sallower than the other, and softer. Her English was the most British-accented.

Clem showed them. "Ah," the man said, "a scarab."

"The incarnation of Khepri," the green-eyed woman said. "The symbol of immortality. You will live forever." She smiled at everything she said; he remembered her smiling with the word "remonstrate."

"They're jolly things," the other woman pronounced, in her stately way. "Dung beetles. They roll a ball of dung along ahead of them, which appealed to the ancient Egyptians. Reminded them of themselves, I suppose."

"Life is that," the man said. "A ball of dung we push along."

The waiter came and Clem said, "Another whiskey sour. And another round of whatever they're having." Beer for the man, Scotch for the taller lady, lemonade for his first friend.

Having bought, he felt, the right to some education, Clem asked, "Seriously. Has the"—he couldn't bring himself to call it a war, and he had noticed that in Egypt the word Israeli was never pronounced—"trouble cut down on tourism?"

"Oh, immensely," the taller lady said. "Before the war, one had to book for this boat months ahead. Now, my husband was granted two weeks and we were able to come at the last moment. It is pathetic."

"What do you do?" Clem asked.

The man made a self-deprecatory and evasive gesture, as a deity might have, asked for employment papers.

"My brother," the green-eyed woman stated, smiling, "works for the government. In, what do you call it, planning?"

As if in apology for having been reticent, her brother abruptly said, "The shoeshine boys and the dragomen suffer for us all. In everyone in my country, you have now a deep distress."

His wife put her hand on his to silence him while the waiter brought the drinks. His sister said to Clem, "Are you enjoying our temples?"

"Quite." But the temples within him, giant slices of limestone and sun, lay mute. "I also quite like," he went on, "our guide. I admire the way he says everything in English to some of us and then in French to the rest."

"Most Egyptians are trilingual," the wife stated. "Arabic, English, French."

"Which do you think in?" Clem was concerned, for he was conscious in himself of an absence of verbal thoughts; instead, there were merely glints and reflections.

The sister smiled. "In English, the thoughts are clearest. French is better for passion."

"And Arabic?"

"Also for passion. Is it not so, Amina?"

"What so, Leila?" She had been murmuring with her husband.

The question was restated in French.

"Oh, *c'est vrai, vrai.*"

"How strange," Clem said. "English doesn't seem precise to me; quite the contrary. It's a mess of synonyms and lazy grammar."

"No," the wife said firmly—she never, he suddenly

noticed, smiled—"English is clear and cold, but not *nuancé* in the emotions, as is French."

"And is Arabic *nuancé* in the same way?"

The green-eyed sister considered. "More *angoisse*."

Her brother said, "We have ninety-nine words for camel dung. All different states of camel dung. Camel dung, we understand."

"Of course," Leila said to Clem, "Arabic here is nothing compared with the pure Arabic you would hear among the Saudis. The language of the Koran is so much more—can I say it?—gutsy. So guttural, nasal; strange, wonderful sounds. Amina, does it still affect you inwardly, to hear it chanted? The Koran."

Amina solemnly agreed, "It is terrible. It tears me all apart. It is too much passion."

Italian rock music had entered the bar via an unseen radio and one of the middle-aged English couples was trying to waltz to it. Noticing how intently Clem watched, the sister asked him, "Do you like to dance?"

He took it as an invitation; he blushed. "No, thanks, the fact is I can't."

"Can't dance? Not at all?"

"I've never been able to learn. My mother says I have Methodist feet."

"Your mother says that?" She laughed; a short shocking noise, the bark of a fox. She called to Amina, *"Sa mère dit que l'Américain a les pieds méthodistes!"*

"Les pieds méthodiques?"

"Non, non, aucune méthode, la secte chrétienne—métho-disme!"

Both barked, and the man grunted. Clem sat there rigidly, immaculate in his embarrassment. The girl's green eyes, curious, pressed on him like gems scratching glass. The three Egyptians became overanimated, beginning sentences in one language and ending in another, and Clem understood that he was being laughed at. Yet the sensation, like the blurred plucking of the scarab salesmen, was better than untouched emptiness. He had another drink before dinner, the drink that was one too many, and when he went in to his single table, everything—the tablecloths, the little red lamps, the waiting droves of waiters in blue, the black windows beyond which the Nile glided—looked triumphant and glazed.

COMMENTARIES

Stanley Kunitz

This morning I heard the remark from one of the speakers that a 100 percent American is somebody with six or seven ethnic strains in his blood. That struck home. Here I am, an American, writing in English, the first generation of my family to be born here, descended from Russian, Spanish, German, and Jewish forebears, participating in a conference on Arab and American cultures. What a mishmash that is. Undeniably, civilization is a complex and polymorphous tissue.

Mr. Updike has made a brilliant and cogent presentation of the cultural situation of the American writer. In American baseball lingo, it touches all of the bases.

It has its sunny and its dark sides. It begins sunny, and it ends in, or at least moves toward, the dark. I feel closer to the dark side than to the sunny aspects. I take particular exception, however, to Mr. Updike's view that the American writer shares in the affluence of his society, and that a single best-seller, prudently managed, can guarantee him financial security for life. I doubt that this is an accurate picture of the situation of the typical American writer.

I have in my hand the September/October 1976 issue of *Coda,* the newsletter of Poets & Writers, Inc., a service organization supported by the National Endowment for the Arts. "Can Fiction Writers Make a Living?" is the theme of this issue. Here is the gist of the answer. It says that everyone knows poets have a tough life financially—few magazines pay to publish poetry, and commercial book publishers shy away from poetry collections. A widely published poet who gets a contract with a commercial publisher is luckly to get a $500 advance against royalties.

On the other hand, according to this article, rumor has it that novelists make a good living from their writing. They get thousands of dollars in advance, and book clubs and mass-market paperback sales pay them thousands more. Their books are optioned for the movies, and they often write the screenplays themselves. Look at Philip Roth, John Barth, and Saul Bellow. Not to mention John Updike, Norman Mailer and E. L. Doctorow. Erica Jong and James Dickey struggled as poets but they made it big as novelists, according to *Coda,* and these are among the few writers most people think of when asked to name an American novelist.

John Leonard of the *New York Times* says there are only a hundred or so writers in this country who can actually make a living from their books, and that includes everybody from Gore Vidal to John D. MacDonald. That's covering a lot of ground. According to Leonard, 1,300 to 1,400 serious novels are nevertheless published every year by trade publishers (2,000 if you count westerns, mysteries, science fiction, and gothics). *A Directory of American Fiction Writers* lists over 800 writers of serious fiction. There are 200 more in a recent supplement, so that makes 1,000. As to the question whether fiction writers can make a living, Aaron Ascher, the editor-in-chief of Farrar, Straus, & Giroux, one of the most prominent of American publishers, says it is "flukey" when a serious literary book becomes a number one best-seller. I think that is sad and true.

So there is a question of the survival of the writer as a representative of the serious imagination. Works of entertainment are something else again, but serious writing in this country is not particularly rewarding, except in every rare circumstances. That is a reflection on our culture.

Poets, of course, are much worse off than novelists. As far as I know, not a single serious American poet today can live off his work. I cannot think of an exception. Nor can he live with the expectation of some day coming through with a best-seller. Professor Laroui's talk this morning was entitled, "Sands and Dreams." American poets have plenty of experience with both. What I am leading to is the assertion that the poet stands outside the mainstream of the American success story. Nobody who wants money or power would choose to be a poet within the boundaries of this culture. Essentially, the poet represents the dissenting spirit, the individual's resistance to the imperatives of a highly advanced technological state with its computer will to reduce everybody to a statistic. He is a remnant of that persistent individualism which Professor Conkin described as being at the core of the American experience.

In general—now I am making very broad generalizations—the poet is suspicious of nation-states, of organized religion, of monopoly capitalism, of tyranny in any form, even when it claims to be benign. He distrusts anyone who chooses to spend his life in the pursuit of power. That generally reflects his attitude towards most politicians, politicians as a class.

So what is the function of the poet in this country, then? I see it under three main headings. One, to preserve the purity and energy of the language. Two, to record the sensibility of an age. Three, to serve as the conscience of the tribe. They are important functions, all of them.

I do not think it can be denied that America today seems to have a wavering sense of purpose and destiny. It is reflected in every aspect of our experience, and it is certainly reflected in our literature, which is less coherent, less visionary, less optimistic than it has been in the past.

No doubt there are advantages in writing in a small country during its revolutionary and formative stages. I think Mr. Updike senses that and touched on that in his paper. The Arab nations are older than the United States, but in a sense they are newer, since they are in the process of rebirth. I visited the West Coast of Africa earlier this year, and there I met with the young African poets. I had almost a sense of envy, not of their general economic condition, or of their circumstances, restricted as they are, but of their identification with a social purpose, a cultural momentum. Their feeling was that they are in the process of making the myths that will sustain their people.

At an advanced stage of a society, one loses that sense. The day of myth-making in this country is over, or at least it is temporarily over. Whether it can be renewed is a question that confronts all persons of imagination.

Even from the beginning, Walt Whitman, who created himself as our myth-maker, the voice of our poetic soul, sensed the contradiction inherent in American life. When he wrote, "One's self I sing—a simple, separate Person,/Yet utter the word Democratic, the word En masse,"/he was expressing the basic conflict between the individual and the collectivity that enters into our whole response to the pressures of existence in this culture.

With his "barbaric yawp," Whitman celebrated the beauties, the glories of this nation of nations. At the same time, in his *Specimen Days,* we find him condemning its hypocrisy and corruptions, its, to use his phrase, "hollowness of heart."

I must say that every time I leave this country for foreign adventure, I return with renewed devotion to my country, with a sense of its greatness. It is great in its promises, great in its opportunities, great in its freedoms. But at the same time, I have a feeling of a certain diminishing of its spiritual life, a feeling of a degree of exhaustion, a fear of its policy as a great power. I sense the dangers of war, of empire. And these are all present in one's imagination as one sits down at one's desk.

I will conclude these remarks by saying that I cannot stress strongly enough how close American writers and artists feel to the aspirations of the emerging peoples of the world. This is particularly true of our young writers, our young poets. Many demonstrate that identification in their translations—we have a whole spate of translations from Latin American writers, Africans, and Asians.

A few years ago, I said that there were more haikus being written in America than in Japan. Well, today everybody is writing *ghazales*— Arabic love poetry. There is an influence in that direction, too.

Let me conclude with a quotation from Marshall McLuhan in the *New York Times*. In a discussion of the presidential debates McLuhan said that young America, in its art and entertainment, now has an empathy with the Third World far exceeding its concern or devotion with the educational and economic establishment of the First World. That is something to think about.

I am happy that our distinguished chairperson has asked me to read my poem "Reflections by a Mailbox," for she told me that she has translated it into Arabic.

I wrote this poem on the eve of our entrance into World War II, when I was waiting to be drafted into the army. It has been remarked that the poem is about the holocaust. That is not entirely so, but certainly the holocaust is a presence in the poem. In moments of crisis, one tends to think back to one's origins, one's whole chain of being. In this case, I am thinking of my European ancestors. The first reference is to Hitler and to the war—the situation in Europe.

"Reflections by a Mailbox"

When I stand in the center of that man's madness,
Deep in his trauma, as in the crater of a wound,
My ancestors step from my American bones.
There's mother in a woven shawl, and that,
No doubt, is father, picking up his pack
For the return voyage through those dreadful years
Into the winter of the raging eye.

One generation past, two days by plane away,
My house is dispossessed, my friends dispersed,
My teeth and pride knocked in, my people game

For the hunters of man-skins in the warrens of Europe,
The impossible creatures of an hysteriac's dream,
Advancing with hatchets sunk into their skulls
To trip the god out of the machine.

Are these the citizens of the new estate
To which the continental shelves aspire;
Or the powerful get of a dying age, corrupt
And passion-smeared, with fluid on their lips,
As if a soul had been given to Petroleum?

How shall we uncreate that lawless energy?

Now I wait under the hemlock by the road,
For the red-haired postman with the smiling hand
To bring me my passport to the war.
Familiarly, his car shifts into gear
Around the curve; he coasts up to my drive; the day
Strikes noon; I think of Pavlov and his dogs
And the motto carved on the broad lintel of his brain:
"Sequence, consequence, and again consequence."

Selected Poems: 1928-1958
New York, Atlantic-Little, Brown, 1959

The next is a much more recent poem, which requires no introductory comment except that perhaps it does illustrate one aspect of American poetry, the identification so many of us feel with the natural universe and the strength we get from it, a strength mixed with compassion and dread.

"Robin Redbreast"

It was the dingiest bird
you ever saw, all the color
washed from him, as if
he had been standing in the rain,
friendless and stiff and cold,
since Eden went wrong.
In the house marked For Sale,
where nobody made a sound,

in the room where I lived
with an empty page, I had heard
the squawking of the jays
under the wild persimmons
tormenting him.
So I scooped him up
after they knocked him down,
in league with that ounce of heart
pounding in my palm,
that dumb beak gaping.
Poor thing! Poor foolish life!
without sense enough to stop
running in desperate circles,
needing my lucky help
to toss him back in his element.
But when I held him high
fear clutched my hand,
for through the hole in his head,
cut whistle-clean . . .
through the old dried wound
between his eyes
where the hunter's brand
had tunneled out his wits . . .
I caught the cold flash of the blue
unappeasable sky.

The Testing Tree
New York, Atlantic-Little Brown, 1971

Nizar Qabbani

I find this meeting especially exciting because I am an Arab poet from
Damascus. When I say Damascus, I do not mean to define poetry in
terms of geography, nor in presenting myself as an Arab poet do I wish
to classify poets according to their race, color, or birthplace, for any
such classification would be a form of segregation.

Poetry is a common nationality embracing all poets, no matter
whether they were born in New York, in Shanghai, or in Mecca. All
poets evoke, despite their different voices, what we call in music
"variations on a theme." That theme, I believe, is humanity.

What about the Arab and poetry, then? Under every Arab's skin, there flows a magical liquid—not oil, as the Western press would have us believe, but poetry. Arab poetry is a unique phenomenon in itself. It is the most treasured heritage of the Arabs. In their pre-Islamic days, the Arabs realized in poetry their only form of aesthetic expression. The vitality of their culture was centered on this single art form, the poem. Arab tribes greeted the coming of a poet with as much fervor as they greeted the coming of a prophet. Arabs today go to a poetry reading with as much enthusiasm as is shown for spectacles or sport events. When the Arab Empire fell, Arabic poetry entered a period of stagnation that lasted 500 years. During this period, poetry was trapped in rigid traditional modes, which were seen as holy and unchangeable. Poetry became a mere rhetorical and linguistic game. At the beginning of this century, with the spread of education and liberal ideas, a new Arab consciousness began to emerge.

While revolutionists sought to reshape the Arab world politically and socially, Arab poets were seeking to create a new poetic language, capable of expressing the new age. These attempts at innovation bore fruit in the 1940s, when Arab poets radically changed the Arabic poem in form and in content.

I began writing poetry at this critical period, when the need for innovation was being recognized and the traditional stance being defended with unprecedented tenacity. It was a long and complex struggle in which I found myself engaged, a struggle that involved an encounter with social, religious, political, and literary institutions.

The first struggle was with a conservative society, upholding the past and condemning any attempt to break through it. The second struggle was with the religious fanatics who consider any departure from their morals and ethics as blasphemy. The third struggle was against the inherited poetic forms that were considered eternal in their perfection. Finally, there was a search for a poetic language that would reconcile spoken and classical Arabic. Through my own experience, I was able to find a poetic language that proved to be a bridge between the two, a language as natural as everyday language. Since the Arab world has been a setting for political upheaval and dramatic change, the Arab poet cannot but reflect in his poetry the explosive and angry nature of his surroundings.

The meeting between American and Arab intellectuals seems to me a very natural thing. What is unnatural is that they have not met until now. Any culture should be open to all other cultures. It should affect them and be affected by them continuously. It goes without saying that the ambition of all writers at all times is to enrich the

world's consciousness. Culture should strive to bring the world together and unify its dreams. Between every artist and the world, there
is a gentleman's agreement that binds him to the service of universal
truth. Science and space discoveries have made the world much
smaller. The slightest tremor of pain in the world is a tremor in the
heart of each artist. Every artist is, by nature, against ugliness and
has as his task to protest against tyranny, discrimination, and injustice.
It is therefore logically and morally impossible for him to side with
the murderer against the murdered, with oppression against freedom,
or with the dagger against human flesh. Freedom is not a double
standard. When we are just in our land, we must be just everywhere.

This meeting gives us an opportunity to introduce ourselves face-
to-face and to converse in our real voices. It also endows us with a
sense of cosmopolitanism, which is so important to every developing
culture.

Now, I shall read two of my poems to illustrate my thoughts.
They were translated from Arabic by my niece, Rana Qabbani, also a
poet. I hope Rana will forgive me if I say that translations are always
only approximations of the original. I happen to believe in the old
axiom that translation of poetry is an act of treason.

"A Poem of Sadness"

Your love has taught me to be sad
And for years
I've been in need
Of a woman to make me sad.
A woman to gather me up
Like bits of broken glass.

Your love has made me
Roam the streets
Looking for your face
In rain, in city lights,
In colored ads
Pasted on the wall.
And I grow lost,
Lost for hours
Searching for a face
That is all faces and a voice
That's every voice.

You take me back to childhood,
And I draw your face in chalk
On fish nets,
On bells,
On crosses

Your love has drawn me deep
Into fairy tales,
And in waking and in sleep
I dream of a king's young daughter
With her eyes as clear as water.
I dream I carry her off
On my fierce dark horse.

I've learned of how I love you
In the smallest things,
In rain,
In trees made bare,
In their yellowed leaves.
I've learned to cry without crying.

Your love has made me seek refuge
In hotels with no names,
In churches,
In cafes with no names.
And how the pulse of earth is faster
And the stars have all grown nameless
Since they learned your name.

Translated by: Rana Qabbani

"Bread, Hashish and Moonlight"

When the moon is born in the East
And white rooftops drift asleep
Under the heaped-up light,
People leave their shops
And go in groups to meet the moon.
They carry bread, and music
And narcotics
To the mountains
Where they trade in fantasies,
And die as the moon is being born.

What does that disc of light do
To my country, the land of the prophets,
And of the simple,
The chewers of tobacco
And merchants of narcosis?
What does that moon do
That we lose our valor
And live to beg from heaven?
And what does heaven have
For the lazy, for the poor?
When the moon out of nowhere comes alive
They become corpses
They shake the tombs of saints
Hoping for rice and children
In our country,
In the country of the simple.
What weakness, what decay
Take hold of us
When the moonlight steeps the carpets
And the teacups and the children
In its flow?
The simple live without their eyes,
They pray,
Commit adultery
And dream of bread
Because there is no bread except in dreams.
They live in resignation, calling to the moon:
O crescent,
O fountain raining diamonds
Hashish and sleepiness,
Unbelievable thing
And marble god,
May you always shine above our East
In these Eastern nights,
Millions who are barefoot,
Who believe in resurrection
And live in houses full of coughing
Fall down before the moon
In my country
Where imbeciles weep and die of weeping
Whenever that crescent shines
And are lulled to sleep by past myths

And dazed dreams
And a lute
Beneath a newborn moon.

Translated by: Rana Qabbani

Salma Jayyusi

What I would like to take up are some of the issues that I think are relevant to this particular meeting of cultures. A conference like this, which aims at bringing together face-to-face two basically different cultures is bound to bring forward the various incompatibilities between them. Unless these are allowed to surface, it would not have served its purpose.

American and Arab writers belong, historically, to two different worlds: the Old World, with its vast inheritance of traditions in literature and society, and its age-old folklore, and the New World, which, although the heir of a long experience in all spheres of human endeavor, has enjoyed a greater capacity to transcend, choose, and reject and has not been weighed down with this inheritance as the Old World has. It could create its own world anew. Moreover, American and Arab writers are the heirs, culturally, of two different *Weltanschauungen*—a Christian versus a Moslem, and a Western versus an Eastern, outlook on man and his universal experiences. Most importantly, the two worlds of the American and the Arab writers belong to two different phases of historical development: the American, enjoying now the fruits of technical progress and an already established secularization of the mind, has a relative political and ideological stability, while the Arab world is passing through a most dynamic and turbulent transformation in all facets of experience. We can speak of Arab society at the turn of this century as being overwhelmingly traditional and agricultural, with a strong religious framework binding its ways of life and its quality of thinking. However, the past three-quarters of the century have been enormously eventful.

The spirit of the twentieth century has invited rejection of the old inherited norms and ways of life. This spirit, which has created the two poles of freedom and responsibility for modern man, has also made sure that developing nations realize they should achieve modernity and progress in the shortest possible time, and gain their freedom from all kinds of constraints, whether internal and traditional or imposed from the outside.

The Arab world, one could say, has been struggling for a long time

75

for this self-realization. In this struggle, the Arab world has been involved in a continuous process of discovering itself and its vast potential, as well as uncovering the complex and intricate realities that kept it so long in chains. All change has been wrought with difficulty and labor. Often a relapse takes place in one sphere or another, stemming sometimes from basic internal contradictions, sometimes from external causes, and so much human endeavor is pathetically wasted. However, the Arab world—indeed all the developing world—can only go forward. These relapses can delay but they cannot deter.

If there is to be any authentic cultural understanding and interaction between contemporary American and Arab cultures, the basic differences both in original cultural patterns and in the kinds of problems confronted within these cultures should be understood, not only with the intellect but also with sympathy and respect.

American art forms have exerted an influence throughout the world, including a strong one on the Arab world. This influence, together with a practical interest in acquiring knowledge of Western culture, has ensured an acquaintance among Arab artists with the more general aspects of American culture. Unfortunately, this influence has not been reciprocated. In the United States, it is still possible to encounter persons with undeniable intelligence who will readily reduce all 1,500 years of Arab experience to the mechanics of desert life and the management of the harem.

Opportunities for serious cultural exchange of the sort we are enjoying in this conference are rare. We should put them to use by making a genuine attempt to live inside the other's world, even for only a few days. We should then seek a basis for a continuous and honest interest in each other's experiences and achievements, and we should seek to understand and feel each other's problems. Mr. Kunitz was right when he said once that the web of the universe is a continuous tissue. Touch it at any point and the whole web shudders.

The Arab writer today is unavoidably enmeshed in myriad problems and conflicts. He knows that in order to survive as a writer he must be the conscience of his people and cannot for a moment ignore the need to express their aspirations and dilemmas. The Arab world is in a state of continuous turmoil as a result not only of the various political problems but also of the sometimes traumatic experience of transforming an agricultural, metaphysically based culture into a modern one. Arab writing, therefore, is often on the point of crisis. It is difficult to imagine an Arab novel based on a theme similar to Mr. Updike's *Rabbit, Run,* which, though highly critical of society, relates its shortcomings to the personal and private experience of the individual, subtly informed by a religious background. Mr. Updike is quoted as having said that he favored middles, never extremes. The contemporary Arab writer, however, particularly the poet, is usually writing about extreme situations. Again, many of Mr. Kunitz's poems reveal a calmness, an aesthetic involvement, and sometimes a joy that are rarely found in contemporary Arabic poetry. Even a poem like his much discussed "Father and Son," on his dead father, is, despite its basic melancholy and anguish, a calmer and more private expression than that of his Arab colleague who tends to be more communal and less personal. It is, in fact, with such poems as his "Reflections by a Mailbox" on the Jewish holocaust in Europe, an extremely moving poem, that a contemporary Arab poet can feel most empathy.

Mr. Updike describes the greatly varied aspects of America as the background of the American writer. The Arab writer, too, has behind him a scene so varied that were it not tragic at times, it would be exhilarating. The great variety of geographical scenery, which stretches from the Arabian desert to cover half the fringes of the Mediterranean, is studded with ancient towns steeped in history and traditions and with new cities aspiring to modernity.

The political and social scene is also astounding in the drastic differences in points of emphasis and pace of development. However, the multiplex divisions of the Arab world into so many countries, each not only with its own vernacular but also with its own political, economic, and, above all, ideological identity, would perhaps lead the observer to expect great differences in the thematic and linguistic elements of literature, as well as in attitudes and world view. However, the general panorama of contemporary Arabic literature does not yield to these frontiers. Poets all over the Arab world, for example, may be divided without much difficulty into traditionalists and avant-garde. The former extol the virtues of the traditional culture, which has been cohesive since time immemorial, as Professor el-Calamawy has so well explained, and the latter meet miraculously even across the borders in their methods, interests, and attitudes. Indeed, contemporary avant-garde poetry has offered the most unified expression of the Arab world's hopes and despair, and several critics have written on avant-garde Arabic poetry since the 1950s as a coherent whole. In the fiction of the Arab world, thematic variations often reflect greater local concerns, but there is a widespread similarity in both the objects of rejection, such as rigid social norms, outdated taboos and habits, and various kinds of oppression and evil, and the objects of aspiration, such as freedom, justice, modernity, progress, and the conquest of contemporary evil. Literature is a central activity of the Arab world.

In his essay, "Poet and State," Mr. Kunitz spoke of the modern crisis of poetry in the West, and the general apathy to it. In the Arab world, however, poetry is still in great demand, and poetry recitals are an important tradition, which seems to flourish even more with the years. In literature more than in any other cultural activity of the Arab world, the deeper currents of thought and the predominant attitudes governing the movement of life are reflected and sometimes anticipated.

The Arabic language, in its modern written form, has also transcended the frontiers. It has been developing steadily towards greater simplicity and modernity all over the Arab world. We see this development not only in prose but also in poetry. Poets like Nizar Qabbani, Abd al-Wahhab al-Bayyati, and Salah Abd al-Sabur were able to arrive at great simplicity, sometimes simulating the intonations of the vernacular. It is not surprising that the first is Syrian, the second Iraqi, and the third Egyptian.

Finally, Mr. Updike spoke of the great freedom of the American writer, in that he enjoys freedom of speech and of the press. The glorious right to speak one's mind, to have the constitutional liberty to describe the truth with honesty and fearlessness, is one of the greatest gifts that man can give himself. However, the absence of such a freedom in certain parts of the Arab world should not be an indictment of Arab culture or the Arab people. Traditionally, the voice of the Arab writer during this last century, a century of change and upheaval, has been the voice of dissent, of protest, of courage and initiative. As I indicated earlier, it has been the voice that crystallized and gave expression to the repressed but very real voice of the people. The freedom of the writer is always intimately related to other freedoms and issues. Because Arab society is at the juncture of great changes, repression is used to contain and control that which promises to be far-reaching. It is the reaction of the old order of things, defending itself against the new order, which is determined to be a part of the twentieth century.

DISCUSSION

JACK HAYS: It struck me during the discussions on literature that there was one category of American writers that was neglected by everyone. I was thinking of songwriters. In the United States, this category is accorded little respect, and it is segregated from literature in general, but I think that is not generally true in the Middle East. Some American songwriters have been enormously powerful and have made a great deal of money with songs like "Joe Hill," "This Land Is My Land," "We Shall Overcome," and "Blowing in the Wind." Songwriters like Bob Dylan are certainly powerful and rich, but are not part of our literary scene. Would anyone care to comment on the role of songwriters in the Middle East?

PROFESSOR EL-CALAMAWY: Songwriters in our literature are of two types. Some of them are very learned poets, who write in the classical or even in the new form of poetry and who also write songs. Then there are those who write in the vernacular and are the more appreciated by the public, but they are not esteemed much as literary men. We call them "songwriters," and their poetry is not registered or studied in the universities or schools. Their poems are sung at home and in the streets but are never recited in schools and are never appreciated as a text.

But again tradition is a factor here. The best singers—the ones most esteemed by the public—are those that sing old classical poetry, like our famous singer Um Kulthum. She built her career on traditional songs, and now that she is dead, she is remembered for them. The songs we sing in our daily life may influence our thinking but they are of temporary value. They never last, and so their effect never lasts.

MR. KUNITZ: How are the songs transmitted? How do the people hear them? Are they presented in public or on television or what?

PROFESSOR EL-CALAMAWY: The singers are very much esteemed by the public, and they are public heroes. Their performances are very well attended by people from every class. But their popularity is ephemeral, and it depends on the singer rather than the song or the words. It is the singer and his voice that make people listen, and I think that is true everywhere.

BRUCE STANLEY, University of Pennsylvania: I spent two years teaching school on the West Bank, and some of my students suffered from something Mr. Updike mentioned—that is, the boob tube or television. I would like some comment on the problems that may arise from the increase in television—and especially American movies—on young Arabs, and especially its effect on poetry.

MS. QABBANI: I think that television is a poisonous medium because it is brought into every home in such a large degree. Most of the films we receive in the Arab world are, of course, commercial films, in which violence and sex are sometimes portrayed in ugly ways. In the Middle East, I think we need a kind of television that would direct the minds of children, especially, into a higher level of culture. Therefore we need programs that are especially fitted to our own culture and our own goals.

KAMAL BOULLATA, a Washington painter: I would like to ask John Updike if he would comment on the period in his life when he wrote his last poem and when he decided to write his first novel.

MR. UPDIKE: The fact is, I still have hopes of writing more poems. I think that there has been in my life a general displacement of the poetry by prose—and not entirely because, as Mr. Kunitz underlined, there is no living in poetry and there is a possible living in prose, although that was a factor. I think that in the United States, in my lifetime at least, all poetry has been somewhat romantic. Poetry depends somewhat upon an intensity of emotion and perception which are more common to young men than to older men. The fact that the poem can be completed in a short time, in a sitting, is inviting to young people, who lead a very broken up kind of life, and it is not dependent so much on observation. It requires some feeling and some verbal facility.

I began by writing poetry that was published in my early twenties, and I think I am proudest of my second book of poems, which came out about 1963. Since then I have not written much poetry. There is an invisible point in time when the poet in one dies, or at least surrenders or retires, and that perhaps has happened to me. If I had to, I would pinpoint it at about the age of thirty-five. This has not happened to Mr. Kunitz, I hasten to add. It need not happen to anyone.

MR. KUNITZ: I was particularly interested in Professor el-Calamawy's comments on the resistance to change in the Arabic tradition. It seems to me this is a profound contrast with American culture. As far as writing is concerned, I think the most popular slogan among young writers of the twentieth century in the United States has been Ezra Pound's dictum, "Make it new." There has been a real cult of novelty. Of course, it is easier to make it new than to make it good, and maybe that is one of the attractions of that slogan.

Change is implicit, it seems to me, in the nature of the American imagination. It is not always change for the better, but there it is, as a phenomenon of the practice of letters in this country. In working with young poets I noticed that contrary to the experience of Arabic poets it has been impossible to interest them in traditional poetry. They do not want to read the poets of the tradition, even though they are planning to be poets themselves. The oldest poet that they will think about is one who is perhaps in his fifties. Beyond that is ancient history, as are the forms in which the poems were written. Prosody—conventional prosody, and all of the conventional forms—have actually been abandoned for years.

As I say, it has been impossible to interest young poets in prosody, but now I notice there is a certain recognition that they have been missing something. This year, for the first time in the last decade, the young poets I have been working with in the writing program in the graduate school at Columbia University have asked for instruction in prosody and in the poetry of the tradition. In fact, they have demanded it and I think that is a very interesting sign. Perhaps it represents a certain shift in values.

PROFESSOR JAYYUSI: In Lebanon, Syria, and Iraq, free verse is an established form, and even in Egypt there is not a single avant-garde poet who writes in the old form now. I have not found any, and I have written at length on this poetry. I do not think there is any established avant-garde poet who is now writing only in the old form of the two hemistichs. I am extremely fond of the old form, but I wonder why many of the old school cannot stomach free verse.

There is no new poet in the Arab world who writes in the old form. These poets write in the new form, in free verse, and some free verse poets are extremely popular. Qabbani and Mahmud Darwish are two of the most popular poets the Arab world has ever known. They are very, very popular. People read them, and there are books of translations in more than one language.

PROFESSOR EL-CALAMAWY: I may have been misunderstood in saying that some of the avant-garde poets—or the poets of free verse as we call them—have gone back to writing classical, old form poetry. I just mentioned that the old forms still exist, and that these poets sometimes resort to them as Qabbani has when he wanted to reach a larger audience. When Adonis (Ali Ahmad Said) was writing an elegy for a distinguished religious scholar, he decided that free verse and the new forms would not sit well with those who came to mourn. I do not think that Qabbani is writing classical poetry now, but I did want to comment that the old form still has an attraction even for those who have so zealously established free verse.

In regard to the fame and renown of the avant-garde or the free verse writers, we should look upon the Arab world as a whole, and it is not small. In Saudi Arabia, for instance, I do not think Qabbani is esteemed.

PROFESSOR JAYYUSI: They have now started writing free verse in Saudi Arabia.

PROFESSOR EL-CALAMAWY: Yes, I don't know that he is considered a great poet in the Maghreb as he is in Syria, Lebanon, Iraq, and Egypt. For example, in the poetry festivals held each year in one of the capitals of the Arab world, Qabbani himself uses the classical form when the country happens to be Iraq—whose capital is very modern in its poetical trends. He considers that the people who come from Najaf and Karbala and so on will not appreciate his new poetry. Ali that I can say in favor of free verse is that it stands a fifty-fifty chance in competition with the old poetry.

PROFESSOR JAYYUSI: That is very kind of you.

PROFESSOR EL-CALAMAWY: A fifty-fifty chance.

MR. KUNITZ: Is there an influential body of modern critical theory on the new poetry?

PROFESSOR EL-CALAMAWY: Yes, there is a body of critical theory. There are critics who defend this new form, scholarly, vehemently, and perhaps emotionally. Still, in Egypt for instance, it is not easy for Salah Abd al-Sabur, our famous free verse poet, to establish himself as the poet of an era. He is knocked down by many classical poets.

PROFESSOR JAYYUSI: Not knocked down.

PROFESSOR EL-CALAMAWY: Well, that is what he feels. Salah Abd al-Sabur sometimes refrains from participating in poetry festivals because of that feeling. He is not sure the audience would appreciate his poetry, and he is not emotionally ready to express himself in old poetry, so he just abstains. There is still a firm stand for the old poetry. That does not mean the new poetry is not solidly accepted and appreciated, especially by a large part of the intelligentsia.

MR. KUNITZ: I have one more question, about publishing. Is publishing privately or officially controlled?

PROFESSOR EL-CALAMAWY: That differs from one part of the Arab world to the other.

PROFESSOR JAYYUSI: Professor el-Calamawy was the chairman of the publishing house.

PROFESSOR EL-CALAMAWY: I am not connected with that any more.

PROFESSOR JAYYUSI: Mr. Qabbani has his own publishing house. I am sure that he is free—

MR. QABBANI: Yes, I am a free publisher.

PROFESSOR EL-CALAMAWY: Do you publish anything but your writing?

MR. QABBANI: No.

PROFESSOR EL-CALAMAWY: He is a personal publisher.

MR. QABBANI: Because that is the best way of publishing. In regard to traditional and new forms, I don't believe that we should be made to feel controlled by the form. Every poet is free to choose any form that he feels is adequate for portraying his feeling and emotions, but we must not forget that the Arab person and the Arabic ear is tuned to a certain kind of music and a certain appreciation of that music in poetry. In Cairo, for example, if I find myself reading an elegy to Taha Hussein, a great figure in Arabic literature, I prefer to use a classical poetic form, because Mr. Hussein taught us discipline and perfection. Therefore, the form I would use to eulogize him would be a disciplined and controlled one.

But, of course, the form is not important. What is important is what expresses the poet. Again, I feel that I am not a poet of the elite or of the intelligentsia. I am a poet of all people. Since most Arab people are more in tune to classical poetry, when I wish to reach a larger audience, I revert to it, as I did when I wrote "Tarsi."

KHALIL SEMAAN, State University of New York at Binghamton: Everybody here has said how important tradition is to an appreciation of Arabic literature, of poetry as well as prose style. Professor Jayyusi, what sort of feeling have you found in your Algerian students for the Arabic literature?

PROFESSOR JAYYUSI: That is a very interesting question. Actually, most Algerian students who study Arabic are not bilingual. They know only Arabic. They might know a little French as a second language. One might have thought that all Algerians know French fluently, but that is not the case. Most of my students in Algeria—and I had very large classes, 80, 100, or 120—had been students only of Arabic. Although many Algerians have grown up speaking colloquial Arabic, they are not yet strongly versed in Arabic literature, so they are not as enthusiastic about poetry and literature as are other students in the Arab world. Some of them are, of course, and, among the Arabic-speaking Algerians who speak no French, some talented writers are appearing now and trying their hand at poetry and the short story in particular.

Of course, in Algeria we have a very long tradition of French writing, in both poetry and prose, some of which is excellent. Arabic, however, is still a problem in Algeria. Sometimes there was not very much rapport between the students and the teacher of literature, but I think that is improving.

MUHAMMAD SITHUM, University of Tunis: I just wanted to make a remark about Mr. Qabbani's popularity in North Africa. I do not know about Algeria, where the problems of the Arabic language, as we just heard, are very complex, but in Tunisia I know that 50 percent of all collections of poetry imported from the Middle East come from Mr. Qabbani's publishing house. There is not a day that passes in Tunisia in which a child is not given Mr. Qabbani's first name.

PART THREE
CULTURE

RATIONAL ASPECTS OF THE CLASSICAL ARABIC CULTURE

Zaki Naguib Mahmoud

"Rational" thinking is meant here to include not only the narrower sense of the word, which limits it to the deductions of a logician or a mathematician, but also the wider meaning, which extends to the procedure of formulating scientific laws or generalized social judgments, through observation, experiment, or just daily experience. It is the kind of thinking which requires proofs for assertions, causes for effects, purposes for action, and principles for conduct. It is thinking in terms of grounds and consequences, or in terms of evidence and conclusions.

What is excluded from rational thinking is knowledge obtained in an immediate way, either from direct revelation, or from intuition—the knowledge that is common among mystics. Not that the classical Arabic culture is void of such immediate sources. On the contrary, revelation and mystic intuitions loom very large in this culture. My intention here, however, is to stress some of the rational aspects, which are too often neglected.

As to the term *Arabic* mentioned in the title, what is meant here is the Arabic-speaking community, whether the people are Arabs by race or not. Indeed, among the so-called Arabic philosophers, scientists, historians, grammarians, and theologians, many were not racially Arabs. They were Persians, Turks, Egyptians, or Berbers by birth, but used the Arabic language as their means of expression. The Arabic language was the common medium of all the Islamic world throughout the centuries known in the history of the West as the Middle Ages. In the history of the Arabs, the period from the seventh to the fifteenth centuries was not their middle ages; it was their zenith.

Rational Approach to Language

Less than a century after the appearance of Islam in the first half of the seventh century, there arose all sorts of problems related to the new religion. The Koran, the sacred book of Islam, is in the Arabic language. Its literary standard has been taken by the Arabs themselves as repre-

87

senting the highest possible peak, demonstrating the real genius of the language. To understand its text satisfactorily, one must first fully grasp the Arabic language as such. It is, therefore, understandable that among the early activities of Arabic scholars was the detailed study of the language. This was done on truly academic bases.

Linguists and grammarians, beginning in the early eighth century, busied themselves with the formulation of rules, as deduced from the actual use of the language in its past literature. Grammar was thus created for the first time. Also created were the rules of linguistic derivation. Perhaps for the first time in history an alphabetical dictionary was compiled. The rules of poesy, including rhyme and meter, were set, based on existing poems composed by the earlier masters of the art.

It is not the intention here to present a table of achievements in the field of language, but rather to indicate the scientific procedure adopted in all those activities.

Rational Approach to Jurisprudence

Next to the study of language came the matter of jurisprudence. Most important was how to deduce rules of behavior from the Koranic text. In so doing, it was not language alone that was needed, but a logical method of deduction as well. The codification of such rules, using, as they did, the stringent procedure of logic, may be the masterpiece of all Arabic rational activity. It is even tempting to say that the method adopted by the leading jurists was rather Euclidean in form. A jurist would start in the way Euclid did, with a certain number of assumptions, including definitions, axioms, and postulates.

Jurists differed, however, either in the details of their procedure, or, a fortiori, in their conclusions. There were two principal schools of thought. Of course there was no difference between them whenever a case was explicitly mentioned in the Koranic text or in the prophet's traditions. Their difference arose with regard to cases for which there was no precedent. One of the schools would say that in such cases the opinion of an experienced judge would do. In this view, values were objective truths. A man of wisdom could intuit what was right and what was wrong.

The other school thought differently. It held that cases not covered by the sacred text should be judged only by way of analogy. Such cases had to be assimilated by others mentioned explicitly either in the Koran or in a Tradition (Hadīth) of the Prophet. What concerns us here, it will be remembered, is the logical approach to problems. Jurisprudence in the classical Arabic culture was nothing less than a sort of applied logic.

The Influence of Greek Writings

In 832, an academy was founded in Baghdad for the translation into Arabic of Greek philosophy and science. Significantly, the academy was called the House of Wisdom. In about half a century, the Arabic-speaking world possessed, in its own language, almost all the works of Aristotle, a considerable part of Plato's dialogues, a large part of the Neoplatonic commentary, the works of Galen, and large portions of the works of other medical writers.

While the ancient Arabs were keen on translating Greek philosophic and scientific material into Arabic, they did not give even a cursory glance at Greek literature. They were too proud of their own literature to think that any other literature could be worth their while. Also, they apparently believed that whereas philosophy and science were the business of humanity at large, literature was of only local interest.

This is a suitable place to mention the high importance of Aristotle's *Organon* in the classical Arabic culture. Aristotle's logic together with the Arabic grammar were indispensable parts of any educational curriculum. No matter what the subject matter, logic and grammar were included.

It is common knowledge that Greek philosophy, Aristotelian philosophy in particular, passed to Latin Christendom through the Arabic version of that philosophy. Averroes is known among students of philosophy in Europe and America as the Commentator, that is, the commentator and the chief interpreter of Aristotle.

The Peripatetic (Aristotelian) school of classical Arabic philosophers, which includes such prominent figures as Avicenna and Averroes, is too well known to need comment. What should be noted is that there is a close similarity in the mental framework between the Greek philosophers and the Arabic thinkers, and this is evidence of a rational tendency among the latter.

The principal theme of the Arabic philosophers was the search for a compromise between Greek philosophy, as representing the human intellect, and Islam, a revealed religion. The quest for a link between religion and philosophy resulted in a masterpiece of Arabic philosophical literature, a book by Ibn Tufayl called *Hayy Ibn Yaqzan* (The Living [person] being the son of the Vigilant [God]). It is a story about a baby left alone on a deserted island. He possessed nothing more than his innate ability to get to know his environment and to make use of it. When Defoe's Robinson Crusoe set foot on his island, he had been reared among civilized fellow human beings; he had secured some education and this guided him in his solitary life. But "The Living" in the

Arabic story was left on the deserted island when he was only a few days old. While he was a helpless baby, a deer fed him and looked after him. He found himself face to face with nature, without any former knowledge. From observation and contemplation, he got to know something about natural phenomena, and about the things around him. In the end he discovered the existence of God, together with a large body of ethical values. In other words, he independently reached the main principles of Islam. This meant to the author that philosophy and religion were one. The human mind and divine revelation converged on a single point.

Mathematics and Science

These fields were no less conspicuous in the rational sphere of the Arabic culture than philosophy proper. Distinguished among mathematicians was the family of Thabit ibn Qorra, which lived in the ninth century. It was the Arabic culture that created algebra; the very word *algebra* is an Arabic word. *Logarithm* is so called after its Arabic author. The numbers used today are the Arabic numbers. Although the numbers may have been taken from India, the Arabic-speaking community used them and transferred them to the world in general. The number zero was created by Arabic mathematicians. Its Arabic name, *cipher,* is still used in many languages.

As to science, let it suffice to mention one name: Jabir ibn Hayyan. It was said by a historian of science that Jabir was to chemistry what Aristotle had been to logic. Each was the originator of his field. Initially, chemical research was concerned with the transmutation of metals, but it soon came to serve medicine. The process of changing baser metals into gold, considered alchemy and not deserving the modern name chemistry, is no longer regarded an impossible dream. Many treatises by Jabir on chemistry were translated into Latin, his name appearing as Geber.

Rationality in Theology

Two eminent groups of rationalists appeared during the first four centuries of Islamic history. One was the Mutazilites (secessionists), and the other was the Brethren of Purity.

The Mutazilites were theologians who considered reason to be the only basis for interpreting the Koranic text. Wherever the text seemed to contradict logical reasoning, it would be interpreted in such a way as to remove the contradiction. An example is the problem of freedom of the will. A number of verses in the Koran explicitly refer to the predestination of man. If true, man's moral responsibility would be meaningless. The Mutazilites, therefore, tried to find a way of explaining such verses so that they would not cancel out human freedom. In attempting to save man's freedom without encroaching upon the divine omniscience, they showed high analytical abilities, and were aided by the Greek logic and philosophy that had just been introduced into their language.

Opposed to the Mutazilites, there appeared a moderate group led by al-Ash'ari. The Ash'arites did not want to carry reasoning too far. Rationality, they felt, should extend only as far as the human intellect can go; beyond that limit one should depend on faith. This Ash'arite position with respect to rationality in religious matters has recently been revived in the contemporary Muslim world by Mohammed Abdu, one of the most distinguished intellectuals of modern Egypt.

The other group of rationalists, the Brethren of Purity, appeared in the tenth century. Like the Encyclopedists of eighteenth-century France, they aimed at public enlightenment based on science and rational philosophy. They cooperatively created a four-volume encyclopedia, consisting of fifty-one lengthy chapters, to which they added a separate general summary of their point of view. This work contains most of the then known material in mathematics, physics, psychology, and jurisprudence.

The brethren joined the attempt to find a compromise between religious teachings and scientific truths. In case of discrepancy, they gave priority to science or philosophy. "Religion," they said, "is a medicine for the sick, but philosophy is food for the healthy. Prophets deal with the morally defective, helping to set them right, or at least to keep them from getting worse. But philosophers deal with sound people, helping them to keep their mental health at its highest level."

Other Writings

Even in history and literary criticism one can easily see the rational bent. Historians often related events to their social or environmental causes. Although I have made it a point to avoid unfamiliar names, one name in the field of sociological history should be mentioned. It is Ibn Khaldun, the philosopher of history, who, in his famous *Prolegomena,* founded the field of sociology.

In literary criticism the scientific approach was stressed, that is, the criticism took the form of linguistic analysis of the text to explain literary values causally.

It is my hope that the few examples I have given are sufficient to show the nature and extent of the rational thinking in the classical Arabic culture.

AMERICAN CULTURE AND THE IDEA OF COMMUNITY

Robert Nisbet

"In what fundamental ways, if any," asks Professor Leo Marx, "is American life unique?" This question, as he acknowledges, has been a persisting one in American life and letters for more than two centuries.[1] We find it, along with proposed answers, in a wide variety of American writing—philosophical, literary, autobiographical, and political. We find the same question, along with efforts to answer it, in a great diversity of works written by foreigners on the subject of American culture. From the time Crevecoeur wrote his *Letters from an American Farmer,* published in London in 1782, and only after some rather distressing experiences in wartorn America, the question "What is an American?" has proved to be an engrossing one to luminaries in Europe and, equally, to Americans themselves. At least two authentic classics in the literature of political philosophy have been produced by Crevecoeur's question: Tocqueville's *Democracy in America* and Lord Bryce's *The American Commonwealth.* Almost without number are the essays, memoirs, and travel accounts of Europeans and Americans alike seeking to plumb the depths of American character: warts, idiosyncrasies, and vices, as well as ornaments and virtues.

Leo Marx, commenting on the diversity of answers to the question, wonders if the uniqueness of American culture may not consist simply in the presence and persistence of the concept itself: "the powerful hold on national consciousness of the concept itself, the pervasive, slow-dying American belief in the nation's unique, not to say, providential destiny."[2] He may well be correct. Certainly, it is impossible to scan the nearly three centuries of American writing without being made aware of how powerful this belief, this concept, has been. Only in our own day, since approximately World War I, has there been a conspicuous waning of confidence, by Americans and others, in the providential character of our destiny. Whether this erosion of belief is to prove a permanent process, one set in the contexts of disenchantment and disillusion, which

---

[1] Leo Marx in *The New York Times Book Review,* February 1, 1976, p. 21.
[2] Ibid.

have been so obvious in recent decades and not likely soon to become reversed, is too difficult a question to seek to answer here.

I want, in any case, to turn to another important element of American culture, one that has been present from the beginnings of American history and has at no time been more conspicuous than at the present moment. This is the idea of community. It has been more than an idea, as I shall indicate; it has been, from earliest times, a quest. Indeed, much of the thought and passion which have gone into the concept of American uniqueness, and of American progress, is derived from a preoccupation with community.

By community I mean much more than local community, or for that matter national community, although both of these are not to be ignored. I have reference, rather, to any form of sustained relationship—religious, social, political, economic, local, occupational—in which the dominant values are a strong sense of individual membership, of cohesion, moral solidarity, continuity in time, a feeling of distinctive function or mission, along with a heightened regard for "we-ness" in contrast to "they-ness." Americans have been on the whole much more prone to celebrate the themes radiating from individuality and self than those connected with community. I would not diminish these; they are clearly parts of American culture and have many manifestations. But I am nevertheless inclined to think that the quest for community has been a powerful, and relatively neglected, aspect of American cultural history, and it will be the subject of these pages.[3]

Errand into the Wilderness

The quest for community is evident in the writings and works of our Puritan ancestors in New England. The ideal of community is luminous in the lines of John Winthrop, written in 1630 on the *Arabella* bound for New England, in which he refers to "our Communion and Community in the work, our Community as members of the same body." Despite all that has been written on Puritan individualism, itself largely an assault on Romanist corporatism, there is a conspicuous emphasis in Puritanism on community, visible as well as invisible, from the very beginning.[4]

---

[3] In my *The Quest for Community* (New York: Oxford, 1953), I dealt with the general, largely political and philosophical aspects of the subject, but with little if any reference to American cultural history. R. Jackson Wilson, in his *In Quest of Community* (New York: Oxford Univ. Press, 1968), dealt with the subject but confined his attention to a half-dozen philosophers at the end of the nineteenth century in America, Peirce, Royce, and Baldwin, among others.

[4] The literary historian, Robert Spiller, correctly stresses the medieval inheritance in the Puritan mind; it was powerful.

To be sure, as Perry Miller informs us in his splendidly clarifying essay "Errand into the Wilderness," much of the initial Puritan interest in community in Massachusetts sprang less from a desire to civilize the American continent, to sow on it communities conceived in the likeness of those villages and towns the New Englanders had known in the land they had left, than it did from a deep conviction (soon to become, alas, a vain hope) that the Puritan experience in the New World would be redemptive, not just for those directly engaged but, far more important, for all those left behind in the England of the wicked Stuarts, and even for all of mankind.[5] It was in this light that Winthrop enjoined his comrades: "For wee must Consider that wee shall be as a Citty upon a Hill, the eies of all people are upon us."

Unhappily for the American Puritans, the eyes of all people were not upon them, and it was the gradual realization of this fact, as Perry Miller points out, that produced a very deep and agonizing crisis of mind among the New Englanders in the middle of the seventeenth century.

It is the central point of Perry Miller's essay that there are, and were in the English seventeenth century, two distinct meanings to the word *errand*. The word can mean a short journey on which an inferior is sent to convey a message or perform a service for his superior. But there is another and deeper sense: the actual business on which the actor goes, the purpose itself, the conscious intention in his mind. Distinction between the two senses is of course vital.

As Miller tells us, it was in the first sense of the word *errand* that the early Puritans settled Massachusetts. Physical settlement was not so much an end in itself as it was an errand, a spiritual errand, for the larger body of Puritans left behind, indeed for all of the elect. Much more was at stake than building a community in Massachusetts. There was the galvanizing belief that God, the whole Body of Christ, the future of the Kingdom was being served. Should this little community in Massachusetts fail, Miller notes, much more would be involved than the destinies of those actually present there. The whole world would be let down. Not only would God's wrath descend upon the tiny Massachusetts community but God would make the community "a story and by-word through the world."

The real purpose of the errand into the wilderness had, then, little if anything to do with the community of New Englanders and its relation to the New World. It had everything to do with God and his angels, and all of the chosen on earth, for whom the doughty Puritans had undertaken the errand.

---

[5] "Errand into the Wilderness" was first presented by Perry Miller as an address at Brown University on May 16, 1952. It is included as Chapter 1 in his *Errand into the Wilderness* (Cambridge: Harvard University Press, 1956).

But alas for the dreams of Winthrop and his brave band, this initial meaning of the word *errand* simply could not be supported for very long. As the years passed, it became steadily more evident, and more galling to the souls of the New England Puritans, that they were not in fact engaged in an errand for their brethren back home. For how many in England among the Puritans could be counted upon to remember the God-inspired, redemption-bound, earth-shaking errand that had been undertaken by Winthrop and the others? After all there were pressing events taking place in England: the Long Parliament, the Civil War, the Regicide, the Commonwealth, the New Model Army, Cromwell the Protector, and whole fresh visions of salvation issuing from the tracts of Levellers, Diggers, Fifth Monarchy men, and others.

There is no wonder at all, then, as Perry Miller suggests, that a crisis of mind should have settled upon the Puritans in Massachusetts by the 1660s. Through Miller we are treated to the contents of a long series of "election sermons" preached at appropriate intervals by the New England divines. One, the key sermon from our point of view, was given in 1670 by the Reverend Samuel Danforth; its title: "A Brief Recognition of New England's Errand into the Wilderness." There had been earlier ones, the mere titles of which provide insight into the torment of mind that produced them: "The Cause of God and His People in New England" (1663), "New England's True Interest, Not to Lie" (1668), and Increase Mather's "A Discourse Concerning the Danger of Apostasy" (1677).

But of them all, as Perry Miller shows us, the most fateful, and also the most brilliantly perceptive, was Danforth's sermon of 1670. For it is in this sermon that there is unfolded for us the poignant, the profoundly shattering, distinction between the two meanings of *errand*. There is much in Danforth's sermon about the iniquities which had grown up among the New Englanders; not merely sins of pride and spirit but of flesh, including the breakdown of family government, with sons and daughters prowling at night, militia days becoming orgies of sex and alcohol, women displaying "naked arms and necks . . . and, what is more abominable, naked Breasts," and even the appearance of brothels. How does the Reverend Samuel Danforth account for these eruptions of wickedness? By calling attention to the confusion in New England minds concerning the errand they were involved in. His great sermon may be taken, as Perry Miller himself takes it, in the light of the more general realization that the initial purpose of the settlement of Massachusetts had proved futile, with consequent disillusionment and breakdown of morality and community. Only too evident, as more and more of the New England Puritans realized, was the fact that (early pious, millennialist hopes notwithstanding) this group was *not* as a city upon a hill for all the world to gaze at, *not* messengers on an errand of God. I can do no better than summarize in the words with which Perry Miller closes his essay:

> They looked in vain to history for an explanation of themselves; more and more it appeared that the meaning was not to be found in theology, even with the help of the covenantal dialectic. Thereupon, these citizens found that they had no other place to search but within themselves—even though, at first sight, that repository appeared to be nothing but a sink of iniquity. Their errand having failed in the first sense of the term, they were left with the second, and required to fill it with meaning by themselves and out of themselves. Having failed to rivet the eyes of the world upon their city on the hill, they were left alone with America.

The Influence of the Puritan Community

"Left alone with America," Perry Miller's haunting phrase, serves admirably to epitomize the plight, not only of the Puritans in New England in the late seventeenth century, but of a long succession of Americans, especially intellectuals, down to our own day. Now, I am aware of the large and impressive literature that takes the Puritan crisis of the 1660s as its point of departure for an analysis of American thought and culture in terms of the search for self. This is a literature in which, inevitably, Emerson becomes the hero, so to speak, of the nineteenth century mind, and the self-made businessman the hero of the nineteenth century economy.

I do not question the fact that individualism in one or another of its forms can be traced back to a good deal of early Puritan consciousness of being "left alone with America." But there is another aspect of the matter, as I have already intimated, and this is the communal. I find it interesting that Sacvan Bercovitch, in his recent *The Puritan Origins of the American Self,* can write, in referring to the Puritans and their intellectual issue: "The American enterprise, unlike all others, interweaves personal and corporate fulfillment." It is the corporate, or as I prefer, the communal, that must be recognized as a powerful theme in American culture, one deriving in no small measure from the early experience of the Puritans in New England.

In the beginning, the idea of religious community dominated, sometimes taking the form of repressive theocracy, with politics made little more than a handmaiden to church. By the end of the seventeenth century, however, there is no mistaking the actuality of social, economic, and political community, given representation in literally hundreds of places, all of which would in one way or other leave an imprint on the American mind. Robert Spiller wrote that Puritanism at its height was a religious connection which resulted in stability of government, of economic conditions, and of individual conduct. To read the Puritan literature of the early eighteenth century, that of Cotton Mather and of Jonathan Edwards particularly, is to see little if any slackening of religious passion but a great deal of concern for the nature of visible community, its economic, social, and political, as well as its spiritual attributes. Mather's own life, characterized by a bold recognition of science, medicine, and education, is indicative of this.

It would be hard to exaggerate the imprint that was left on the American mind, literary and political alike, by the early Puritan community. I shall refer presently to the literary aspect. Politically, town-meeting democracy, though far more evident in New England than anywhere else, would come to seem to many observers the very essence of American democracy. Jefferson adored it and, in his later years, wished it had been incorporated in the Constitution. Tocqueville, in 1831, admired it almost above any other aspect of American democracy. There were also the Puritan-inspired voluntary associations, each as communal in character as it was self-help in inspiration. Even in our infant cities— Charlestown, Philadelphia, Boston, Newport, and New York—a sense of close community existed during the eighteenth century, at least prior to the Revolutionary War, that seemed remarkable to European visitors and to Americans themselves after returning from visits to the capitals of Europe with their appalling spectacles of poverty, division between rich and poor, and squalor everywhere.

I must not exaggerate or romanticize here. It would be negligent to pass over the side of America that had reached grim reality by the middle of the eighteenth century: the America of the impoverished settlers of the western reaches, of the frequently exploited indentured servants, of the black slaves in ever-increasing numbers, and of the increasingly real division between the wealthy and the poor. Despite the early and still extant myth, America in the eighteenth century was by no means a homogeneous setting of middle-class, egalitarian democracy. Very real social classes were in evidence, ranging from the wealthy, quasi-feudal landholders of New York and Virginia, with often vast estates governed along European, aristocratic lines, down through the merchants and shopkeepers to the artisans, the indentured, and the enslaved at the bottom of the pyramid.

None of this is to be doubted. But there is not and never has been a community worthy of the word that cannot be seen to contain diversity, hierarchy, tension, and even conflict. Only in the minds of the psyche-delically oriented, the seekers for instant and therapeutic community, is the word a synonym for total harmony. To any historian or sociologist, community is built around the sense of cohesion and continuity, and must convey a feeling of distinctive function as well as of personal membership, but even the closest and stoutest of communities is never free of tension and latent conflict, with the occasional eruption of divergent individuality.

None knew this better than the authors of *The Federalist*. The greatness of that essay in political community lies in the authors' realization that what was needed was a form of government suited to those less than angels: free government, but government under no illusions of the perfectibility of man, then or at any time in the future. The Constitution had established that kind of government, that kind of political community. What was needed, however, was a document that would do what Locke's *Second Treatise* had done—give clarity, meaning, and justification to a signal event. This *The Federalist* accomplished with rare genius.

In a sense, then, the crisis of mind that had tormented the Puritans of the 1660s, that plagued Cotton Mather in his *Magnalia Christi Americana,* published at the beginning of the eighteenth century, achieved a high degree of resolution, through political rather than religious measures, in the Constitution. Out of many communities had come one sovereign community, its Constitution the object of worldwide admiration. The quest for community, however, became only stronger in America during the century following.

Community in the Nineteenth and Twentieth Centuries

Tocqueville, on his visit to America in 1831, was struck by the combination of economic and political prosperity on the one hand, and, on the other, by an underlying restlessness, a disquiet of mind that could not be assuaged. "In America I saw the freest and most enlightened men placed in the happiest circumstances that the world affords; it seemed to me as if a cloud hung upon their brow, and I thought them serious and almost sad in their pleasures." [6] Tocqueville explains this in part by reference to equality and to the inability of human beings ever to fulfill expectations once egalitarianism becomes the law of life. But, as

---

[6] Alexis de Tocqueville, *Democracy in America,* vol. 2, part 2, chap. 13.

Tocqueville realized, there was something else involved, something that sprang from tension between religion and politics—with people attempting to find religious truth in the dogma of the sovereignty of the people and yet at the same time to keep religion as separate as possible from affairs of state—and also from a craving for community that sprang in substantial measure from the erosive effects of equality upon the time-worn communities of class, family, and the sacred. The spirit of individualism could be, as Tocqueville stressed repeatedly, tonic and creative. But all too easiiy it could rust into mere egoism, selfishness, and the feeling of being separated from other human beings.

There are several major manifestations of the American search for community in the nineteenth century. Far from least is that which we find in some of the great literary works of the century, beginning with the novels of Hawthorne, Melville, and Cooper, continuing through many of the writings of Mark Twain, and coming down in our own century to the extraordinary works of William Faulkner. The theme of community, of community violated, of community sought, of community experienced, and of community lost, is a powerful theme in some of the greatest American literary works. I am not expert in these matters, but I do not think we have, in our commentaries, given sufficient emphasis to the idea of community in the great tradition of American letters. Over and over we read about the spirit of individualism, of escape, of self-reliance, and of the achievement of self. This spirit, to be sure, exists. But it is well to keep in mind the kind of community, of individual to individual, of individual to nature, of individual to the moral order, that we find in *The Scarlet Letter, Typee, Omoo,* and, far from least *Moby Dick,* and in the novels of Fenimore Cooper. The relation of Natty Bumppo and Chingachgook, of Ishmael and Queequeg, and of Huck and Jim on the raft tells us more about community—personal, moral, and also ecological—than we are likely to realize on first reading.[7]

In this century, as I have noted, it is to William Faulkner that we turn for preoccupation, at high level of genius, with the nature of community. From Faulkner's first novel, *Soldiers' Pay,* which is the story of a wounded flyer brought back to his native Georgia, through *Mosquitoes,* in which he voiced his almost venomous dislike of intellectual destroyers of American tradition, down through the great novels set in Yoknapatawpha County, the theme of community is central in Faulkner. Like Edmund Burke, whom Faulkner may or may not have read, he makes community an organic binding of place, history, and the sense of

---

[7] N. H. Pearson, in "The American Writer and the Feeling for Community" (*English Studies,* October 12, 1962) dealt perceptively with the thematic role of community in Hawthorne, Melville, and others.

membership. Conflict, hatred, exploitation, degradation: all of these exist in abundance in Faulkner's novels and stories, but they are set nevertheless in the context of a community that transcends that which is merely individual.

The city novel represents another major area of American literature that may be seen in the light of the communal ethic. There must be significant exceptions, but on the whole American writers have dealt with the city as a kind of social and moral void, as anti-community. From Howells through Crane, Phillips, Norris, Herrick, and Dreiser down to Dos Passos, Farrell, and Algren, the city is given a special kind of prominence that is largely lacking, I believe, in the works of Europeans. Rare in the American city novel is anything like the portrayal of the urban scene presented in Dickens, Balzac, Hugo, Proust, or Mann. It is not that the Europeans are blind to vices and depravities in the urban scene; it is that these tend to be accepted as a part of the human condition. They are not woven into the very texture of the city as they so often are by American novelists. In the American city novel—as indeed in so much American sociology—the city is the very epitome of anonymity, of anomie, estrangement, and alienation. Frank Cowperwood, Maggie, Studs Lonigan, and Frankie Machine are made by their authors to seem the very consequence of the anticommunal forces dominating the metropolis. I am aware of an American literature that can find a great deal of meanness, bigotry, and mind-numbing dullness in the village or small town, that can celebrate escape from the village. But it is still difficult to find in American writing, as Morton and Lucia White have shown in their study of the subject, *The Intellectual vs. the City,* very much acceptance of the city by the American intellectual. Certainly not the kind of acceptance that is to be seen in some degree in Europe and a probably larger degree in Asia.[8]

This leads me to still another pattern of concern with community in American culture and thought, one that has to be expressed more negatively, in the accents of nostalgia. I have reference to the work of a number of thinkers who flourished around the turn of the century: Mr. Justice Holmes (who, of course, lived well beyond the turn), Henry Adams, and William Graham Sumner, among others. All of them were born before the Civil War, had come into early manhood indeed just before the outbreak of that convulsive, transforming event. It is plain from what they wrote in the aftermath of the war that they

---

[8] Blanche Gelfant, in *The American City Novel* (Norman, Okla.: University of Oklahoma Press, 1952), wrote with breadth and insight on the alienation from the city that is found in so much American literature.

hated everything economic, social, political, and cultural that they could see emanating from the war, or from forces generated by it.

In a recent work on the Civil War, Bruce Catton writes

> The American people in 1860 believed that they were the happiest and luckiest people in the world, and in a way they were right. Most of them lived on farms or in small towns, they lived better than their forefathers had, and they knew their children would do still better. . . . The average American was then in fact what he since has been in legend, an independent small farmer, and in 1860—for the last time in American history—the products of the nation's farms were worth more than the output of all its factories.[9]

The year 1860, Bruce Catton concludes, "was the final, haunted moment of America's age of innocence." Very probably the nearest the American people have ever come to a sense of community achieved was during the period leading up to 1860, although Tocqueville, in 1831, was struck by contrary signs and, as I shall indicate momentarily, even in that age of innocence there were a great many Americans seeking community in almost desperately utopian ways.

Even so, I know of no other way of accounting for the blend of hatred, disillusionment, cynicism, and blunted idealism—and also very evident nostalgia—that we find in so many of the writings of the individuals I have mentioned, Holmes, Sumner, and Adams, and to these Mark Twain could most certainly be added. All, as I say, had grown up in that halcyon period cited by Catton—in little Hannibal or Hartford, or in the still-quiet, restrained, and simple Boston—and all shared a hatred of what the Civil War and its consequences had done to the America of their birth. They hated industrialism, the new rich, the financial speculators, and the culture (political, as well as moral and social) that went with these forces. But it must not be forgotten that they hated with almost equal intensity the increasingly characteristic responses to the problems spawned by industrialism and megalopolis, the responses of a socialist or egalitarian kind.

In his *In Quest of Community,* R. Jackson Wilson has shown convincingly the degree to which analogous longings and nostalgic recreations could affect the philosophical systems of such scholars as Peirce, Baldwin, Ross, Hall, and Royce. Wilson is no doubt right when he concludes: "The difficulty they faced was as insoluble as it was simple— there probably *was* no form of community which could be efficient and

---

[9] Bruce Catton, *The American Heritage Picture History of the Civil War* (New York: American Heritage, 1960), p. 9.

powerful enough to cope with modern America and still be spiritually bound together by what Peirce called love and Royce loyalty." [10] I dare say the same could be said of the others I have mentioned, Adams, Holmes, Sumner, and Mark Twain. Henry Adams, as we know, was driven back to the Middle Ages, and if this was not true of many of his contemporaries, it cannot be said that they ever found redemptive community elsewhere. Sumner, Adams, Holmes, and their kind, their very exalted kind, believed that loss of community, community of every type, at every level, coupled with loss of the moral authority that is the warp of community, was America's curse. But, then, this had been the burning conviction of the Reverend Samuel Danforth in 1670, of Cotton Mather a generation later, and it was the haunted belief, the preoccupation of Hawthorne, Melville, Cooper, and others in the nineteenth century.

Utopian Communities. There is one other manifestation of the quest for community in the history of American culture that deserves consideration. Here we are dealing with something outside the pages of literature, philosophy, or social science; with something very practical indeed. I refer to the wave of community-building in the nineteenth century and later that we commonly think of as the utopian movement. From New England to California these communities could be found at one time or other, some with present-day remains still to be seen. Many were religious, but many others were secular in the ordinary sense of the word. It would be unfair to omit reference to the European intellectual roots of many of these communities: the visions of such minds as Saint-Simon, Owen, Comte, Cabet, and especially Fourier. And there were indeed Europeans caught up in the fever of community-building, of utopia-constructing. But so far as I know none of this compares to the extent and intensity of utopian communalism in America, beginning very early in the nineteenth century. Brook Farm and New Harmony, as names, quickly come to mind, and with good reason. But in some ways the most successful of the experiments in community were not so conceived by their makers; they were, instead, eruptions of evangelical religion, such as Latter Day Saints. The Mormon community, one of the strongest and tightest, with Deseret its geographical designation, had a great deal of the communal ethic in it, and still does.

Nor were these utopian communities, odd though some of them were, altogether out of character with the mainstream of American movement westward. It is all very well to speak of the spirit of individualism in the settlement and development of the Western frontier,

---

[10] R. Jackson Wilson, *In Quest of Community* (New York: Oxford University Press, 1968), p. 174.

but it is to tightly knit groups, associations, and communities that we look even when we are studying the fur trade in the Rockies or gold mining in California. In so many communities the first buildings to be constructed were a school house and a church, each a context of, as well as symbol of, the very real spirit of cooperativeness that existed. The so-called bees—logging bees, housing bees, quilting bees, and scores of others—attest to something rather different from anything that can properly be conjured up from individualism. If by the 1920s, following the catalytic experience of military service in Europe, many American intellectuals could take some pleasure in fleeing the American small town, in pillorying Main Street, this is only testimony to how cohesive— even to the point of suffocation—these small towns and villages could be. And, as I noted above, many of those who fled the village or small town, to settle in a Chicago or St. Louis or New York, seemingly paid penance in the form of their renderings of the urban void.

The Current Community Impulse. No one, I think, would argue that the American preoccupation with community—lost or to be regained—has diminished during recent decades. It is said by students of the matter that no fewer than 12,000 communes, rural and urban, exist in this country at the present time. Some are degraded and squalid; others are profoundly religious in theme. Some succeed, some fail, to be succeeded by new ones. But what they all have in common is an ethic that is communal to the core. They are lineal descendants of, not only the utopian communities in nineteenth century America, but, also in one form or other, the Puritan communities in the seventeenth century, and the Puritan passion for community, invisible or visible, can often be seen in these frequently bizarre groupings. But there are other signs of the communal impulse in American culture: in the recrudescence of the ethnic community, the renewed sense of both pride and protection in ethnic identification, with all the rituals, folkways, and customs which attend this identification; in the renewal of neighborhood, at least as a value, and in large measure as a response to what has been widely perceived as federal-collectivist invasion of this form of community, through forced ethnic busing, or whatever; and in the clear success of some of the pentecostal or evangelical faiths—their proclaimed individualism of faith and rebirth in no way disguising the deeply associative character of so many of them. These are some of the more vivid, frequently exotic, upthrusts of the communal spirit in America. Without number are those quests for community—in suburbs, condominium developments, singles bars, encounter groups, street festivals—which make up so much of American popular living at the present time. The spirit of restlessness amid riches, of deprivation or alienation in the presence of prosperity, that so struck Tocqueville is much in evidence at the present time.

Quite possibly the presidential election of 1976 may be seen in this spirit. Is it not evident how deeply Jimmy Carter's roots lie in the spirit I have just mentioned: the spirit of moral community lost, of need for moral community to be regained? It is one thing for an individual to meet, or seem to meet, the demand for community through the ordinary channels of localism, regionalism, religion, and voluntary association. It is something else when the desire for moral or social community is met through the immense powers of the presidency. That, however, is not a subject that falls properly into this paper.

COMMENTARIES

Laura Nader

It is interesting that these two papers were presented together. On the one hand, we heard about Arabic culture, rational thinking, and the kind of linear logic that has led to the present level of development in world civilization. Americans, on the other hand, are concerned with the question of individualism and community institutions, such as communes, which are antilogical and antilinear and go back to the kind of contextual situationalism that Max Weber's description of Middle Eastern law has so celebrated.

Professor Nisbet's paper was very interesting and at the same time most elusive. It reminded me, in a way, of Professor Said's comment in the Round Table that one must always go back to a verse in the Koran to understand what is happening in Arab culture today. So too, Professor Nisbet suggests, in this country. If we are to understand what is happening in America, we have to go back to our English Puritan ancestors, but a few things have happened since the Puritans came. A number of people of other ethnicities arrived, enriching our culture, and increasing its diversity. The people who were here before the English also enriched it and gave us the idea of bees.

In order to answer the question, "What is distinctly American?" or "What is uniquely American?" we have to take a comparative look. Bees are American Indian, and we find this kind of cooperative working pattern throughout the New World, but these kinds of work groups are also found in small communities all around the world.

When we say that the quest for community might be distinctly American, then again we have to go back to our primate origins. We are all primates. That is, we have a basic need for community. When the English Puritans came to this country, the people who boarded the boats did not all know each other before they started, and they did not all know each other when they arrived here. They had to do something to develop ties. This was the essence of the quest for community.

They found themselves in a frontier society, and one of the main characteristics of a frontier society is self-reliance. From this came the idea of depending on oneself, the concept of individualism.

Taking as a base Professor Nisbet's comments, I would like to draw your attention to some of the things that have led to the development of the need for community, beginning with work. One of the most extraordinary happenings in this country has been the shift from a society of self-employed workers to a society of employees—a shift that has not received adequate scholarly attention. Around 1840, between 60 and 75 percent of the population was self-employed, and in the 1970 census 7 percent was self-employed. By contrast, in Egypt, of those people that are working, something like 70 or 75 percent are self-employed.

This means that, in the United States, the salaried workers (and vice presidents and presidents of corporations are salaried workers) depend on others for a living. They develop, along with this pattern, a competition between the loyalty that they have to their work and the loyalty they have to their community. How is this illustrated? Millions of American families are moved every year by corporations. Anyone who wants to move up has to move around. The result is that the leadership that could be present in one community is moved to another community. This policy of geographic mobility is probably appropriate for the military and for diplomatic personnel, but inappropriate for building community.

Something else has happened. Schools used to be places where one built community. Recent studies indicate that schools train students in patterns that can be described as egoistic, or individualistic, rather than altruistic. We are training our young people to think in terms of developing themselves and not of giving to the community. We ask Johnny what he will be when he grows up, but nobody ever asks what he will do for his society. He is trained to be a salaried employee and not a citizen.

Another issue in education is busing. We really do not know, and probably will not know for a long time to come, the effect of busing in this country. We have practiced a philosophy that if we mix everybody together we will somehow achieve something like egalitarianism. When children are mixed together, however, they act like monkeys in laboratories. They are fragmented, upset, hostile and aggressive. There has been an increase in violence in the schools that may be related to the nervousness that results from mixing.

The idea of egalitarianism has been confused with the idea of equal opportunity. What we want for people is equal opportunity, not just mixing people together. In my home town of Winsted, Connecticut, the people decided to bus because everybody else was busing. Since they have no black families, they decided to bus on the basis of age. They were going to put all of the first and second graders in one school, all third and fourth graders in another school, et cetera.

What has happened to the family in this country? It has changed dramatically. The home used to be a place where parents taught their children. They taught them what they needed to know to farm, read, and write. Now the school has taken over these jobs, and everybody in a family claims equal rights as an individual. If children want to do something, they do it. If they do something wrong, the parents are at a loss to know what to do about it. A pattern has developed in American society —probably in the last sixty to eighty years, certainly since the work laws—under which parents pay their children to participate in their own community. It may come as a surprise to our Middle Eastern friends in the audience that, when children do tasks around the house in America, more often than not, they are paid to do them.

With respect to the attitudes towards the city that Professor Nisbet spoke about, I would like to comment that the Eastern city has always been a decentralized city, a series of villages, of small communities, of small quarters. It has never been as big and as centralized as Western cities have been. Probably scale is important in building and maintaining a community. If the scale is too large, a community cannot be built. The centralization that has occurred in Boston and New York must not occur in the Middle East. In modernizing, we have eliminated the small ethnic communities, and, as Jane Jacobs pointed out in *The Death and Life of Great American Cities,* the people who lived in these small neighborhoods gave the soul to the city.

We need to nourish diversity in America, to build neighborhoods, as is being done in communes. I would guess that a large proportion of young people going to communes come from suburban "communities." There have been communities in cities in the United States, and there have been communities in the rural areas, but these have never been suburban communities, though, interestingly enough, that is what they call themselves.

In Berkeley something curious is happening in the building of neighborhoods. The biggest issue in Berkeley over the past year and a half is the traffic barriers that were put up in the middle of the streets to prevent through traffic in certain areas. This was supposed to build communities and local areas in Berkeley. It was to be supplemented by such things as "brier patch" urban networks, designed to help build new businesses in the area and support the city. It is a modern version of the rural bee. There is a tremendous amount of vitality in the movement to do something within present neighborhoods rather than exiting into the counterculture. I know that people say that what happens in Berkeley is not necessarily what will happen elsewhere, but, in the past fifteen years, it has not been a bad precursor.

Mustafa Safwan

Dr. Mahmoud's paper has a style that shows the rationalistic approach that he described so beautifully. Its main characteristic is precision. In deductive thought, we start by defining the terms, and then we use these terms to prove our point. But what will happen if we want common speech to comply with these definitions? That would make common speech impossible—not merely wit but speech in general. Suppose, for example, Dr. Mahmoud had felt obliged to start by defining his terms. If he had put himself under this obligation, we would have never had this chance to hear him. The kind of precision he obtains is of a different sort. He places every word in its context in such a way that all ambiguity is removed. It is a kind of precision that is obtained afterwards, not beforehand. It makes the task of a discussant difficult. All that the discussant can do is testify to his knowledge.

Dr. Mahmoud gave us an honest, faithful portrait of Arabic culture. One of the privileges of this way of presenting a case is that it brings together the main characteristics of the object described. The main characteristics of Arabic culture are the following:

The first is that it is centered on the Koran.

Second, it is a culture that assimilated, enriched, and transmitted Greek science and Greek philosophy. Here I would like to digress to say that the Arabs achieved this task so well because the only medium between them and the Greeks was the book. They did not have television, radio, or other means of communication, or, rather, miscommunication. This remark may seem strange, but imagine that somebody in Egypt, for example, were to forbid the entry of all American motion pictures and devoted the money instead to translations of American writers—I mean translations acceptable by men of letters, that conveyed, for example, the biblical strain and the elegance of Melville, the calculated flatness of Hemingway, the humor and gentle madness of a Thurber, and so on (but not the business of putting Sartre or Camus into some Arab jargon in a day or two). If proper translations were made, they would facilitate communication between Arabs and Americans. In the case of Arab translations of the Greek, it was not necessary to make a choice. The only medium through which they could communicate with the Greek was the book.

The third characteristic of Arabic culture is a qualification of the second. Here, to express myself in the terminology of my master Dr. Aziz Atiya, I would say the main contribution of the Arabs to humanity was the lifting of all the barriers between the Sassanid Persian culture and the Greek culture except for literature.

And the fourth characteristic is that the leading personalities were not specifically Arabs. Most of them belonged to the east and south of the Mediterranean—they were mainly Persians.

One is tempted to ask whether these four characteristics are related to each other, and then answer, yes, and construct a hypothesis showing the relationship. My starting point will be to call your attention to a distinction concerning levels of rationality. The first level of rationality is common speech. Everybody knows the story of the man who complained that his friend told him he was going to Hamburg in such a way as to suggest he was going to Kraków, when in reality he was going to Hamburg. The man was complaining because his friend was telling him the truth. Common speech is always addressed to somebody, who uses it as the starting point of some deduction. There cannot be any human communication without some argumentation and refutation, the arts that Aristotle canonized and codified in his *Topics*. Common speech, then, is the first level of rationality.

The second level of rationality only came with the invention of writing. There could be no science and no history, in the sense we understand it, if there were no writing.

The third level of rationality is characterized by the invention of another kind of writing, the symbolic writing that prevails, for example, in logic. It was invented by Aristotle, when he symbolized propositions by letters.

After these distinctions between levels of rationality, I must mention a book which was published recently and edited by one of the most able scholars in France. The scholar is Monsieur J. Pierre Vernant, and the book is *Divination et Rationalité*. He contributed an article to it, in which he develops an interesting idea. He says that rationality was achieved in high degree by the Greeks because they were not the people who had invented writing. The point is that the act of inventing writing had the effect of bestowing sacredness upon the written word. (I think I could feel similar awe of certain matter-of-fact objects such as a pair of gloves, a book, or a feather revealed for what they are by the genius of a Rembrandt or Vermeer.) Vernant says the very fact that the Greeks did not invent writing, but merely took the Phoenician form and perfected it, had the effect of making the written word an instrument—a vehicle for thought or for the spoken word. This was the main factor in the development of rationality among them.

Dr. Dillon mentioned Professor Dodds. In *The Greeks and the Irrational,* Professor Dodds demonstrated that the irrational was not a strange element to the Greeks. Their language was full of the irrational and their ideas were full of irrational creeds. He illustrates his idea by the notion of Ātē, which can be translated as infatuation or divine temptation. As an illustration, Dodds evokes a scene in the nineteenth book of the *Iliad.* Agamemnon, having inexplicably taken the mistress of Achilles, has to explain himself. He says it was not he who did the act, but Ātē, the divine temptation, his fate. The irrational realm did exist among the Greeks, and it does not diminish the force of Professor Dodds's thesis if I add some remarks.

I have said that common speech is the soil of rationality, but is common speech also the soil of irrationality? How can man explain his unexpected actions, except by recalling notions like Ātē or "it was written." Among the most poetic moments are those when the poetic imagination grapples with the fundamental relationship between man and language.

Take another example: responsibility and its paradoxes. If the results of an action are all known beforehand, there can be no responsibility because they are all foreordained. And, if the results of an action are not known, there can be no responsibility either, because they were not anticipated. These are the kinds of problems dealt with by the tragedians and the poets in Greek literature. Literature is the laboratory of rationality. This thesis is corroborated by modern writings on the origin of Greek tragedy, such as *The Origin and Early Form of Greek Tragedy,* by Gerald Else.

Grappling with the irrational can be done only by free minds, literary minds, poetic minds. Arabic culture, as I said, lifted the barriers (except for literature) between the Sassanid Persian culture and the Greek culture, but it remained an Eastern culture. That means that it belongs to the area where writing was invented. I think that this thesis would be corroborated by someone like Norman O. Brown, who wrote about the world of antiquity. His thesis is that the Mediterranean was a vital field of conflict between the Persians and the Greeks.

The Greeks were victorious in the Persian Wars, and they ushered in the unity of this area. Whenever we look at a map giving the centers of the wheat trade or the wine trade or the production of vases, we feel that the whole of this area is one. The ultimate Arabic conquest of the area may be regarded, in some sense, as a revenge of the Persians.

I would not put it that way, but those who do so corroborate my feeling that Arabic culture belongs to the East, and that this fact explains its characteristics.

I must emphasize that there are free minds and free thought, but there is no rational society. Every society, whatever it may be, is based on beliefs, and societies do not readily accept discussion of these beliefs. Societies progress precisely because there are free minds and rational minds, but they are never much admired.

Having talked about mind and society, we may ask about policy. Here I may differ slightly with my master, Dr. Atiya. I agree with him that policy, after all, is a temporary matter. Temporary as it may be, however, it is of absolute importance to the living being. There are policies that forbid the development of free minds, of rational minds. The prevailing policy in the Arab world forbids the development of all rational thought.

Having spoken about thought and society and policy, what about community? I find community a very mysterious thing. It is very easy to draw an apple. It is just as easy to draw two apples that touch each other. But two apples that touch each other willingly are more difficult. The apples of Cezanne, for example, are miraculous because they have community, community that stands in opposition to nothing else. That is the miracle. With the single exception of Cezanne's apples, I would say that the quest for community could be called a quest for segregation.

I wonder about the basis of community. It is related to the human image, which is surely the basis of the feeling Professor Nisbet describes as "we-ness." I can have a friendship for a horse, a dog, or a monkey, but I cannot develop a sense of we-ness with any of them. The human image is the basis of "we-ness," but it is also the basis of division, so if there is some "we-ness," it must come from something other than the human image. I also wonder what beliefs or ideas govern the constitution of communities in the American society.

DISCUSSION

DR. DILLON: Despite the vast diversity in American and Arab cultures, there must be some unity, too. What I realized in listening just now is that the Greeks gave both to Arab civilization and to the United States something that we all should try to get rid of—categories that lead us to confuse words with things. These constructs tend to make us victims of our own classification systems.

They should make all of us, Arabs and Americans alike, want to rush off to read the Zen Buddhist masters to find out what to do with those dichotomies. One might just as well recognize a unity in a whole range of human experience that will not tolerate rationality or irrationality. Even the Buddhist civilizations, however, had to have categories in order to get on with the art of life and living and to speculate about the known and the unknown.

Certainly one could conclude from the discussions this morning that culture must be understood in its largest sense, its literary and humanistic as well as its anthropological senses. The modern world could not function without writing, that gift of civilization which originated in the East. But along with that came a certain literalism and a terrible dependence on what people have written down, and the error of judging people, or expecting them to behave, according to the rules attributed to them. Certainly, propaganda thrives on this literalism. People expect others to behave according to their political theories or their religious theories. The curse of literalism is dependence on the word and the book.

Dr. Nader has given us another area of discourse in the legal arrangements she discussed. Extra-legal rules are continually being codified as we search for community in an unstructured world. Such rules include those governing the right of segregation and the right of withdrawal from that community.

Because we are guests today of an institute that has the word *policy* in its name, and because I am a victim of the policy-oriented culture of the city of Washington, I would like to put a very loose question to my fellow participants. What traditional Islamic-Arabic ideas of brotherhood or sisterhood would contribute to an international community with the kind of diversity we have been celebrating here today? Specifically, on questions of energy and the survival of industrial societies, we might ask what bases we have for creating an international community to help us when we reach the end of fossil fuels to make greater use of solar energy and photosynthesis.

DR. MAHMOUD: I hope Dr. Safwan will agree that there is no conflict between us. In culture one does not find rationality on the one hand and irrationality on the other. They are mingled, but if we are going to talk of either one, we must dissect this entity to get at its components artificially. In classical Arabic culture, every book contains the elements mingled. But in this paper, I was concerned with one aspect only, so I had to make a dissection. I asked myself on what basis to dissect this culture when I looked at it posthumously. My answer was to select those parts of Arabic culture characterized by cause and sequence, whatever the field may be. I did not mention literature or Arabic poetry because poetry is not concerned here. A poet does not compose his poem on the basis of causal connections. Mystics loom very large in the Arabic culture, but they also are not concerned here because mystics do not connect things causally. A philosopher would, a literary critic would, a scientist would, and so on. I selected examples to conform to the definition I set.

Dr. Safwan said that it was natural for the Arabs to translate Greek works because there was no other medium than the book. If that is the case, why did India not translate the Greeks? The fact that the Arabs did shows a kind of relationship, a similarity, between the mental attitudes of the Arabs and the Greeks, whereas there is a dissimilarity between the attitudes of the Indians and the Greeks. Greek culture was available to whoever wanted to take it. Why did the Arabs take it, but not the Indians or the Chinese? In 832, we started translating Greek scientific and philosophical works but not literature, because what is common to us and the Greeks lies in the realm of the rational. We differ in the literary realm.

The fact that the medium was the book—the only medium of that time—makes no difference. The significant fact is that we did not find Greek philosophy and Greek science foreign to our nature. The Arab mind is deeply rational, and picks up rational concepts and the rational procedures wherever it finds them.

Dr. Safwan analyzed rationality at various levels. In speech and writing, he has selected the raw material out of which culture grows: literature, science, philosophy, and the rest. There are levels of rationality, but the levels that concern me are two: the level of science and the level of philosophy. There are degrees of universality or generalization: the more we generalize, the higher the standard of rationality.

We took both strata, the stratum of science and the stratum of philosophy, from the Greeks. Speech is the soil of both rationality and irrationality, but, if the same garden gives oranges and apples, does that mean that oranges are apples? Saying that speech is the soil of both types of production proves nothing and disproves nothing. It just states a primary fact.

I wonder how Dr. Safwan can refer to symbols—logical and mathematical symbols and so on—as a third stage. What are speech and writing if not symbols?

He made the interesting point that, though the Arabs removed the barrier between the Eastern and the Greek civilizations, they remained Eastern. I would say rather that they removed the barrier between the two cultures and made of them one organic unity, which is the Arab culture. This is the point to stress here if we want to understand the Arab culture. They broke the barrier between the Eastern and the Greek cultures, and made them one. In a book of mine, published in 1961, I made the point that historically we find two extremes: in the Far East, the traditional culture was intuitive, and there was little argument in it. At the other extreme, we have the Greeks, who argued and did not depend on intuition. The Arabs are in the Middle East, and they are really in the "middle" in the sense of what is brought together in the Arab culture. We have had the greatest mystics, and, at the same time, the greatest scientists.

The Middle East has the capacity to absorb the two extremes, and no other place has had this capacity. If one follows European culture, one finds an almost purely logical culture, a scientific culture. There are, of course, mystics, but they are not part of the mainstream. And, in India and China we find a mainstream that is quite different.

In the Arab culture, we do not draw the line between these two extremes, because they are one. Any eminent person in Arabic culture has both elements, as does the culture in general. Therefore, I cannot easily accept Dr. Safwan's assertion that the Arabs broke the barriers but remained Eastern and unaffected, presumably, by the mixture. I believe that the Arabs, together with being religious, mystic, and metaphysical, are highly rational. I am not underestimating the metaphysical attitude of the Arab culture, but there is also a high degree of rational thinking.

DR. DILLON: In the few remaining moments, we should hear some post-Puritan and post-Aristotelian dialogues between the natives of the New World. We have moved fairly far from Greece. Few of us learned Greek or Latin, and many of us have not had the benefits of Arabic literature even in translation.

Professor Nisbet, could we have your comments?

PROFESSOR NISBET: The coexistence of the mystical and the rational is certainly not foreign to the long medieval period of Western society. There have been many, many books on Christian mysticism, which reached its height in the twelfth and thirteenth centuries. But, as Lynn T. White, the historian of science and technology of the Middle Ages, has pointed out, the idea of invention occurred in Western thinking in the twelfth century, not in the later and much overrated period of the so-called Renaissance.

Mysticism and logical thinking have certainly been cardinal elements in Western thought, though I am not capable of commenting on their relative importance. Whether this coexistence is a more splendid one in Arabic culture than in Western medieval culture, I do not know, but it certainly existed. Christian mysticism was a very powerful vein of thought, for a long time, and it still is.

As to the matter of community, I quite agree that it is a "spongelike" word; it probably became somewhat corrupted in the 1960s, when there was a search for "instant" community—a community that became symbolized, alas, by the Woodstock rock festival rather than by a group of people living together, working together, and following some kind of distinctive function and purpose. The Spanish philosopher Ortega y Gasset says somewhere that people do not come together just to be together; they come together to do something together. That is little more than a half-truth. People do come together to be together, but I do not think communities of that kind prove durable. If the present communal movement in the United States survives, and I hope it does, it will be because these communes, or a large number of them, have become identified with something basic—economic, social, structural— a perceived sense of function. Many of them will blow away in the first strong wind; many of them have already blown away, because they were based on the idea of how nice it is to be together and hold hands and smoke pot together and have happy communal imaginings. This is a debasement.

The Latin language, which I used to know quite well, was quite right in putting *communitas* and *societas* in two quite different declensions. The difference between *societas* in the Latin and *communitas* is great, and I think probably we are experiencing at the present time a recrudescence of a genuine form of communalism. How long it will last I do not know. No one can predict the future—all one can do is guess and be intuitive. The rediscovery of ethnicity among Poles, Jews, Chicanos, and others, however, is a phenomenon that cannot be ignored. The rediscovery—or "renaissance"—of ethnicity contains an in-built sense of community, real or imagined. Neighborhoods will probably begin to come back. They have somehow remained in a few places in the United States, particularly the large cities, such as New York. Living in New York made me become aware of how powerful a neighborhood can be. I agree with Dr. Nader on the difference between the Western city and the Eastern city. Max Weber pointed this out in his great study of the city, noting as the chief difference that, even in the Middle Ages (an intensely communalistic period), the individual citizen was the unit of Western urban life. In the Eastern city concepts such as "quarter" counted more and there was a kind of concentric relationship.

If the problems of politics, power, war, and ecology are somehow contained in the next twenty-five to thirty-five years, we will see a genuine revival, a shoring up, of communal influences in American culture. Legal, philosophical, and political atomism will assume a less and less magisterial place then they have had in the past. Somehow, we will reach a balance between the national community, which most Americans cherish and must have, and the kinds of community that spring up from the common pursuit of some objective, a common feeling of purpose. This balance is tremendously important, and there are moments when I become optimistic about its coming about.

DR. DILLON: Have you something optimistic as well, Dr. Nader?

DR. NADER: There are just two points I would like to make. First, as I have had more and more experience with our energy agency, the Energy Research and Development Administration, I realize that we are not as rational and scientific as we like to feel. If I were to name an agency in Washington that is full of mystics, that would be my choice. [Laughter.]

My second comment comes back to Dr. Dillon's comment on policy. We can speak only artificially of two discrete cultures, the American culture and Arabic culture. We must begin to focus our attention on the process of cultural development in the entire world. I stress the word *process*. There is an interdependence in the world today that is accelerating at a rapid rate. We spoke about multinational corporations yesterday. We could speak of many other institutions that help in this acceleration, some of them are based in the private sector, and some are government based. What happens in the United States affects the Arab world. When cyclamates were taken off the shelf here,

119

they were put on the shelf in other places, such as the Arab Middle East. The Middle East is accepting ideas that have originated, partly at least, in the West, such as the idea of expert knowledge. I would suggest that the Arab world be aware of the Western overuse of expertise as we have used it, but I would hope that Arab concepts of situationalism and contextualization are not lost in the process.

On the other hand, what happens in the Middle East clearly affects American society. We would be naive to think the Palestinian problem has not had a major effect on the availability of resources for the whole world, not just American society. The availability of oil resources is clearly having an effect on American society and how we organize our lives. Other resources, such as uranium, are found in different parts of the world. We are not discrete cultures any longer— we are interdependent. If we had a conference spanning the period from 5000 B.C. to 1976, we would find we were all intimately related. And, that is something we should not forget.

PART
FOUR
POLITICS

THE SOCIOCULTURAL DETERMINANTS OF ARAB DIPLOMACY

Mansour Khalid

I begin my paper with definitions. Words mean different things to different people if they do not have a common medium of communication. I think we are all aware of the origin of the word *kangaroo* as a name for an Australian animal. The story has it that when the first white settlers set foot in Australia, they were amused at this funny looking animal. They asked a group of Aborigines what this animal was called, and the answer was, "kangaroo." A few years later they realized that in the language of the Aborigines kangaroo meant "What do you mean?"

Dictionaries define *diplomacy* as "the management of a country's affairs by its agents abroad (ambassadors and ministers), and their direction by the Ministry of Foreign Affairs at home," [1] or the "conduct by government officials of negotiations and other relations between nations, the art or science of conducting such negotiations, skill in managing negotiations." [2]

Those definitions deal with diplomacy as an artifice; the diplomacy of the diplomatist. But what we mean by diplomacy for the purpose of this discourse, and indeed the essence of diplomacy today, is something much wider than simply the art of negotiation. Clemenceau's remark that war is much too serious a matter to be entrusted to the military may be applied to diplomacy. Diplomacy is much too serious a matter to be entrusted to diplomats alone.

In modern-day diplomacy, there cannot and should not be a distinction between the function of a diplomatist and that of a foreign-policy maker. Diplomacy has come to involve too much interplay between domestic and external factors to allow for such a separation. Without a proper understanding of all the internal and external influences on foreign policy there can be no effective conduct of diplomacy by a state or a proper analysis of that diplomacy by other states. This

---

[1] *Advanced Learner's Dictionary of Current English* (Oxford: Oxford University Press, 1956).
[2] *Random House Dictionary of the English Language* (New York: Random House, 1973).

new vision of diplomacy impels states today to "introspect, to re-examine their own roles, to raise questions such as whether perception by States of other States is efficient, feedback is leading to adjustment, or whether there are blockages in the information, decision and implementation processes." [3]

Foreign-policy makers, in order to undertake such introspection and reassessment, are obliged to educate themselves on the factors and variables that influence the thinking and action of states. Those variables—political, economic, sociocultural, and so forth—are interacting and variegated, and in one manner or another they affect the setting within which diplomacy is exercised and the content of that diplomacy. *Setting* here refers to the political and functional structures as well as the actors in the play. *Content* refers to the goals and values.

It is fair to assume that, of all those factors and variables, the sociocultural influence plays a determining role, if only for its effect in fashioning the personality, disposition, and orientation of the actors in the diplomatic scene, be they individuals or groups, and in determining the value system of those individuals and groups. This is in no way intended to underrate the importance of political factors, which admittedly play an important role in focusing the issues.

Sociologists maintain that sociocultural factors have a pervading impact on man's perception of political realities, since they help shape the cognitive orientation of the community and individuals within that community, that is, their feeling of attachment, involvement, or rejection of political objects and beliefs; and their evaluative orientation, that is, their judgments and opinions about other opinions and beliefs, which usually involve applying value standards to political objects and events.[4] In other words, the decision makers in any community always act in accordance with their perception of reality, not in response to reality itself. Reality is seldom as objective as it seems, or rather as it is made to seem. Reality and its image are not always congruous. Worse still, images are often a distortion of, a deviation from, or simply a misconstruction of, reality. It is, therefore, necessary to understand the cultural influences that give all those shades to reality to the point of being an impediment to communication.

Dealing with the sociocultural setting of Arab diplomacy, let us start by defining who is an Arab. What are the values for which Arabs have an effective regard? And, how do those values relate to some

---

[3] J. W. Burton, *Systems, States, Diplomacy and Rules* (Cambridge: Cambridge University Press, 1972), p. 205.
[4] Michel Brecher, *The Foreign Policy System of Israel* (London: Oxford University Press, 1972), p. 229.

concepts and practices of Arab diplomacy? This attempt—as indeed is the case with all sociological studies, which are replete with intuitive judgments and subjective experiences—cannot claim to be completely scientific. Man is too complex an animal to allow the science of man to postulate hard-and-fast rules. However, one does not have to go as far as Lord Acton's dictum—that all sociological studies are purposeless since they cannot be pursued with chastity like mathematics.

Who Is an Arab?

Inspired by prejudice or romanticism, Westerners developed an image of the Arab that includes the nomad, the camel, the mosque, the desert, and the palm tree. To the Westerner, an Arab is sensual, pugnacious, emotional, and irrational. This image of the Arab as nomad may have had a Biblical origin, which was perpetuated by the heritage of bitterness from the olden days of the Crusades and the modern days of the colonial wars. However, there is no evading the fact that the present-day caricature of the Arabs has been deliberately amplified by a prejudiced, and often uninstructed, media.

The term *Arab,* perhaps since the heyday of the Islamic Empire, came to mean something different from simply an ethnic group living in the Arabian Peninsula. *Arab* denotes a specific ethnocultural group inhabiting that part of North Africa and the Middle East which was permanently Arabized by the Muslim Arab conquests of the seventh and eighth centuries A.D. Arab migration from the peninsula into the neighboring verdant lands of Mesopotamia and the Mediterranean was known before Islam and gave rise to the celebrated kingdoms of Palmyra, Petra, Ghassan, and Hira. But the impact of the Islamic conquests was more pervading and permanent. Arabization was achieved either through intermarriage between Arab conquerors and the inhabitants of the conquered land or through conversion to Islam and the establishment of Arabic as the universal language of the converts.[5]

Arabism today does not refer only to the inhabitants of geographic Arabia. And it is far from being a purely ethnic concept, defined by the purity of Arab stock—otherwise the Arabo-Negroid and the Arabo-Hamitic groups would not qualify. These groups represent over two-thirds of what is known today as the Arab world.

Arabism should also not be confused with Islamism. The term *mussulman* was invariably used during the French colonial era in the

---

[5] Edward S. Atiyah, *The Arabs* (Harmondsworth, Middlesex: Penguin Books, 1955), p. 8.

125

Maghreb to denote the autochthonous Arabic-speaking populace. Although Islam has played a cardinal role in the expansion of Arab civilization, the terms *Arab* and *Muslim* are not interchangeable, though they refer to things that are conterminous. The non-Arabic-speaking Muslims of West Africa, Turkey, and Persia are not Arabs, and the Arabic-speaking Christians of Lebanon are not non-Arabs. For this reason it is important, while recognizing the important role Islam played in shaping Arab culture, not to lose sight of the extra-Arab characteristics of Islam.

Arab Culture and Personality Disposition

Arab culture, more than any other culture, is a condensation of the content of Arab history. The term *culture* here is used to signify the sum total of the modes of life of a people which were built up through ages and transmitted from one generation to another, as well as the values which sustained that life. Values, on the other hand, refer to the attributes universally desired and considered worth striving for because they give the community a sense of purpose. They are generally pursued either for their social desirability or for their moral excellence.

The study of any culture requires the study of language and religion—the two basic components of any culture. The impact of any religion on the development of a people's culture is fundamental. Culture and religion are not the same thing, but they are not different things either. To T. S. Eliot, no culture can develop except in relation to a religion. Culture cannot be considered more comprehensive than religion, nor should religion be considered only as an element supplying the ethical framework to culture which is the ultimate value.[6] Eliot in so saying was trying to avoid two errors: first, that religion and culture are two different things between which there is only a loose relationship, and, second, that religion and culture may be completely identified with each other.[7] This paradox is easily discerned in the relationship between Islam and Arab culture.

As to languages, it is assumed that they are the basis of all civilization, since they constitute the principal sign system that made intellectual interaction and transmission among nations and generations possible. This is more true of the Arabic language than of any other.

---

[6] T. S. Eliot, *Notes Towards the Definition of Culture* (New York: Harcourt, Brace, 1949), p. 28.
[7] Ibid., p. 33.

Arabic, being the language of the Koran, has acquired a certain sanctity. For that reason alone, the Arabic language was the greatest cohesive force among the Arabs. This idea of the sanctity of Arabic was underscored by Prophet Muhammad when he said (in the words of al-Tabarani): "I love the Arabs for three things: because I am Arab, because the Koran is Arabic and because the tongue of those who go to paradise, once in paradise, is Arabic." [8]

Apart from its role in Arab cohesion, we will also see that the speech patterns of the language had a great impact on Arab communication, particularly with non-Arabs.

Desired Arab Values

Within the Arab value system some values rank higher than others; for example, endurance, communal cohesion, honor, and rectitude.

Endurance is one of those values imposed by the condition of life of the nomadic Arabs of olden days. Arnold Toynbee viewed the institution of nomadism as a "tour de force" in response to the vicissitudes of nature and recurring desiccation. Nomadism gave Arabs both stamina and strength of will. To Toynbee, no patriarch could survive in the nomadic environment "without exercising and exacting from the human beings and animals under his patriarchal authority those virtues of forethought, self-control and physical and moral endurance which a military commander exercises and exacts from his troops." [9] Traces of those conditions are still to be found among the Bedouin Arabs of the peninsula, North Africa, and Western Sudan. [10]

Communal cohesion, within the Arab value system, is undoubtedly the most desired value. It is a corollary of endurance if endurance is meant as one way of mobilizing all the forces of the community against the challenges of nature and strangers. Cohesion exists in different degrees within different strata of the community. The more central the group within the community, the greater is the cohesion. This cohesion is sometimes carried to the extreme of communal aggression in retaliation for injury suffered by kith and kin; this should not be viewed as evidence of a propensity for fighting but as a natural consequence of the

---

[8] Quoted in the introduction to *Lisan al-Arab*, by Ibn Manzur (Beirut: Dar Sadir, 1955), p. 7.
[9] Quoted in W. Montgomery Watt, *What is Islam?* (London: Longmans, 1968), p. 23.
[10] Talal Asad, *The Kababish Arabs* (London: C. Hurst, 1970); and Tore Nordenstam, *Sudanese Ethics* (Uppsala: Scandinavian Institute of African Studies, 1968).

law of retribution. This ethos, which is a pre-Islamic heritage, was well
described by the great pre-Islamic poet al-Shanfara:

> Yonder, on the mountain pass of Sala'a lay a dead man
> whose blood shall not remain unavenged.
> On me he bequeathed the burden and passed away,
> and that burden I shall assume.
> If gone, behind me is a cousin, resilient and unflinching,
> in pursuit of retribution.

Honor is another cherished value among Arabs. To an Arab,
honor and respect by the community are interchangeable concepts.
Honorable behavior can be reflected in manifestations of manliness,
attitudes toward the old and weak, sexual conduct, particularly in the
case of women, and so on. But here again there is a strong correlation
between honor and group cohesion and group survival. Honorable
behavior is that "which strengthens the group and serves its interests;
while shameful behavior is that which tends to disrupt, endanger,
impair or weaken the social aggregate." [11]

Because of this correlation between personal honor and social
approbation, some students of Arab society claim that loss of face often
impinges on honor.[12] An Arab considers it an affront to his honor to
suffer loss of face. This "tyranny of the face" leads an Arab to do everything possible not to show his troubles to those close to him, let alone
his enemies.[13]

Rectitude is one of those values highly desired by any community,
being the bedrock on which social and personal equilibrium are based.
Religion emerged as the *prime* source of rectitude in the life of man, not
only because of its earthly benefits but also for its heavenly reward.
In that regard Islam is a simple religion "whose tenets do not involve the
unattainable and are well within the grasp of the least tutored understanding." [14]

Islam and Arab Culture

Without Islam and Arabic language there would have been no Arab
civilization. In the words of Edward Atiyah, the great Arab civiliza-
tional achievement could not have been realized but for "the possession
of one of the finest and most expressive forms of speech ever fashioned

---

[11] Raphael Patai, *The Arab Mind* (New York: Charles Scribner's Sons, 1973),
p. 90.
[12] Ibid.
[13] Ibid., p. 105.
[14] Atiyah, *The Arabs,* p. 29.

by the mind and tongue of man. Islam itself is unthinkable except in terms of the spoken Arab word." [15]

Islamic influence permeates Arab society because the realms of God and Caesar are neither divided nor delineated in it as they are in Christianity. Islam, like Judaism, provides "a complete system of social legislation based on divine sanctions. Islam comes nearer to Judaism than to Christianity." On the other hand, like Christianity, it delivers "a universal rather than a tribal message." [16]

Because of the dual character of Islamic faith, which is not divorced from everyday life, a secular domain in non-Muslim culture emerged to become the most potent normative force in Arab society. Islamic legislation firmly established on the edicts of the Koran and the Shari'ah (example or experience of Prophet Muhammad) evolved to cover all areas of human activity. An elaborate body of jurisprudence in the social and ethical and the civil and criminal fields was developed through processes of deduction and analogy. The works of Abu Hanifah, al-Shafi'i, Abu Yusuf, and others abound with legal precedents and rules to be followed by Muslim lawyers. It is, therefore, not surprising to note that several new Arab constitutions stipulate that "Shari'ah" is to be considered the major source of legislation.[17]

Islam was also a great cohesive force, both within Arabia (Arabian tribes) and outside it (Arabized and non-Arabized Muslim communities), because it generated among them an extraordinary sentiment of brotherhood. On the other hand, without the influence of Islam, Arabic language and culture could not have found their way, and permanently implanted themselves, in countries so far and wide. This implantation has happened, in some cases, at the expense of almost erasing the autochthonous languages, such as the Coptic, Berber, or Syriac.

Islam also was the one major factor that saved the Arabic language from degeneration. The Arabian Peninsula, in the pre-Islamic era, knew diverse dialects of Arabic. Some of those dialects found their way to the early recordings of the Koran. Aware of the dangers of adulteration of the holy book, Caliph Uthman was prompted to make the daring decision to burn all the versions of the Koran except the one eventually known as "Uthman Book." That version was distributed, by the order of the caliph, within Arabia as well as to all outside Muslim territories, as the only authenticated version of the Koran.

A consequence of this sentiment of Islamic brotherhood is the

---

[15] Ibid., p. 22.
[16] Ibid., p. 14.
[17] Egyptian Constitution; Sudanese Permanent Constitution.

concept of Islamic union, which loomed high on the horizons of Muslim politics during the anticolonial wars, which were seen by the general populace as a continuation of the religious wars (the Crusades). The religious undertones in the liberation wars in Egypt, North Africa, and the Fertile Crescent were too obvious to be disguised or denied.

The attempt to establish religion (Islam) as the only viable force for Arab unity met with resistance from those claiming that language and culture are the most important formative forces of national unity. Needless to say, many adherents of the latter view were Christian Arabs.

The Right Accent and the Right Word

"Give me the right accent and the right word and I will move the world." This is not an Arab speaking. It is Joseph Conrad. But students of Arabic would say that, more than any other living language, Arabic works like magic on its listeners. In the words of Philip Hitti, "No people in the world has such enthusiastic admiration for literary expression and is so moved by the word, spoken or written, as the Arabs. Hardly any language seems capable of exercising over the minds of its users such irresistible influence as Arabic." [18]

The great mystique that surrounds the Arabic language and its great potential for rhetoric, rhythmic cadences, and hyperbole [19] are a source of both strength and weakness of the language. Language is an important vehicle not only for reporting experiences but also for defining those experiences. So, inasmuch as the structure of the language is conducive to graceful and adorned reporting of experiences and emotions, it also encourages exaggeration in expression, which is not conducive to scientific precision.

In Arabic, sometimes, words become an end in themselves. This is much more true of poetry, which is the "most distinctive creation of Arab aesthetic genius." [20] It is also true of Arabic prose, particularly when it comes to public utterances. Imam al-Jurjani, in his classical treatise on eloquence, contends that "words give sciences their place, define their standing and reveal their secrets." [21] It is words, not facts or theorems, that reveal the secrets of science. Al-Qalqashandi, in his major work on Arabic composition, prefaces his great opus by saying

---

[18] Philip K. Hitti, *The Arabs: A Short History* (Princeton, N. J.: Princeton University Press, 1943), p. 21.
[19] Patai, *The Arab Mind*, p. 48.
[20] Atiyah, *The Arabs*, p. 60.
[21] Abd al-Qahir al-Jurjani, *Asrar al-Balaghah* [The secrets of eloquence] (Cairo: Maktabat al-Qahirah, 1972).

that the speaker's ability should be gauged by his oratory and fluency.[22] It is the grace of the words and fluency of the expression rather than the logic of the argument and veracity of the statement that count.

Arabs and Modern European Influences

Modern Arabism is not a creation of those traditional factors alone. The new contact with Europe and what ensued from it—the anti-colonial wars, the exposure to new concepts of government and social structures, the adoption of new techniques, and so on—had their impact, too, on Arab culture and personality. Arabs have come in contact with Europe since the eighth century. The early contacts, basically intellectual, were less pervasive. The contact with Europe in the last two centuries, however, has had a more profound effect in shaping the Arab personality. The European implantation has been all-embracing (cultural, economic, political, and social), and the impact has been enhanced by a revolution in communication that has shortened distances and amplified experiences.

The study of Arab Westernization is important not only for tracing the impact of modern European values and ethos on the Arabs but also for properly understanding the Arab personality. Personality is defined not only by a description of its inherent traits of character but also by a determination of what it is not. The definition of a specific personality is at the same time a negation of another. In their attempt to define their personality configuration within the last seventy-five years, the Arabs were almost always comparing themselves with Europeans.[23]

The fiercest reactions to implantation of European culture in the Arab world occurred in countries where the political domination was accompanied by the establishment of European colonies. Algeria is a case in point. Westernization in Algeria, and indeed in the whole Maghreb, was viewed as a war of cultural extermination, and for that reason people clung to the very few things left to them by the colonizers. Religion was the most important of those institutions. To the Algerian the Frenchman was always a *Gawri* (from a Turkish word for *infidel*). The French, on the other hand, continued to call the original inhabitants of the land, not in relation to their *patria* but in relation to their religion, *les mussulmans*.

---

[22] Abu al-Abbas Ahmad al-Qalqashandi, *Subh al-A'sha fi Sina'at al'Insha* [The light of the night-blind in the art of composition] (Cairo: The Book Organization, 1964).

[23] Abdallah Laroui, *L'Idéologie Arabe contemporaine* (Paris: Maspero, 1967), p. 15. See also Jacques Berque, *Les Arabes d'hier à demain* (Paris: Maspero, 1967).

The impact of the West is understandably much more noticeable on the elite in the Arab world. The elite, who were more exposed to Western culture through education, came not only to enjoy the products of that culture but sometimes to emulate its ethos and institutions. The same people, however, remained emotionally rooted in their own tradition. A revealing insight into this ambivalent attitude can be discerned in an intriguing novel written by the modern Sudanese author El Tayeb Saleh.[24]

The Arab elite are torn between two cultures, indeed torn from within. As a result of this split personality, they become victims of what some writers describe as "double ambivalence." On the one hand, they want to enjoy the products of Western scientific achievement while rejecting the values that inspired those achievements; on the other hand, they are fiercely patriotic while exasperated at the backwardness of their people, to the point, sometimes, of failing to relate to them.[25] This is true only up to a point, however—the history of the Arab wars of liberation, social reform, and emancipation reveals that, in spite of this frustration, the elite did not entirely disdain the hopes and sufferings of humbler men.

Students of Arab history are often intrigued by this fierce love-hate relationship between the Arabs and the European colonizers, which is not matched by any other relationship between a colonized people and their erstwhile colonizers. This is described as either an inferiority or a superiority complex, depending on your vantage point. The modern Arab society, which accepts gladly the products and tools of Western civilization, often rejects the values that made the manufacturing of those tools possible. Arabs see in those values and that ethos an element corrupting their "superior" cultural values. Not only is political domination resented but also the values of the dominator are considered unwholesome vagaries and a source of exasperation.

Some even claim that this rejection also applies to political institutions, like democracy, liberty, and socialism. Arabs often talk about Arab socialism, authentic democracy, and liberty that is congenial to their society, meaning that those political and social concepts and institutions must be adapted to Arab conditions. They maintain that Europe has no monopoly of wisdom and that the European pattern of government and society is not necessarily the best suited to all societies.

There can be no denial that the emerging contemporary Arab ideology has been greatly influenced by Western thought, including Marxism—Marxism being an outgrowth of the libertarian ideas of

---

[24] Tayeb Saleh, *Season of Migration to the North* (London: Heinemann, 1970).
[25] Patai, *The Arab Mind,* p. 198.

Christian Europe. In many cases the influence is not one of interaction; rather it is an action and reaction. This is true even of the religious revivalists like Mohamed Abdu, who was greatly influenced in his thinking by the precursors of the French Revolution. Abdallah Laroui finds in this new ideology both a progressive and a retrograde element. It is progressive because it offers a model that is conceptually and emotionally advanced enough to cope with objective realities in the Arab world. It is backward because it is a copied model, which did not penetrate to the core of Arab society; instead, it attempted to copy a model from a European society which is itself changing.[26]

On the other hand, the Arabs, who have a powerful sense of history and tradition (which often degenerates into resigned nostalgia), are aware of the role their forefathers played in the evolution of modern European culture. They accuse European historians of distorting Arab history and of being ignorant of the great legacy left by Arab historians. Some European writers even reject the existence of any analytical approach to history by the Arabs, on the ground that the concept of time in the Arab mind is simply an undifferentiated quantum.[27] Others claim that the Arab historical perspective is distorted because of the absence of any concept of chronology. "To understand the historical perspective of the Arabs we should realise that they were very interested in persons and relations of persons, but not at all in quasi-mathematical time, conceived as flowing regularly in a straight line." [28] There is also the claim that because Arabs know their ancestors for many generations, their historical perspective is given by genealogy and anecdotes.[29]

All those claims, of course, lose sight of the great legacy left by Arab historians, like al-Mas'udi, al-Maqrizi, al-Qayrawani, and Ibn Khaldun. Al-Mas'udi, prefacing his celebrated work on history *Meadows of Gold,*[30] enumerated one hundred-fifty Arab historians and maintained that he wanted to follow their path. He described history as a science with defined rules and criticized historians like Thabit Ibn Qurrah al-Harrani who approached the science of history without adhering to those rules.

It is revealing that European encyclopedias still say that Emile Durkheim was the first social scientist to subject everyday life to a rigorous sociological study and that Saint Simon and Auguste Comte,

[26] Laroui, *L'Idéologie Arabe,* p. 212.
[27] Patai, *The Arab Mind,* p. 295.
[28] Watt, *What is Islam?* p. 78.
[29] Ibid., p. 79.
[30] Abu al-Hassan al-Mas'udi, *Muruj al-Dhahab* [Meadows of gold] (Beirut: The Lebanese University, Dept. of History, 1965).

133

to whose methodology Durkheim's is related, were his only two predecessors in the investigation of society. The fact is, the first philosophy of history and the first systematic sociological interpretation of history were formulated by Ibn Khaldun in his *Prolegomena* (*Muqqadimat*).

Some European historians of Arab civilization tend to find dogmatism and tyranny in Arab history and tolerance and libertarianism in European history. Those historians, while elaborating on the great achievements of the period of the Enlightenment, deliberately gloss over the suffering of Descartes and Rousseau.[31] The contrary is true when the same historians write about the Arabs.

Abdallah Laroui has rightly pointed out that those historical incongruities, misrepresentations, and distortions of fact are not a European monopoly. The picture of Europe painted in some of the Arab classical history works was very dim indeed.[32] On the other hand, those same historians glorified the golden eras of Arab history—the eras of al-Mutwakkil and al-Mamun—while understating the persecutions of the "Mutazilites" and the sufferings of Ikhwan al-Safa (Brethren of Purity). As a result of such historical claims and attitudes, according to Laroui, the East and West, instead of being only two directions on the globe, almost became two metaphysical purposes or tendencies.[33]

Several other contemporary Arab thinkers advocate a more rational approach to modern European culture, not marred by prejudices and complexes. Zaki Naguib Mahmoud believes that such an end can be achieved by approaching reality with analytical reason rather than viewing it through the prism of myth and dreams, by relating phenomena to their natural causes rather than seeking metaphysical explanations for human action, and by developing a sense of proportion so that things can be viewed within their proper perspective.[34] Such an approach of cultural relativity, we maintain, is the only one that can help build bridges between peoples of differing cultures.

Cultural Attitudes and Diplomacy

Sad as this may sound, foreign-policy decisions are hardly dictated by an enlightened vision of the world. They are, instead, always influenced by domestic considerations and by domestic cultural attitudes.

---

[31] Laroui, *L'Idéologie Arabe,* p. 20.
[32] Ibid., p. 16.
[33] Ibid.
[34] Zaki Naguib Mahmoud, *Thaqafatuna fi muwajahat al-'asr* [Our culture faces the modern age] (Cairo: Dar al-Shuruq, 1976), p. 54.

Generally speaking, attitudes toward the outside world are not necessarily rational since they depend on traditions derived from cumulative historical legacies. These attitudes may take the shape of hostility, jealousy, emulation, suspicion, affinity, or cultural and ideological exclusiveness.

This is not to deny that those attitudes are prompted by what states consider to be their vital interests. Those interests range from the augmentation of power to cooperation and interdependence with the outside world. In this sense the content of foreign policy is, and will always be, determined by the self-interest of states. National interest, however, has always been a loosely used epithet in political parlance, often implying opportunism. Experts say that foreign policy in a changing world has to be opportunistic because "national interests become concrete in foreign policy objectives when opportunity is recognized and evaluated as worth pursuing in terms of cost and value." [35] Trying to attribute a humanistic value to foreign policy is simply flying in the face of reality. Humanism by definition is not national since it transcends both natural and manmade barriers.

Through bitter experience, states have learned to accept that their domestic groups must agree to act in concert in relation to the outside world. With this understanding, the bounds of propriety in interstate relations are set. But states consist of domestic groups with conflicting interests, be they regional, occupational, or ideological, and each group has the means of expressing itself and exercising its influence on the decision maker. Therefore, it often becomes difficult for policy makers to articulate a meaningful policy. [36]

Going from generalities to specifics, what are the objectives of Arab diplomacy, what is the effect of Arab culture on conceptual formulation and modes of communication, and who are the groups most effective in influencing foreign policy within the Arab community? In our discussion of Arab culture, we found the recurring themes within the Arab value system to be those of group cohesion, honor and self-respect, and the idolization of Arab culture and all its constituents, tradition, language, and creed. Looking at the evolution of Arab diplomacy one can trace the manifestations of those cultural attributes. In inter-Arab relations and in relations between the Muslim world and Europe, for example, one can identify those cultural attributes at the origin of specific policies.

---

[35] Klaus E. Knorr, *Power and Wealth: The Political Economy of International Power* (New York: Basic Books, 1973), p. 147.

[36] Ivo J. Lederer, ed., *Russian Foreign Policy* (New Haven, Conn.: Yale University Press, 1962), p. 147.

Inter-Arab Diplomacy

The dominant theme in contemporary Arab politics is that of Arab unity. Arab unity is the corollary of that most cherished value, group cohesion. The idea of Arab unity is so powerful that it has found its way into the constitution or charter of almost every Arab state. In many political utterances and declarations, Arab unity is referred to as God-ordained and predestined. It endows a political movement with a sanctity that turns it into a moral crusade. A political objective is no longer an idea subject to reason but a sacred rite to be followed religiously. Dissension is no longer a difference of opinion but heresy and treason.

In the nineteenth century, the modern concept of Arab unity (otherwise called Arab nationalism) was born as a reaction to Ottoman rule in Greater Syria. It was first articulated as a systematic Arab philosophy of government by a young elite that emerged in that part of the Arab world—an elite educated in France and exposed to the new ideas of nation-states (which transcended religious denominations), liberty, and social justice. The Baathist can justly claim the fatherhood of the concept of a rejuvenated Arabism with a secular face. The very appellation *Baath,* which means "revival," is revealing.

But what is more revealing in the emergence of the new secular concept of unity is the very motto the Baathists have adopted: "One Arab nation with an immortal message." The motto is paradoxical, because the only timeless or immortal message of the Arab nation has been, and still is, Islam. For the secular Baath, the paradox is compounded by the fact that many of the forefathers of the movement were Christian Arabs, though there might not be many in the Baath today. Baathists continue to brandish secularism, in a sense denying the importance of the only factor that has made all the countries of the periphery indelibly Arabic, that is, religion.

Protagonists of Arab unity, an objective and just cause, have proliferated, each one claiming to be the inheritor of the faith and the charisma, and each claiming that the idea of unity is a destiny and a given reality. Unity among peoples with a common language, geography, and cumulative cultural heritage is a natural objective. This is much more so today when the world is moving toward greater union among nations for reasons of survival, cooperation, and pursuit of happiness. But while accepting those objective realities which make unity a necessity, one also has to accept other objective realities that make the attainment of such a goal a matter for rational calculation and design. By *rational* we mean the sound use of means to reach a given end. Defective knowledge of a situation and a limited capacity to analyze facts will not lead very far. Such a rational approach is certainly not a concomitant of the belief that political institutions are predestined. It is not without reason that sovereign Arab states exist today. It is not without reason that they exist with differing political and economic structures and with varying degrees of social and economic development and of communal homogeneity. Overstating those differences is politically negative, but understating them is politically disastrous.

Arab unity is a political necessity, and, rationally approached, it is a feasible objective. One rational way of achieving such unity is through a systematic building up of functional institutions, first within Arab countries that have the most in common and then within the larger League of Arab States. Development of unity in the economic, cultural, and political fields will help provide the ground for a deeper unity and a common sense of purpose. There is evidence to show that, after the bitter experiences of the past, Arab states are learning their lesson. However, on the Arab political stage are those who suffer from the myth of grandeur, the worst addiction of politicians, some of whom continue to sway the untutored.

Islamic Unity

The brotherhood of Islam has been a tremendous force for cohesion among Muslims. Loyalty to religion was often overriding, to the point of generating a sentiment of fraternity among all Muslims, a feeling of belonging to one community.

The experience of the Arab-Ottoman conflict revealed that other bases of social cohesion are also still in play. This proposition is maintained in spite of claims by some historians that the Ottoman had become too spiritually destitute to be considered a defender of the faith. Indeed, if Islamic brotherhood is to supersede more existential allegiances, sociopolitical organizations and institutions must sustain it, otherwise the centrifugal forces of other political and economic fragmentations will come into play. No such institution existed before the creation of the League of Islamic States.[37] This new revival and institutionalization of Islamic brotherhood is evidence not only of the resilience of the creed but also of the determination of Muslims to maintain what they consider the greatest supporting value of their society.

Here again, it is necessary to recognize that, in spite of religious fraternity, in the domain of politics there are different conceptions of

[37] P. J. Vatikiotis, *Conflict in the Middle East* (London: Allen and Unwin, 1971), p. 17.

what is just and correct within the Islamic world. A political objective cannot be defined by its sanctity, nor can it be attained through preaching. Differences among Muslim countries are natural since the political evolution has not been identical in all of those countries. Some of them grew through peaceful evolution, others were the offspring of radical revolutions. And, where domestic structures are based on fundamentally different conceptions of what is just, the conduct of diplomacy grows complex, and it becomes difficult even to define the nature of disagreement because what is obvious to one is problematic to another.[38]

East-West Relationship

Relations between the Arabs and the West have always had emotional strands. The Arabs were indignant at European exploitation of their resources. They resented European domination. They have never forgotten or forgiven the raw deal they received from Europe (which includes America) in the Arab-Israeli conflict, a conflict viewed as an extension of the anticolonial wars. They are ever aware of their glorious past and of the premeditated effort of European historians to deny the existence of any relation between that past and present-day Arabs. On the other hand, the Arabs have always been aware of the Judeo-Christian nexus with Islam. They recognize the impact of European education, administration, science and technology, and ideas of socialism and democracy that came through contact with colonizing powers.

Arab feeling toward the West is one of complexes and ambivalence. Policy and diplomacy continue to be conducted with the logic of reaction. That reaction leads to the belief that some Arab cultural values are timeless and thereby negate the role of the social laws of history. Cultures, like people, are dynamic, and no culture can claim exclusiveness and specificity to the point of having nothing to do with other cultures. Such an attitude tends to consign countries to a political limbo, remote from reality.

One positive aspect of the East-West confrontation, evidenced in the colonial wars but heightened and focused by the Arab-Israeli wars (to the Arabs, Israel is an annex of Europe), is its effect on the Arab approach to Western culture. Arab-Israeli wars, particularly that of 1967, caused an agonizing reappraisal by the Arabs of both their thinking and their methods. The 1967 war, in particular, was a traumatizing experience. It led to much self-examination. Professor Constantine

---

[38] Henry A. Kissinger, *American Foreign Policy* (New York: Norton, 1974), pp. 11-12.

Zurayk, who wrote ably and openly on the social consequences of the Palestinian wars, came to the conclusion that

> The Arab society and the Israeli society with which we are faced, belong to two different civilisations, or to two different phases of civilisation. This is the basic cause of our weakness despite our large numbers, and of the strength of the Israelis despite their small numbers. When we shall reach their level, the problem will be solved by itself.[39]

No longer are the yearnings only those of Salama Musa and Muhammad Mandur, or of Abbas al-Aqqad. Governments are now aware that the only way out of the social rut and stagnation is through science and technology—that planning and development are the only way to achieve social betterment. There are no short cuts in history, though slogans abound.

This traumatic experience has already had consequences in Arab politics. The prime example is the conduct of the October War. The war involved mastery of sophisticated weaponry, therefore, proficiency in technology. It involved avoidance of propaganda and gullibility—secretiveness had not been the hallmark of Arab diplomacy in the past. The importance of the October War lay not so much in what it achieved on the ground as in what it achieved psychologically, by restoring the faith of a people in themselves.

Another aspect of change is the dexterous use of the Arab economic potential as a bargaining counter in diplomacy. The oil embargo set in motion one of the most fundamental changes in international economic relations in decades. Its direct results include the wide-ranging review of the international economic order, the North-South debate, the Arab-European dialogue, and the new concept of triangular cooperation among those who have the technology, those who have the financial assets, and the proletarian nations of the world that own tremendous untapped resources. In spite of bickerings in international conferences, a hangover from the past, one cannot fail to discern a new sophisticated trend in Arab negotiations aimed at winning friends and persuading people.

The majority of Arab statesmen today, except for the revolutionary romantic, the infantile purist, and the charlatan (all of whom must be contended with), are aware of the necessity of a more rational approach to diplomacy, based on a better understanding of one's interlocutor, rather than on *idées fixes* and a priori positions. A realization may be

---

[39] Constantine Zurayk, *Ma'na al-nakbah mujadadan* [The meaning of catastrophe reconsidered] (Beirut: Dar al-'Ilm lil-Malayyin, 1967).

emerging that foreign policies of states are nothing more than actions, or strategies for action, designed to terminate, reduce, sustain, or expand cooperation or conflict. And policies should be viewed as attempts either to adapt goals to external environments or to help adjust those environments to goals—nothing more, nothing less. Diplomacy is called upon to relate the means to the end.[40]

Who Determines Foreign-Policy Decisions?

Diplomacy, in both conception and conduct, is a very complex domain. For that reason alone, decision making in foreign policy cannot be an exercise available to everyone. To have any influence on foreign policy, a group must be aware of what difference foreign policy makes in terms of wealth, peace and tranquility, prestige, welfare, and so on. In addition, it must have the ability to articulate this knowledge in a coherent manner.

In the Arab world, there is such a high degree of illiteracy and such a disconcerting ignorance by the general public of the outside world that those attributes are to be found only in the educated class. And even among the educated, they are found only among the more outward-looking. For the rest, a vision of the outside world is formed by myths, prejudices, irrational axioms, and ideological stances.

The outward-looking educated groups in the Arab world include the political scientists, the professional diplomats, the military strategists, the business complexes, and the few enlightened men of the media. Sometimes those groups view themselves as the trustees of the society, and its relentless educators on foreign policy. But those elite groups are, by and large, a product of two cultures—their own and that bestowed upon them by European education. It is, therefore, not surprising that all the ambivalence that characterizes their modes of thinking is reflected in their attitude toward the outside world.

Problems in formulating foreign policy are not characteristic of Arab diplomacy alone. Even in countries with a high degree of literacy, many among the educated are uninstructed in foreign policy. According to George Kennan, because of the "egocentricity" of the participants in the American domestic political struggle, it has been difficult for the United States to devise a sensible national foreign policy. Often, whatever happens internally is viewed as much more important than what is happening elsewhere in the world, or indeed in the relations with the rest of the world.[41] Such an attitude is hardly conducive to the conduct

---

[40] Knorr, *Power and Wealth*, p. 34.
[41] George F. Kennan, *Memoirs,* vol. 2 (Boston: Little, Brown, 1967-72), p. 319.

of enlightened diplomacy, though it may be rational within the bounds of its own irrationality. Professor Galbraith, in his *Journals,* comments on diplomats who choose the easy way of adjusting requirements of a sensible and enlightened foreign policy to domestic policy considerations only to continue enjoying their prestige of office: "To a considerable extent they succeeded in their effort, their life was tranquil, their enjoyment undiluted. But for posterity to grant these men similar exemption from adversity would be too kind. The price of an easy time in the present must, surely, be a low score in the history books." [42]

Problems of Communication

In the conduct of diplomacy, ability to communicate with others in defining objectives, framing issues, and analyzing actions and reactions, plays an important role in the determination of positions. Language has always had a profound influence on ways of reasoning and, indeed, on ways of conceiving the universe.

Arabic is a language with such a great potential for rhetoric, exaggeration, and rhythmic exigencies that words are sometimes used for their own sake more than for what they are understood to mean. Disraeli, one of the greatest masters of the English language, said: "With words we govern men." Within a different cultural context, Confucius taught us that "without knowing the force of words it is impossible to know men."

A student of Arabic realizes that exaggerations are used not necessarily to emphasize a point but rather because of the linguistic exigencies of the *tawkid,* that is, the rule of emphatic assertion. A vehement reaction, loaded with threats, far from betraying a propensity to conflict, might be meant only to insult and humiliate the adversary, in the best tradition of the *hijā',* that is, poetic invective, an important institution of Arabic poetry (Abu al-Tayyib al-Mutanabbi is its foremost master). Nobody believed that Mutanabbi meant a single word of what he said in his celebrated praise of Sayf al-Dawlah, the prince of Aleppo, or in his *hijā'* of Kafur the Akhshedite, prince of Egypt. The truth and untruth of the statement in the *hijā'* is irrelevant. What is relevant is the potency of the insult as conveyed by the words and similes used. [43] To a Western ear accustomed to subtle understatements all this might sound uncouth. Not so for an Arab listener.

---

[42] John Kenneth Galbraith, *Ambassador's Journal* (Boston: Houghton Mifflin, 1969), p. xv.
[43] Jacques Berque and J. P. Charnay, *L'Ambivalence dans la culture arabe* (Paris: Editions Anthropes, 1967).

The tendency toward sloganeering in contemporary Arab politics is an outgrowth of this linguistic heritage. Slogans are repeated as if they would eventually be made to come true by the very dint of repeating them.

In spite of all its verbal redundancies, the Arabic language is also very rich in modes of subtle expression. The tradition of homonymous expressions, or *Aḍḍād,* on which a lot has been written by Ibn al-Anbari, is one example. Homonymous expressions lend themselves to the use of euphemism and variegated verbal undertones.

Modern Arab thinkers are aware of the communication problems, of their tendency to resort to repetitions and exaggerations to make a point. They also know that modern technological culture requires precision and a rationalization of the modes of expression.[44] The new schools of Arabic literature, in poetry and prose, betray a new trend in content and style. To be authentic,. writing no longer has to be traditional. The works of Tayeb Saleh, Salah Abd al-Sabur, and Muhammad Ibrahim Abu Sinnah among the literary writers, and Abdallah Laroui, Malek Bennabi, and Lewis Awad among the social scientists and social critics are examples of the new trend.

Conclusion

Not all images are true. The Arab stereotype is false, as are the European and American stereotypes. But to understand the true nature of a subject, the veil of imagery must be pierced. Otherwise we shall always be victims of prejudices and misconceptions born out of ignorance. In the words of William Hazlitt, "Prejudice is the child of ignorance."

---

[44] Zaki Naguib Mahmoud, *Tajdid al-fikr al-'arabi* [Renovation of Arab thought] (Beirut: Dar al-Shuruq, 1971); *al-Ma'qul wa al-la-ma'qul* [The rational and the irrational] (Cairo: Dar al-Shuruq, 1975); and *Thaqafatuna fi muwajahat al-'asr* [Our culture faces the modern age] (Cairo: Dar al-Shuruq, 1976).

THE AMERICAN OPPOSITION
TO GOVERNMENT AND ITS
INTERNATIONAL IMPLICATIONS

Samuel P. Huntington

For most countries, the identity of their people as a people is the product of a long process of historical evolution out of shared ethnic origins, blood ties, shared experience, and a common culture. But such is not the case with the United States. "Before the 1770s, with a few minor exceptions," as Austin Ranney nicely puts it, "no political system had ever been deliberately created at a single point in time to maximize certain general principles." [1] On July 4, 1776, however, the United States came into existence as the product of a conscious political act based on explicitly set forth political principles. From the start, national identity was defined not in the terms familiar to other societies but in terms of what in one century Abraham Lincoln labeled a "political religion" and in the next Gunnar Myrdal termed "the American creed." One does not speak of Britishism, Frenchism, Germanism, Japanesism, or even Russianism as a set of principles, but one does speak of Americanism in this way. It is, in effect, an ideology or rather, since it is unsystematic, the substitute for an ideology. "Americanism," as Leon Samson observed, "is to the American not a tradition or a territory, not what France is to a Frenchman or England to an Englishman, but a doctrine —what socialism is to a socialist." And this, he suggested, was why socialism as an ideology got nowhere in America: the ground had been preempted. [2]

Not only are national origins and national identity bound up with a particular set of political principles, but throughout most of American history there has been overwhelming agreement among the major elements of the American people on those principles. To those, from Tocqueville to Louis Hartz, who have looked at the patterns of political belief in America in comparison with those in Europe, this consensus has been a dramatic and overpowering fact. Nor have the critics of

---

[1] Austin Ranney, "'The Divine Science': Political Engineering in American Culture," *American Political Science Review,* vol. 70 (March 1976), p. 140.
[2] Leon Samson, *Toward a United Front* (New York: Farrar and Rinehart, 1935), p. 16, excerpted in John H. M. Laslett and Seymour Martin Lipset, *Failure of a Dream?* (Garden City, N.Y.: Anchor Books, 1974), p. 426.

143

consensus theory been able to explain away that fact. The agreement is one on general principles and values. It does not mean that there has been an absence of violence in American history; as Richard Hofstadter has suggested, Americans do not need ideological differences to engage in bloody brutalities against each other.[3] Nor does it mean that Americans have agreed how these principles should be applied in practice; indeed, the struggles of American history have often been precisely over that issue. But it does mean that at the level of general principle there has been a remarkable degree of political homogeneity—and consensus—in American society, particularly as compared with the societies of Western Europe.

Of what, then, do these principles consist? Three of the most notable European observers of the American scene provide answers at three very different points in American history.

> The Americans [said Tocqueville] are unanimous upon the general principles that ought to rule human society. From Maine to the Floridas, and from the Missouri to the Atlantic Ocean, the people are held to be the source of all legitimate power. The same notions are entertained respecting liberty and equality, the liberty of the press, the right of association, the jury and the responsibility of the agents of government. . . .
>
> The Anglo-Americans acknowledge the moral authority of the reason of the community as they acknowledge the political authority of the mass of citizens; and they hold that public opinion is the surest arbiter of what is lawful or forbidden, true or false. The majority of them believe that a man by following his own interest, rightly understood, will be led to do what is just and good. They hold that every man is born in possession of the right of self-government, and that no one has the right of constraining his fellow creatures to be happy. They have all a lively faith in the perfectibility of man. . . .[4]

A half-century after Tocqueville, Bryce summed up the principal elements of the creed in strikingly similar fashion. The key dogmas of American thinking, according to Bryce, were: (1) the individual has sacred rights; (2) the source of political power is the people; (3) all governments are limited by law and the people; (4) local government is

---

[3] Richard Hofstadter, *The Progressive Historians* (New York: Vintage, 1970), p. 461.

[4] Alexis de Tocqueville, *Democracy in America,* vol. 1 (New York: Vintage, 1955), p. 409.

to be preferred to national government; (5) the majority is wiser than the minority; (6) the less government, the better.[5]

A half-century after Bryce, in turn, Gunnar Myrdal remarked that "Americans of all national origins, classes, regions, creeds, and colors, have something in common: a social *ethos,* a political creed." "The American creed," he said, was a creed of "humanistic liberalism," which developed out of the Enlightenment and which embodied the "ideals of the essential dignity of the individual human being, of the fundamental equality of all men, and of certain inalienable rights to freedom, justice, and a fair opportunity. . . ."[6]

The basic ideas of the American creed thus include liberty, individualism, equality, constitutionalism, and democracy. These ideas clearly do not constitute a systematic ideology, and they do not necessarily have any logical consistency. At some point, indeed, as has often been pointed out, liberty and equality clash. So also individualism can run counter to constitutionalism, and democracy or majority rule may infringe on both. Precisely because it is not an intellectualized ideology, the American creed can live with such inconsistencies. Logically inconsistent as they may seem to philosophers, however, these ideas do have a single common thrust and import for the relations between society and government. All the varying elements in the American creed unite in imposing limits on the power and institutions of government. The essence of constitutionalism is the legal restraint of government through a fundamental law. The essence of liberalism is freedom from governmental control, the vindication of liberty against power, as Bernard Bailyn summed up the argument for the American Revolution. The essence of individualism is the right of each person to act in terms of his own conscience and to control his own destiny free of external restraint, except insofar as such restraint is necessary to insure comparable rights to others. The essence of egalitarianism is rejection of the idea that one man has the right to exercise power over another. The essence of democracy is popular control over government, directly or through representatives, and the responsiveness of governmental officials to public opinion.

In sum, the distinctive thing about the American creed is its antigovernmental character. Together its key ideas form a standing—and powerful—indictment of almost any political institutions, including

---

[5] James Bryce, *The American Commonwealth,* vol. 1 (London: Macmillan, 1891), pp. 417-418. In this paragraph and subsequently, I have borrowed a few sentences from my "Paradigms of American Politics: Beyond the One, the Two, and the Many," *Political Science Quarterly,* vol. 89 (March 1974), pp. 1-26.
[6] Gunnar Myrdal, *An American Dilemma,* vol. 1 (New York: Harper, 1943), pp. 3-12.

American ones. No government can exist without some measure of hierarchy, inequality, arbitrary power, secrecy, deception, and established patterns of superordination and subordination. The American creed, however, challenges the legitimacy of all these characteristics of government. Its ideas run counter to the nature of government in general. They run counter to the nature of highly bureaucratized and centralized modern government. They run counter to both the original and the inherited nature of American government.

Therein lies the dilemma. In the United States, government is legitimate to the extent to which it reflects the basic principles of the American creed. Government can never, however, reflect those principles perfectly. Consequently, government is illegitimate to the extent to which people take seriously the principles of the American creed. If people then try to make government more legitimate by bringing political practice more into accord with political principle, such efforts normally have the effect of weakening government rather than strengthening it. Because of the inherently antigovernmental character of the American creed, government which is strong is illegitimate, and government which is legitimate is weak.

In fact, in comparison with European societies, government has always been weak in America. This weakness was the product originally of the fact that no need existed in the United States to centralize power and establish a strong government in order to overthrow feudalism. In this sense, as Tocqueville pointed out and Hartz emphasized, Americans "arrived at a state of democracy without having to endure a democratic revolution, and . . . are born equal instead of becoming so." The absence of feudalism thus eliminated a major negative impetus to strong government. The presence in its place of a pervasive consensus on liberal and democratic values furnished an additional, positive incentive to limit government. In the absence of a consensus, in turn, strong government would have been necessary; as Hartz pointed out, it was only because the images of American society held by the framers of the Constitution were erroneous that the system of divided and checked government which they created was able to last.[7] The fact of consensus thus made possible weak political institutions; the content of the consensus reinforced the weakness of those institutions.

Strong government has historically emerged in response to the need either to destroy a traditional society or to fight against foreign enemies. In the seventeenth-century era of state-building in Europe, the absolute monarchs engaged in both activities simultaneously and unremittingly.

---

[7] Louis Hartz, *The Liberal Tradition in America* (New York: Harcourt, Brace, 1955), pp. 83-86.

From the start the United States was spared the need to do the first, and shortly after its birth, it was spared the need to do the second in any serious way until well into the twentieth century. The United States was able to maintain national independence and national security without having to create a strong apparatus. When this situation seemed to change in the 1940s and 1950s, many of the instrumentalities of a strong state apparatus were created. This development took place, however, only because Americans at that time were not terribly concerned about realizing their political values in their domestic political practice, however much they might have been concerned about protecting those institutions from foreign threats. Once Americans became concerned about the gap between their political ideals and their political institutions in the 1960s, they began to eviscerate the political and governmental institutions which had been developed to deal with foreign enemies.

"If there is one message I have gotten from the Pentagon Papers," Daniel Ellsberg told a cheering crowd of MIT students in the fall of 1971, "it is to distrust authority, distrust the President, distrust the men in power, because power does corrupt, even in America." [8] And if there were any who did not get the message from the Pentagon Papers they almost surely must have gotten the message very shortly thereafter from the Watergate tapes. That, however, is an old message: it is a refrain constantly repeated through more than two hundred years of American history.

The central—and the oldest—theme of the American political tradition is opposition to concentrated power. The revolutionaries of 1776 opposed monarchical power and defined the issue as liberty against power. The Jacksonians attacked the financial-commercial power of the national bank. The following generation zeroed in on the slave power. The Progressives saw the threat in the organized power of the trust and the machine. The generation of the 1960s found the enemy in the concentration of power in the executive branch of government. The deeply rooted suspicion of power has been shared by radicals and reactionaries, liberals and conservatives. The extent of this hostility is a distinguishing characteristic of American political culture compared with that of other societies. Among peoples, Americans have clearly been the most fervent and consistent believers in Acton's dictum.

In rather striking fashion, Americans have tended to interpret those two potentially conflicting values of the American creed—equality and social mobility—in such a way as to be compatible with opposition to authority. In a variety of ways, as Cora Du Bois has pointed out, the

---

[8] *Boston Globe,* October 14, 1971, p. 8.

"American hostility to figures in authority" has operated "to play down status differences" and to produce an informality and familiarity in manners. Success is valued, but some forms of success, particularly those which do not involve hierarchical authority relationships, are valued considerably more than others.

> [U]pward mobility is valued as successful activity, but when it reaches a point where it outstrips the premise of equality and the focal value of conformity it borders on *hubris*. . . . It is the boss, the politician, the teacher, the "big shots" who are disvalued figures to the extent that their superordinate position implies authority. It is the movie star and the baseball hero who are valued figures since their pre-eminence connotes no authority but at the same time dramatizes the meteoric rise to fame and popularity through hard work and youthful striving. [9]

Winning the race against others is good; exercising power over others is bad. The American attitude toward "bigness" is similarly ambivalent; in objects it is good; in organizations—which involve the structuring of power—it is bad. Big buildings, big automobiles, and "big" wealth in the sense of individual wealth have been generally viewed favorably. Big business, big labor, and, most particularly, big government are viewed unfavorably.

Underlining this point is the striking difference in American attitudes toward inequalities in wealth and American attitudes toward inequalities in power. When major inequalities in wealth emerged in the latter part of the nineteenth century a "gospel of wealth" was also developed to justify and legitimize them. Great wealth was hailed as the reward for great effort, great merit, great risks. People could and did make the case that wealth was evidence of virtue. That attitude remains widespread even in the late twentieth century.

Inequalities in power in the United States are almost as prevalent as inequalities in wealth. They will continue to exist, as in part a consequence of inequalities of wealth but also more generally as an inherent concomitant of a highly complex and bureaucratized society. In contrast to the case of wealth, however, American society has never developed a justification for differences in power. The United States has had and still has a gospel of wealth. It has never had and, in the nature of things, cannot have a gospel of power. Instead it has a pervasive antipower ethic.

---

[9] Cora Du Bois, "The Dominant Value Profile of American Culture," in Michael McGiffert, ed., *The Character of Americans* (Homewood, Ill.: Dorsey Press, 1964), p. 230.

In his classic study of race relations in the United States, Gunnar Myrdal brilliantly pinpointed "an American dilemma" which existed between the deep beliefs in the concepts of liberty, equality, and individualism of "the American creed" and the actual treatment of the Negro in American society. What he probed, however, was only one manifestation, albeit the most dramatic one, of the widespread gap between political ideals and institutions in America. What he termed *an* American dilemma is really *the* American dilemma, the central agony of American politics.

In any society, of course, some gap exists between political ideals and political practice. In a society in which the dominant ideology was one of absolute monarchy, and in which in theory there were no restraints whatsoever on the power of the ruler, political practice would, of course, reveal very real limits on his power. "Unofficial" reality would deviate from "official" ideology. Efforts to bridge this gap, however, would tend to reinforce the power and authority of the existing institution; they would be efforts to make the incomplete absolutism which did exist into the more complete absolutism which should exist. Such efforts would enhance the legitimacy of the state by strengthening the state. Contrast this relationship with that which prevails in the United States. One function of an ideology in a political system is to legitimate rule, to furnish a persuasive and compelling answer to the question: why obey? The American creed, however, provides the rationale for restraints on rule: it is a much more fruitful source of reasons for questioning and resisting government than for obedience to government. "Credibility gaps" develop in American politics in part because the American people believe that government ought not to do things which it has to do in order to be a government and that it ought to do things which it cannot do without undermining itself as a government.

The ideological challenge to American government thus comes not from abroad but from at home, not from imported Marxist doctrines but from homegrown American principles. The stability of political institutions is threatened not by deep-rooted cleavages but by deeply felt consensus. Americans cannot be themselves unless they believe in the creed, but they also must be against themselves if they believe in the creed. The more intensely Americans commit themselves to their national political beliefs, the more hostile and cynical they become about their political institutions. The legitimacy of American government varies inversely with belief in American political ideals.

The United States is unique among countries in the scope and intensity of its commitment to liberal, democratic, and egalitarian values.

As a result, the United States is also unique among modern societies in the nature of the gap which exists between prevailing political ideals and existing political institutions. As in no other society, the dominant political creed constitutes a standing challenge to the legitimacy of political institutions.

Consider, for instance, the contrast between American and European societies. Most Western European societies have inherited patterns of ideological pluralism, giving rise to interclass and interparty ideological conflict. As a result, the political institutions in such societies reflect a variety of ideological influences. In contrast to the situation in the United States, in Europe the adherents of particular ideologies typically have distinctive and continuing affinities with particular political institutions. Conservatives support the monarchy (if there is one), the executive, the aristocracy, upper houses in the legislature, the courts, and, usually, the bureaucracy. Liberalism and republicanism are identified with parliaments and parties. Socialists and Marxists support trade unions, working-class parties, universal suffrage, and, in some circumstances, popularly elected legislatures. As a result, when the legitimacy of an institution is challenged in terms of one ideology, it can usually be defended in terms of another ideology that has significant appeal within the society. In Third and Fourth Republic France, the republicans and the Left challenged and the Right defended the power of the executive; their roles were reversed with respect to the power of the Assembly. In the United Kingdom, a Marxist attack on the Crown or Parliament will lead to liberal, democratic, socialist, or conservative defenses of these institutions.

In America, on the other hand, if an institution or practice is illegitimate by the democratic and liberal norms of the American creed, it has no alternative defenses available in conservative, aristocratic, Marxist, or Christian Democratic traditions, as there would be in most Western European countries. There is only one source of legitimacy, and if it is taken seriously, much of what is inherent in any government—including government in America—verges on illegitimacy. Political institutions and practices stand alone and defenseless before the overpowering liberal consensus.

The ideological pluralism in Europe also means that, by and large, liberal, democratic, and egalitarian norms are weaker in European countries than they are in the United States, and non-liberal, nondemocratic norms stressing hierarchy, authority, and deference are stronger. Comparisons of political culture in the United States and European countries consistently document those differences. From Crèvecoeur and Tocqueville to the present, almost without exception, European observers have focused upon egalitarianism, openness, absence of social hierarchy, suspicion of political authority, and belief in popular sovereignty as critical characteristics distinguishing American from European politics.

In contrast to Western Europe, the Soviet Union, China, and Japan lack traditions of class-based ideological pluralism. To a much greater extent, indeed, these societies resemble the United States in being historically characterized by a high degree of homogeneity in political values and ideology. What distinguishes these societies from the United States, of course, is the content of that consensus. In Japan, despite the import of Western democratic, socialist, and Marxist ideologies, major continuities in basic norms of social and political organization have been maintained from the late feudal Tokugawa era into the modern, post-World War II period.[10] In the Soviet Union, a successful revolutionary party eliminated the liberal tendencies which had appeared in the late nineteenth century and imposed ideological homogeneity on a reconstructed society. In China, the Communist conquest of power produced a new political culture combining elements of both revolutionary and traditional (Confucian) political culture. In all three societies, however, the dominant values and norms of the political culture differ fundamentally from the liberal, democratic, egalitarian, and individualistic values which prevail in the United States. The tradition of middle-class liberalism, which preempts the scene in the United States and shares the stage in Western Europe, has been totally absent or has had only a marginal or aborted existence in these non-Western societies. In all three societies, the stress, in one form or another, has been on the pervasiveness of inequality in social relationships, the "sanctity of authority," in the phrase Lucian Pye used to describe China,[11] the subordination of the individual to the group and the state, the dubious legitimacy of dissent or challenges to the powers that be. American ideas of openness, liberalism, freedom to dissent, the right of opposition, and the norm of equality in human relationships stand in striking contrast.

This contrast could pose difficult international problems for the American political system. In the Soviet Union, China, and Japan, the prevailing political values and social norms reinforce the power and authority of the central political and governmental institutions of society. In the United States, the prevailing norms, insofar as Americans take them seriously, work to undermine and to weaken the power and authority of government. Yet the Soviet Union, China, and Japan are precisely the states with which the United States will have increasing inter-

---

[10] See especially Chie Nakane, *Japanese Society* (Berkeley: University of California Press, 1970), *passim*.
[11] Lucian W. Pye, *The Spirit of Chinese Politics* (Cambridge, Mass.: M.I.T. Press, 1968), pp. 91ff.

actions, both cooperative and competitive, in the future. Given the "disharmonic" element in the American political system, the continuing challenge, latent or overt, which lies in the American mind to the authority of American government, how well will the United States be able to conduct its affairs in this "league" of powers to whose historical traditions basic American values are almost entirely alien?

During the first part of the twentieth century, American external relations were largely focused on Western Europe. In most countries in Western Europe, there were almost always significant political groups whose political values were similar to American ones. Even more important, perhaps, lodged deeply in the consciousness of Western European statesmen and intellectuals was the thought, impregnated there by Tocqueville if by no one else, that American political values, in some measure, embodied the wave of the future, that what America believed in would at some point be what the entire civilized world would believe in. This sympathy, partial or latent as it may have been, nonetheless gave the United States a diplomatic resource of some significance. European societies might resent American moral or moralistic loftiness, but they knew, and the Americans knew, that the moral values Americans set forth (sincerely or hypocritically) would have a resonance in their own societies and could at times be linked with social and political movements in their own societies which could not be ignored. Both this at least partial sense of identification and the more general sense of future convergence in political values are absent in relations between the United States and the Soviet Union and China, and, to a lesser degree, Japan. Japan has, to be sure, been a working democracy for over a quarter century, but, as we pointed out, the continuity of the long-standing values stressing hierarchy, vertical ranking, and submissiveness creates in some measure a degree of "disharmony," which has resemblances to, but is just the reverse of, what prevails in American society.

In practice, American government is more permeable, less authoritative, and weaker in relation to the society it purports to govern than the governments of all the other major powers. American government was designed to be weak, and, comparatively speaking, it has remained weak. The mystique of "The State," so prevalent in European societies, has been happily absent from the American experience. But the Lockeian virtues of American political institutions do not necessarily help the United States to compete effectively in a Hobbesian world of "hard states." In addition, traditional American values impose a variety of moral and political restraints on governmental behavior, which are notably absent in the case of most other major countries. It is, for instance, inconceivable that any other society would dismantle and demoralize its foreign intelligence agencies in an "orgy of self-destruction" (in Kissinger's phrase), as the United States did in the early 1970s. In the post-Watergate era, in particular, governmental officials whose behavior transgresses liberal morality will pay a political price which would never be demanded in any other society. The widespread consensus on liberal values in the United States also means that Americans may well attribute to other governments inhibitions and goals quite foreign to the cultures in which those governments operate. Such misperceptions can greatly reduce the ability of American officialdom to come to realistic grips with the world as it is. The great problem for Americans in the coming decade is to retain their traditional ideals and values in a world in which those ideals and values may well be unique and be viewed as irrelevant.

COMMENTARIES

Boutros Boutros-Ghali

The best way to discuss the paper of Dr. Mansour Khalid and the socio-cultural determinants of Arab diplomacy is to present a short summary of my paper,* and to relate it to Arab diplomacy—its failures and suc-cesses. That should illuminate the two different approaches on the same subjects.

Before World War II, there was no Arab diplomacy, but rather many various diplomacies working at cross purposes. The separation between the Arabs in Asia and the Arabs in Africa was absolute. The Palestine problem put an end to this lack of coordination among the Arab diplomacies, and the London conference, or the Palestine con-ference in London in 1939, was the first formal international recognition of a common Arab diplomacy. The creation of the Arab League, in March 1945, offered the Arab states an institutional framework for a common Arab diplomacy.

How should the word *Arab* be understood? The matter was dis-cussed during the meeting which preceded the drafting of the pact of the Arab League in 1944. The official interpretation of the word *Arab* was that it implies a civilization with "a common culture, a common lan-guage, and a common aspiration to create an Arab nation." When the Arab League decided to amend its charter, the leaders again discussed the concept and agreed that Arabism involves a common language and common civilization.

I agree with Dr. Khalid that a common mistake is to confuse Arabs with Muslims. Not all Arabs are Muslims, and not all Muslims are Arabs. There were Arab Jews in Egypt, in the Yemen, and in Baghdad. There are Christian Arabs in Lebanon, in Syria, in Palestine, in the Sudan, and in Egypt. On the other hand, the Iranians, the Indonesians, the Senegalese, and the Nigerians are Muslim but not Arab. Only Arab

---

* See Appendix C.

155

states can join the Arab League. Muslim states that are not Arab cannot become part of the Arab League.

A second mistake is that the Arab states and Arab diplomacy are based on a racist concept. This confusion is related to the Arab anti-Zionist policy, which is sometimes wrongly considered to be anti-Semitic. Indeed, to the extent that they can be counted, the so-called pure Arabs number no more than 10 million, and the remaining 100 million are simply Arabized or Arabic-speaking Nubians, Somalians, Berbers, and others—a mosaic of ethnic groups that is sometimes called the "Arab melting pot." Arabism is based on the concept of an open society, and Arabization is a dynamic and continuous process. Somalia, an African country that embraced Islam, has adopted Arabic as the official language and become an Arabic country, and it was admitted to the Arab League. This same Arabization will probably occur in the Comoro Islands as a result of its obtaining its independence. Here I find a comparison with the concept of Americanization presented by Professor Samuel Huntington. Arabism, like Americanism, is an unsystematic ideology.

The failures of Arab diplomacy are reflected in four fields of activity. First is the failure to establish joint diplomatic representation. There is no provision for the Arab League to represent all the Arab states, nor is there any common diplomatic representation for several member states in a foreign country. There is a great need for such representation, given the increase in new states in the world and the difficulties young Arab states encounter in the arena of bilateral and parliamentary diplomacy. The Arab League tried to adopt a resolution calling for diplomatic coordination among the Arab nations, but it failed. The only result was that an Arab Bureau was established in several countries.

The second failure lies in the projection of the Arab image. African diplomacy in the 1960s succeeded in reinforcing the position and the image of Africa throughout the world, but Arab diplomacy has failed to promote a positive Arab image during the past twenty years, even though the Arab and the African countries belong to the same community and are confronted with the same diplomatic problems.

The third failure is the lack of control of treaties signed by the individual Arab states. Because they failed to develop machinery to control treaties, the different Arab countries concluded different treaties with the Soviet Union, for example, leading to a major dispute in 1954-1955 during the creation of the Baghdad Pact.

The fourth failure of Arab diplomacy, and one of the most important, has been the failure to settle inter-Arab disputes in an Arab framework. The Arab League failed completely to settle inter-Arab disputes, and the Arabs went directly to the Security Council to settle them.

Arab diplomacy has succeeded, however, in other fields of activity. The first is the decolonization of the Arab world. Although the fight for the decolonization of Palestine has been marked by a series of spectacular defeats, decolonization of the other Arab countries was achieved by common Arab diplomacy. It could be argued that decolonization would have taken place without Arab solidarity, Arab League action, and Arab diplomacy, but such assumptions are incorrect. A common Arab diplomacy offered a framework for the claims of the dependent Arab states and for collective intervention by independent Arab states. Within such a framework, the intervention could not be condemned as a kind of Arab neocolonialism by any Arab state. A regional international organization gave legitimacy to Arab action in the face of the colonialists' dialectic, which viewed any liberation movement as sedition. Arab diplomacy contributed to making decolonialization a doctrine and a principle of international law, and it succeeded in coordinating Arab policy within various international organizations. The Arab group in the United Nations, in a certain way, preceded the formation of the United Nations, and led to the creation of the Arab-Asian group and, later, the Afro-Asian group.

A second success of Arab diplomacy lay in the development of the concept of nonalignment. The Arab League was represented at the Bandung Conference in 1954, where the concept of nonalignment was promulgated, and the Arab League tried to become the permanent secretariat of the nonalignment movement. It failed, but Arab diplomacy has continued to play a very important role in nonalignment.

And the third positive contribution of Arab diplomacy is the establishment of an Afro-Arab dialogue. This has been the greatest success scored by Arab diplomacy in the last thirty years. It has been a success not only for the Arab and African countries, but also for all the developing countries of the world—in particular, the producers of raw materials. The Arab countries decided to recycle oil profits in the developing countries of Africa and created institutions to send Arab money or petrodollars throughout the Arab world. Even if some feel the amount of money is not enough, it is the first time that two groups of underdeveloped countries have decided to collaborate on their development.

In conclusion, I will say that Arab diplomacy has been an avant-garde diplomacy, a model for Asia, for Africa, and for the Third World as a whole. It has been a forerunner in opposing the colonial powers, and it was the first to make political, economic, and cultural decolonization its supreme objective. It was also the first to elevate anticolonial struggle to the level of a doctrine of regional international law. Within the framework of the United Nations and other specialized international agencies, Arab diplomacy has contributed to the creation of the Afro-Asian group—the first institutional voice speaking for the under-developed countries to the rich, industrialized world.

We must also recognize, however, that Arab diplomacy has failed to settle disputes among the Arab countries. Arab diplomacy has proved incapable of dealing with the creation of the Zionist state. This dynamic state represents a national contradiction within the Arab world, and has added a dimension to the Cold War.

Arab diplomacy can further an integration and, later, a federation of the Arab world. Only a common Arab diplomacy can save the Arab world from division into zones of influence. One of the saddest episodes in modern history is that of a rich and promising region of the world, with an ancient and authentic civilization, giving way to internal dispute because of the lack of imagination, generosity, and diplomacy shown by its elites.

Helen Thomas

Among scholars, I feel like a fish out of water—strictly out of my element. I could not even begin to deliver rebuttals on either of the two eloquent papers, but observations, perhaps. I think Dr. Khalid said that diplomacy was too important to be left to diplomats. It is not. It is all left to Henry Kissinger.

I have always wondered what an "Arab" was. My father and mother came from Tripoli. It was in Syria then, and now it is in Lebanon. In our family, we always say we are glad he did not miss the boat, and I have always felt that way. I spent a morning in Philadelphia with President Ford, who addressed the Polish-American Congress and then went to the Italian-American market section. He said they should keep their "Little Italy" intact, with their local schools, their local shops, and their local churches.

In the neighborhood I grew up in, in Detroit, there were German families and Italian families, and there was a Lebanese-Syrian section. No presidential candidate ever went there, though, probably because they knew we felt we should be assimilated. Our whole intent was to try to be Americans, whatever that meant.

I do not mean to de-emphasize our cultural background—no one loves the music, the food, the customs, the great generosity and hospitality of these ethnic groups more than I do. But most of us strongly desired to have a sense of belonging, and at times we did not have that sense.

When I came to Washington during World War II, I suddenly became aware that there was an Arab awakening. I began to learn about the beginnings, the articulation of this awakening, in Western terms, and the attempts by Arab nationalists to overthrow the rule of the Ottoman Empire, the French, the British, and others. I understood their yearnings because I related it to our own—to American independence from Great Britain. But then came the Palestinian War and the struggle in North Africa, and I thought there was tremendous sympathy in our country for Morocco, Algeria, and Tunisia in their effort to win independence. That struggle and the massacres that followed were very painful.

What I am trying to say is that I honestly do not know what an Arab is. I think an attempt has been made here to explain it, and I still do not know. It disturbs me as a so-called communicator to see the headline, "Christians Fighting in Lebanon," because I think a lot of Christians are not fighting on one side or the other.

I agree with much of what Mr. Huntington has said. I have had a vantage point at the White House since the Kennedy era, and I have not liked the tremendous growth of power in the presidency, especially not the President's pushbutton power of life and death over us. Vietnam has proved that without credibility a President cannot govern, and the lack of trust in that era—and maybe again in the Nixon era—was, I suppose, justified.

I do not feel that the American people have a deep and all-pervading lack of trust in their government. In fact, I see just the opposite: I think they have a tremendous yearning to believe and a will to believe again. They are almost quick to believe now, and perhaps they ought to keep a little skepticism.

As for the "orgy of recrimination," I remember that remark very well. It came about April 1974, I think, when President Nixon's departure from office was in sight, and everybody knew it but Kissinger. Kissinger made a speech about how Nixon's departure would divide and hurt us, how it would hurt diplomacy in the world because people would no longer believe that we were capable or that there was anyone in charge here, and he said that we should not indulge in an orgy of recrimination.

I disagree. I think we should indulge in orgies of recrimination to make this a better country. I think we did that—we took it down to the depths and brought it up again. I think we showed that no man, not even a President, is above the law. There is always a yearning for individuality against strong government; may it ever be so. I think governments should be challenged as ours was in regard to Vietnam. Eventually, everybody got together and saw the light. Kissinger now says that Vietnam was a disaster. *Now* he tells us—four and a half years later. Of course, everybody says it was a disaster now, but the kids were saying it a lot earlier.

There are times when the government should be challenged. We should have a strong government, but it should be a government that truly reflects the will of the people. Only then can this government really prevail or endure.

DISCUSSION

PROFESSOR LANEY: Anyone who seeks to understand the United States and its peculiarities, its strengths and its weaknesses, could do a very good deal worse than to start by reading the collected works of Professor Huntington on the subject. In my view he has put his finger squarely on perhaps the key to understanding American culture, though he might have stressed a little more the mixed bag of that culture. Even the opposition to strong government or to a concentration of power is encased with a lot of other notions, but this opposition to power seemed to me particularly apt in understanding what Sir Denis W. Brogan once called the American way in war, and perhaps in understanding the American way in foreign policy. I have in mind the alternation of American policy, between total moral war on behalf of great principles, on the one hand, and, on the other, isolation and leaving all those "foreigners" alone, together with our notorious and continuing inability to sustain a limited war, as in Korea and in Vietnam, and as may very well be the case in some future war. In your view, Professor Huntington, is the objection to concentrated power the most general case of the mixed bag of American beliefs? And is the first thing to understand about American political culture that it consists of a number of beliefs which are mutually inconsistent?

PROFESSOR HUNTINGTON: I agree with what Professor Laney has said. I think he pointed to one very important consequence of the dichotomy I was stressing between our political values, beliefs, and political practice and our governmental institutions.

The existence of that dichotomy leads to moralism, which is certainly a trait that is at times widely prevalent in the United States. Moralism often leads to cynicism, and cynicism leads to hypocrisy. We tend at times to go around in a circle, going from one to the other in an effort to try to come to terms with ourselves. This phenomenon does manifest itself, as Professor Laney mentioned, in the way we conduct wars. By and large, our successful wars were the wars which we seemed to be pleased with after we had fought them—wars which we not only

161

won, but won in a righteous cause. And I think, as many foreign observers both of American wars and of American diplomacy have commented, this element of moralism is always there, even if it is at times beneath the surface.

MR. BAULLATA: I am suspicious of generalized definitions, whether they be of Arabs, of blacks, or of Jews, especially if expressed by outsiders. Dr. Khalid builds a thesis according to the definitions of the so-called Orientalists, such as Raphael Patai, who lacks sociological training and whose book, *The Arab Mind,* which has been quoted from, offers a distorted if not a blatantly racist definition of the Arab. This is not only dangerous but also very regrettable coming from a person with the stature of Dr. Khalid. The Third World has known native intellectuals who mimic ideas of such Western Orientalists, but recently it has also known a new generation of concerned intellectuals, who are giving an insider's definition of the Arab character. Hisham Sharabi's book, *Arā fi al-Mujtama' al-'Arabi* (Thoughts on Arab society), is only one example among many. I would like to recommend this book to Dr. Khalid with the hope that in future talks he would be able to speak of the Arab peoples as an insider and not mimic ideas of outsiders.

I also regret having to have said that.

DONALD TANNENBAUM, Gettysburg College: I almost hesitate in light of what the previous speaker said about generalization, but nevertheless I will forge ahead and ask for a comment on the following: It seems to me that the notion of interdependence in international relations is a concept that might be useful for drawing together the threads of what I perceive to be two separate views—the American view and the Arab view. I wonder if Professor Huntington might comment on the value of the idea of interdependence and what it might mean in bringing together these two views.

PROFESSOR HUNTINGTON: Obviously we are becoming more interdependent in a variety of ways. This is perhaps particularly a traumatic affair for the United States, because the trends toward interdependence, developing especially in the past decade or so, have in large part resulted in greater dependence by the United States and other states in regard to resources, trade, and a variety of means of support. I am not sure that interdependence is a way of insuring that Arabs and Americans will communicate better or understand each other better. It simply provides the reason why it will be necessary and desirable for Americans and Arabs and most other peoples in the world to communicate and to understand each other better.

162

SPEAKER: As a European, I am struck by the biased view on the Middle East given by the American media. Ms. Thomas, knowing the role of the press in the decision-making process in the United States, which differs from that in Europe, and considering how the press here molds public opinion, would you comment on the statement that the American press, with the possible exception of the *Christian Science Monitor,* lacks the intellectual stature of the European press in regard to the Middle East?

MS. THOMAS: That may be your point of view. I suppose that Europe is closer to the Middle East. Europeans have dominated the Middle East much longer than we have tried to, so maybe they have a closer affiliation. I have not seen so much of the intellectual stature. Because of the French mandate over Syria, Lebanon, and elsewhere, maybe the French do have a deeper understanding. But at the same time I do think that the American press is trying to understand, and that more interesting articles are being printed now on the Middle East.

DR. MAKSOUD: Dr. Khalid, would you respond to the observation that was made earlier by Mr. Baullata?

DR. KHALID: My only comment is that Mr. Baullata's statement decries generalizations, but it contains a gross generalization about Orientalists. I mentioned in my speech that many of those Orientalists are responsible for the misconstruction and distortion of Arab culture and of Arab history. I referred to many of the contemporary Arab historians and to some of the traditional historians. At the same time, there are schools of Orientalists who had some very piercing insights into Arab culture. I mentioned people like Jacques Berque and Maxime Rodinson. Those people are Orientalists, if we can use that term, and I think they understand the Arab culture perhaps much better than many of the so-called insiders.

The question of insiders and outsiders depends on where you draw the circle. There are underlying assumptions in all of these statements; they start from some ideological bias. A Marxist wants to view things within that prism. An anti-Marxist wants to view them within a different prism. We should accept some interpretations of Arab culture and Arab personality by non-Arabs if they fall within the bounds of objective analysis. As I said, this is not to say that all that has been written by Orientalists is right or that it cannot be dismissed. There is a lot of misrepresentation in their interpretations of certain aspects of Islamic culture and the Arab concept of history. We must avoid those generalizations, if only for the sake of objectivity.

163

DR. JOHN DUKE ANTHONY: To follow on Dr. Khalid's remarks just briefly, the gentleman on my left has an outsider's view on these matters. Most of us here are either Americans or Arabs, but Ambassador Edward F. Henderson is from Great Britain and has been acknowledged as one of Great Britain's foremost Arabists for the better part of thirty years. He fought in North Africa in World War II, served in Syria, served in Amman, Abu Dhabi, and Qatar, and is a principal figure in the so-called Bureimi dispute, which brought about a clash between Great Britain, Saudi Arabia, the Arab states, and the Americans all at once. Inasmuch as he has been a participant in these events and is now a guest in the United States, I thought it fitting that he make a few comments about the themes we have been addressing here.

EDWARD F. HENDERSON: I am very much privileged to be the only non-Arab, non-American to talk to you. My career in several spheres— business, diplomacy, and earlier the army—has brought me in contact with the Arabs. My main problem has always been to try to represent their views to somebody 3,000 or 4,000 miles away. I have never had the slightest trouble on the spot finding out what each of us wanted, but it has been a business trying to tell a company or a government 4,000 miles away what is going on.

In the days when I first went through the Middle East, there was a very big gap in understanding between the West—America, France, Great Britain—and the Arabs. I think that gap has narrowed tremendously. We always, in those days, preached that the British should learn Arabic. We preached, we preached, and we preached. We have had great success because the Arabs have all learned English. It was easier that way. But I do notice, over the period of the thirty years or so during which I have been involved, a very great increase in understanding. This has been due to the people on the spot on both sides and the extraordinary hospitality and friendliness of the Arabs, which I think is their most renowned characteristic.

I have also seen a great improvement in Anglo-American relations there, because in 1948, 1949, and 1950 we were on opposite sides of a fence, and the problem we were arguing about has been happily solved, to the content of all parties concerned.

DR. MAKSOUD: As chairperson, I will use my arbitrary power to call on a very distinguished American—the former chairman of the Foreign Relations Committee, Senator Fulbright—to say a few words.

J. W. FULBRIGHT, former U.S. senator (Democrat, Arkansas): Just to have this conference, I think, is a great step forward. It is only recently that affairs of this kind have been held. I was extremely pleased at Ms. Helen Thomas's comment that she believes the newspapers in this country are now disposed to pay some attention to problems discussed here, and I look forward with a great deal of interest to see how they will report this conference. I have made speeches and I have attended meetings where others made speeches, on the Arab point of view, but rarely has any notice whatever been taken of them. However, I agree that there is a much greater interest and recognition, not so much about the media, but within the circles where I am now working and among some of my former colleagues. Understanding and finding solutions to the problems that have arisen in the Middle East are of vast importance, not only to us as a nation, but to everyone who is trying to make some sense in our international relations.

I do think there has been some improvement, and I am hopeful that the press will assist in that educational process. I have, as you well know, for many reasons been interested in this question of communication. One thing that I have always been reasonably proud of was the initiation of the program to exchange scholars with other countries. That program is designed to do just what this conference is doing—to acquaint Americans with the cultures of other people, and now especially the Middle East.

I hope our Arab friends will understand that we are a very parochial country. I can say that because I especially am an example of this parochialism, having been brought up in the Ozark Mountains, which are about 1,200 miles from here. When I was young, there were no airplanes. It was very difficult to get out of the Ozark Mountains to go anywhere, and we never thought of learning Arabic as Ambassador Henderson did. I was completely ignorant about most of the problems discussed here, and even of the existence of the countries with which we are now so deeply concerned. I had not the slightest idea that I would ever have to speak Arabic. I tried to speak English, but even that was beyond our capacity in many cases. We really spoke a dialect of the Ozark Mountains. But now I think there has been real progress, and I am very encouraged by this conference.

I know there are movements toward the establishment of chairs in Arabic studies in various universities. This I applaud. Foundations have been created, as we have read recently, designed to bring about greater understanding and communication.

In the long run, there is no sleight of hand by diplomats or anyone else that can solve these problems. The only thing I have any confidence in is the gradual process of education, if I may use that word in its broadest sense. When people live and communicate with others of different cultures, they do acquire an understanding of those cultures, and they nearly always find that those differences are not nearly so significant as they had thought, whether they be differences in language or in ideology or in culture. I have seen literally hundreds and hundreds of people that participated in such programs. Although they may not fall in love with everyone from the other culture, and they still may have reservations about certain differences, they invariably develop quite a change in their attitude and their approach toward people from a different culture. I applaud the American Enterprise Institute for organizing this conference, and I look forward to similar programs in the future, in which we can have frank and candid exchanges. Then I hope the American people will all be educated, and I am sure they will, to our mutual benefit. There is no country, really, that needs the kind of education I have in mind more than the United States, because of its size, its physical remoteness, and, above all, its power.

All of us should recognize that with the kind of economic and military power that we have, there comes a great feeling that we can do it ourselves. This has been the history of all such countries. When they became powerful, they thought there was no need for cooperation with lesser powers. Now I think we are at a point where we realize the need for others, and I think we will respond. We can be of great benefit to all the world.

PETER BECHTOLD, Foreign Service Institute: Dr. Mansour Khalid has been very modest in not talking about his very extensive diplomatic experience, and I want to ask him if he would like to make some comparative statements. He has been very active in the highest diplomatic level in the Arab world, with Africans, with Europeans, and with Asians. Are there certain things that are typical of Arabs but not, say, of Africans, Europeans, or Americans? And are there some elements of diplomatic style that are peculiarly Arab?

DR. KHALID: That is a difficult question. What can be considered typically Arab in the conduct of diplomatic activity? In regard to Arab successes in the conduct of diplomacy, I think Professor Boutros Boutros-Ghali referred to a few examples, and one of them, perhaps, can be elaborated upon. That is the concept of Afro-Arab solidarity.

In my thinking, this solidarity is an outgrowth of the results of the October War and the perception of a new relationship between the Arab world and Africa. This colossus has not been recognized very much. As Professor Boutros Boutros-Ghali aptly said, the result of this diplomacy and the new concept of Afro-Arab solidarity is developing into something far-reaching. It is more than just being able to count on the African vote in the United Nations or on the African organization to take a unified position against Israel. A global area of operation is developing, with perhaps a common vision as to the future of both the Arab world and Africa. New institutions are being created, some of them political, some of them economic, and a new charter is being devised for Afro-Arab cooperation. This charter has already been adopted by the Afro-Arab Conference of Ministers and will be put before an Afro-Arab summit. The idea is to put the resources of both groups together in order to help each other. As Professor Boutros-Ghali said, this is perhaps the first experience of developing countries helping each other. From that can emerge another area of cooperation—a triangle of cooperation between the Arab countries, with their tremendous financial assets, the African countries, with their natural resources, and the Western countries, with their knowledge. The Arab-European dialogue in a way is an attempt to use the resources not only of the Arab countries but also of some of the African countries.

Another success of Arab diplomacy is the creation of new institutions. As I said before, perhaps a more rational approach to Arab unity would be through a functional approach—the creation of institutions that will bring people together, that will make the ordinary man in any particular Arab country feel that there is meaning to this unity.

Take an example in my country, the Democratic Republic of the Sudan. We are embarking on a major development project known as the Arab Agricultural Program. The idea is to use Arab resources for agricultural development of the Sudan, which has tremendous potential—something like 200 million acres of fertile and arable land, of which only 8 percent is being used. Within the coming twenty-five years, we hope to invest something like $6 billion in developing this land. This is an example of what can be achieved through a new concept of Arab diplomacy.

DR. MAKSOUD: This conference is a pilot project for the cross-fertilization of ideas. We have discovered shared values here, as well as differences. By finding the extent of these shared values, we can clarify our differences. This is an important part of communication.

The principal speakers today have been very revealing in discussing not only the achievements of their societies but also their problems. In communication, credibility often can be measured by the freedom shown in discussing one's problems. In this seminar, we have established mutual credibility through the critical assessment of our respective attitudes and perceptions. This has been done through the scholarship evidenced by the principal speakers and by the insight and remarks of the discussants and the participants.

At this moment in the Arab world, we realize that our credibility

167

would be enhanced further if our newly discovered wealth were used to relieve poverty. If we can do that, then many of the adverse images of Arab personality held by the world community would be improved. Furthermore, such matters as the hemorrhage experienced by the Lebanese and the Palestinians in the last year and a half must be interpreted as a challenge to Arab collective diplomacy to become more relevant and effective. In this respect, I am very critical of Arab diplomacy.

On this 200th anniversary of the American Republic, we have discovered how much of American decolonization is relevant to our national experience. We have also discovered that the melting-pot theory—the integration of a multiplicity of ethnic and religious backgrounds—is also very similar to the thrust of our national self-expression. That is why, at times, we are perplexed that the United States underwrites an ideology that is the very negation of its own melting-pot theory. Part of the problem of communication is that the Arabs do not understand why the United States underwrites not only the existence of Israel, but also the objectives of Israel. We are also perplexed by the lack of perception the United States has shown of the legitimate aspirations of Palestinian people.

While recognizing these basic failures, this conference has renewed our understanding that our differences should be subordinate to our common approach and common policy.

PART FIVE

CAN CULTURES COMMUNICATE?

ROUND TABLE DISCUSSION

EDWARD STEWART, visiting professor of communications, University of Minnesota, and moderator of the Round Table: The subject of our discussion—"Can Cultures Communicate?"—is a very challenging one. Since this Round Table is part of a two-day conference on Arab and American cultures, sponsored by the American Enterprise Institute, those cultures will probably receive most of our attention, though the discussion should have general application to cross-cultural relations.

For communication to take place, there must be some common ground, but Arab and American cultures are very different from each other. If Arabs and Americans must have some empathy for each other's culture in order to communicate, what conditions do Arabs require to build trust with Americans, and what conditions do Americans require to build trust with Arabs? I wonder if Professor Said would address the question.

EDWARD SAID, Department of English and Comparative Literature, Columbia University: Yes, I am happy to start off by sounding an optimistic note, that it is indeed possible for Arabs and Americans to interact culturally in the fullest possible sense. But, having said that, I should add, realistically, that in the present context there are two principal obstacles to an optimal relationship between the two cultures.

First, cultural relationships do not exist in the abstract: they take place in the world. The relationship between Arab and American cultures is highly politicized for a number of fairly obvious reasons. The Middle East—and, in particular, the Arab Middle East—is a place of great political, economic, and social concern to the United States. Since before World War II, there has been little American cultural involvement in the area, with the exception of isolated missionary and charitable institutions. Relationships between the two cultures are a post-World War II phenomenon, and they have been highly conditioned by a number of very powerful political constraints, which tend to narrow the focus of these relationships.

The second obstacle is that, for reasons both of language and of cultural or religious tradition, Arab culture is not widely known in this country. The problems of translation are many, but that is only part of it. If you were to ask a generally literate American about what is now taking place culturally in the Arab world—in poetry, in fiction, in the arts generally—he would be very hard put to name a single figure of any importance. That is to say, of any importance to the Arabs. He might mention Kahlil Gibran, but he is not of this time. So one feels that the possibilities of intercultural relationships at this moment are severely limited.

PROFESSOR STEWART: You are saying that there is a narrow interface between the two cultures. Professor Huntington, would you like to comment on that?

SAMUEL P. HUNTINGTON, Department of Government, Harvard University: I think that is certainly the case. The problem is one of ignorance—the product of a lack of communication—on the American side, and I can look at this only from the American side. You raise the question of trust—How do we go about establishing trust between Americans and Arabs? One can have trust only where one has communication; communication is a necessary but not a sufficient qualification for trust. In order to establish trust, one has to have dealings among individuals. Trust is something which exists within, or rather between, individuals. The problems of establishing trust between Americans and Arabs are little different from those of establishing trust between any other groups of individuals—between social classes or generations or, for that matter, between different people in different occupations. It is something which has to be done on an individual basis. Related to that is the need to eliminate from American thinking many stereotypes of Arabs, which are based on ignorance.

PROFESSOR STEWART: You have identified the individual basis of intercultural communication. Dr. Safwan, can you concur with that?

MUSTAFA SAFWAN, psychoanalyst: To start with, I must beg your pardon if my English proves to be hesitating or at times incorrect. As a matter of fact, bad pronunciation may be a handicap or an obstacle to communication between individuals, but, as far as cultures are concerned, one of the main obstacles to communication consists in the fact

172

that man always puts some passion in his relationship to his identity—to his national or social identity. Some of this passion must be renounced to facilitate mutual communication. This point requires longer development which can wait until later.

PROFESSOR STEWART: Are you suggesting that Americans might have some difficulty in handling passion?

DR. SAFWAN: No, I meant all of us, all of us, whatever the group. The very fact of *appartenance*—of belonging—has something gratifying in it, a kind of gratification which must be renounced. I mean, every position implies opposition.

LAURA NADER, Department of Anthropology, University of California, Berkeley: In discussing trust between Arabs and Americans, we must determine which Americans and which Arabs are meant. In the relationship between American oil companies and the heads of Arab states, for example, there has been a great deal of mutual trust, and the two groups have had a long relationship. In the attitudes of Lebanese or Syrian villagers, there is also a tremendous amount of trust because they have relatives in this country who are Americans, and the villagers see this as a natural link. The question might even be turned around to ask why Arabs continue to trust Americans in spite of debacles like the situation in 1967 when the United States condoned Israeli aggression against Jordan, Syria, and Egypt.

We should return to the point Professor Said brought up, which has to do with politicization. Several studies carried out in California analyzed the Arab image used in textbooks in the California schools and in films, cartoons, songs, and other media, made since 1920. These studies indicate that stereotyping is a very important technique in building or sabotaging trust between cultures. If we look at the question through time, we find that in this country from 1920 Arabs were perceived as being good fighters and exotic desert lovers with harem girls, and the rest of it. But, over the past several decades, this image has changed to one of the Arab who is cruel, weak, and decadent. It is probably no surprise that this change should have occurred as interest in the development of the state of Israel began to develop.

To sum up, we should specify exactly which Arabs and which Americans are under discussion, at what point in time, and what the function of the images might be.

PROFESSOR STEWART: You have raised the issue of stereotypes, and how the American perception of Arabs has changed in the last twenty or thirty years. Do we have any examples of Arab perceptions or stereotypes of Americans? Perhaps there is a lack of realism in how people perceive us, compared with how we really are.

PROFESSOR SAID: To compare the two sets of perceptions, again one would have to specify the areas precisely. On the whole, there would be an inequality between the two perceptions for the simple reason that America as a cultural entity to the Arab world is rather different from the reverse. That is to say, the relationship of America to the Arab world has been characterized by strength and by great development. The general Arab image of America and the West has been one of wonder and of some admiration, which in the past few decades has, for the most part, soured. There is a long history of cultural attitudes, which could be described as stereotypes, in the West generally, which have filtered into American culture. They are very hard to remove. In time, they may change or be modified, as Professor Nader was saying, but they are not radically changed. Certainly the events of the last two or three years have demonstrated this.

PROFESSOR NADER: I would like to disagree with the pessimism implied there. The image of China changed overnight. We passed from a time when the Chinese could not do anything we considered good, to a time when, to some people, the Chinese cannot do anything bad. The change occurred very dramatically and very rapidly through government leadership. We need not be entirely pessimistic.

PROFESSOR HUNTINGTON: Stereotypes and images can exist on two different levels—we can have stereotypes, first, of individuals and, second, of societies or cultures. Most of our stereotypes are of people in other societies as individuals. As you said, Arabs are viewed as being untrustworthy, weak, cunning, and so forth—all individual characteristics. It is rather striking that what you identified as the recent American stereotype of Arabs is precisely the stereotype which not too long ago Americans had of Jews. The stereotype of Jews has changed, and so has that of Arabs, and you are absolutely correct in saying that these stereotypes can change very quickly as a result of leadership and of images presented in the media. This is because they have little or no basis in reality.

There are, however, real differences, major differences, in cultures and societies in terms of how people relate to each other. Societies differ, people do not. Many years ago, I was a member of a group of ten American scholars and former public officials who went to meet a similar

174

group in Japan. When I arrived in Tokyo, I was met by a Japanese escort, an official from the foreign office. For an incredibly long hour-and-a-half drive into Tokyo from the airport, he wanted to find out who was the leader of our group. We did not have a leader, but this was inconceivable to him. He came back again and again and again trying to find out the hierarchy in the American group of ten.

Ten Americans could get together and cooperate without any defined hierarchy, but in Japan when ten people get together there is a Number One, a Number Two, a Number Three, and so on. The difference is in the way in which individuals organize themselves and perceive their relations to other people in their society.

PROFESSOR STEWART: You are suggesting that there will be differences in society in terms of how people identify with the group. Let me pose a question here. Do any of the differences between "the American identity" and "the Arab identity" block intercultural communications between the two societies? How do the Egyptians feel about that, Dr. Safwan?

DR. SAFWAN: The very idea of stereotypes made me think of an experience I had in Egypt on one of my last visits, two or three years ago. It brings up the question of the effect of American films in building a stereotype of the American image. In Cairo, I saw a film on television about the Korean War, in which an American pilot spread devastation around the country and then got down from his plane and met a child coming from all of this horrid desolation. The pilot was very moved by the spectacle. He took the child in his arms and gave him a piece of chocolate or something like that. It cannot be denied that an image like that distorts one's view of Americans. This image sums up the Egyptian attitude toward Americans. This image of a pilot who can do everything—who can bring evil and good together—is an ideal image, and I think it deforms one's perception. It leads to stereotypes that make authentic or genuine perceptions rather more difficult.

PROFESSOR NADER: Let me give you an example of how stereotypes are being formed today. In discussions of energy in this country, the term *foreign oil* is rarely used. It is usually *Arab oil*. But, among the seven largest oil producers in the world, Arab countries in fact are absent from the top two, which are Russia and the United States. Arab countries rank only third and seventh. And yet when we talk about why we need such things as nuclear power plants, we do not talk about foreign oil but about Arab oil. This creates a certain stereotype of the

175

power of oil-rich Arab lands that does not conform to reality. Also, in these discussions, it is interesting that most people do not differentiate between *Iranian oil* and *Arab oil*. In fact, they do not understand that the two terms imply different cultures.

PROFESSOR STEWART: You have talked about the stereotypes and how they have changed. If we think of a stereotype as a picture in the mind, does this picture tell more about Arabs or about Americans, particularly as it keeps changing?

PROFESSOR HUNTINGTON: I think it tells something about how Americans perceive their interests, or at least how leading groups in American society see their interest, because these stereotypes do change and do reflect changing interests.

PROFESSOR STEWART: So these changes do not necessarily correlate with changes taking place in Arab society. They are more a commentary on American interests and shifts in those interests.

PROFESSOR HUNTINGTON: There may be some relationship to Arab society—obviously, the Arab world is becoming urbanized and is no longer largely peasant or Bedouin. The change in stereotypes which professor Nader mentioned at the beginning has some relationship to what is going on in the Arab world, though undoubtedly it is very far from the reality of those changes. But it is frightening how stereotypes can change overnight.

PROFESSOR SAID: For the last two or three decades at least, Arab society has been going through a tremendous number of changes. To talk about Arab society or Arab culture, as we have, is to wipe out important distinctions between the various societies within the Arab world. In many ways, they are quite different from each other, though they do have points in common. Also, we are not taking into account the fact that these societies are constantly in change and that even an Arab in the midst of this change would be hard put to characterize the present stage of his development. The changes are so fast and so revolutionary that the confusion is almost inevitable.

In addition to that, the political atmosphere is highly charged. At no moment that I can remember in the last two decades could relationships between Arab and American societies or cultures be described as peaceful or normal. There has always been some extra dimension which aggravates a situation and makes the sense of change and confusion even greater. That is one reason why people resort to stereotypes—they need something stable to hang on to. Frequently, stereotypes are generated not only out of ignorance but also out of fear.

PROFESSOR STEWART: Professor Huntington mentioned that we need not only to have trust but also to communicate. In connection with your remarks, can we look at some of the problems of cutting across the stereotypes, cutting across the culture differences? In the area of individual or cultural communication between Americans and Arabs, what might be some of the challenges and some of the problems? One of the things that often comes up, for instance, is that Americans tend to note differences between words and actions, and they often see a greater schism between language and behavior in the Arab world than at home. Does this kind of culture difference present a problem in terms of communication?

PROFESSOR SAID: It is curious that many generalizations about this "schism" between words and actions or reality in Arab culture have been made by people who do not know the language. These generalizations about the way Arabs think and the way Arabs speak, and the difference between them are made on the basis of a few free-floating generalizations about Arab society and Arab mentality. In any other situation, one would openly call this racist. You cannot characterize a culture according to some norm that you impose on the relationships between words and actions and say, "It is perfectly clear that Arabs really never mean what they say"—a popular stereotype.

Words and actions differ in all societies—one must allow for such differences. But to make an arbitrary judgment and say it is greater in Arab societies and less great in Sweden and in the United States is perhaps a rather dangerous form of generalization, which leads to nothing productive.

PROFESSOR NADER: Some people have characterized the student movement of the 1960s in the United States as a rebellion of the young because of the gap between what the American government was saying and what it was doing. The difference between word and act has been the crux of the argument between the so-called student movement and the establishment for the last ten years. Looking at this question cross-culturally, one finds no culture has a monopoly on the gap between word and act. The size of the gap reflects the health of a culture, that is, if the gap between word and act becomes too large for the people of that culture, then there is some trouble there. Similarly, if the gap is too large in an individual, that would indicate a mental health problem.

PROFESSOR HUNTINGTON: This gap is not a phenomenon limited to the 1960s in the American experience. It is something which has been with us virtually from the beginning, particularly in the area of politics. We have set forth an impossible set of political goals and ideals and have talked in rhetorical terms about achieving them. Inevitably, we fall very short and compensate by engaging either in moralism or in cynicism or in hypocrisy, trying to bridge the gap between rhetoric and reality. I would find it difficult to believe that the problem is any greater in the Arab world than it is in the United States.

PROFESSOR STEWART: Can anyone guess the source of that stereotype about Arabs? Americans often mention this schism though we have acknowledged it is no greater among Arabs than in American society. What is the source of the notion?

PROFESSOR SAID: I think the specific historical source can be found in the general Western perception of what in the nineteenth century was called the Orient. As early as the first part of the nineteenth century, "scientific" generalizations were made on the distinction between what used to be called the Semitic, or Oriental, languages and the Western languages. This was the moment when comparative linguistics was born as a science. From a scientific discussion of a language, such as one of the Semitic languages, generalizations would be made about the kind of mind that would produce that language. A wholesale identification was made of the language with this generalized mentality, and by the middle of the nineteenth century, "the Semitic mentality" was said to be exemplified in its language, which was considered unable to deal with modern—in this case, European—reality.

Such generalizations have been very, very influential. We still frequently hear that Arabic is a rhetorical language, that Arabic is a language of eloquence, that it is in effect a medieval language, and that it cannot deal with modern reality. By imputation, these generalizations are also supposed to apply to the Arab mentality. There is a respectable pedigree for this kind of nonsense, and it *is* nonsense because no linguist today would ever agree with it. But it persists, as Professor Nader was saying. It is to be found in textbooks, not only in high school textbooks but also in college and so-called scientific texts.

DR. SAFWAN: Rather than two mentalities, two functions of speech have been recognized by many anthropologists—Malinowski, for example. Language or speech as a vehicle of communication, an instrument for the communication of practical needs, has been distinguished from expressive speech. The latter kind of speech would be the kind through which one tries, for example, to get recognition in the Hegelian sense. This second function of speech exists in all societies and in some is the more privileged. To put the matter in a brutally simple way, one can use speech either to make money or to make one's own being. It is the second function which is privileged in Arabic, as one feels in talking with Arab people. In America, communication tends to be codified in view of "practical" ends.

PROFESSOR NADER: The mistake people in one culture often make in dealing with another culture is to transfer their functions to the other culture's functions. A political scientist, for example, went to the Middle East to do some research one summer and analyzed Egyptian newspapers. When he came back, he said to me, "But they are all just full of emotions. There is no data in these newspapers." I said, "What makes you think there should be?"

The other comment that I wanted to make, following up on Professor Said's observation, is that the tendency to see one's culture as the most logical, the most beautiful, the most whatever, is a tendency that anthropologists sometimes refer to as ethnocentrism. In the nineteenth century, it was commonplace to look not only at Semitic languages but also at all other non-Western languages of the world and say, "These people are prelogical, they speak like children," or, "They are illogical, they are prescientific." Many labels were used, and, of course, the culture that always came up on top was that of the person doing the analysis. If we went back into Arab history, as we easily can, and read the historians that described early European culture, we would find them doing the same kinds of things and making the same kinds of judgments.

PROFESSOR STEWART: This phenomenon is similar to that of stereotypes, which say a great deal more about the holder of the stereotype than about the other society. Americans often claim, rightly or wrongly, that there is a difference in how the two societies use information and knowledge. In American society, information and knowledge are treated more as a commodity, whereas in Arab societies, they are more often treated as a source of power, something which is accumulated and not necessarily dispensed with the same freedom found in American society. I wonder if we could look at that.

PROFESSOR NADER: As long as someone has previously used the

179

word *racist,* I can use it again. It is just a nonsensical statement, with absolutely no basis. The government studies that are done in this country are all put on shelves after they are done. They are purely for ceremonial purposes, one study after the other. We gather information supposedly to apply to social problems but we never apply it. There is no evidence whatsoever to buttress the statements that you have quoted.

PROFESSOR SAID: It is curious that whatever knowledge there is in the United States of Arab culture is skewed towards classical culture. If a literate American knows anything about Arab civilization, he is likely to know about Ibn Khaldun, Averroes, and people of that sort— that is to say, medieval philosophers, writers, and poets. This person would know little about what is now taking place in the Arab world. This is one of the most striking and peculiar discrepancies between the two cultures, that the relationship is not between one contemporary culture and another contemporary culture, but between a contemporary culture and a classical culture. In the formal study of Arab culture in this country and in the West generally, a great deal of attention is paid either to the classical period or to current sociopolitical or socio-economic realities, as defined by modern Western political and social scientists. The rather large area of Arab endeavor engaged in ongoing contemporary culture receives no attention whatever, so Americans know nothing about the modern Egyptian novel, for example, or about modern Syrian poetry. A most peculiar sort of time lag exists in the world today.

PROFESSOR STEWART: The other country is always seen out of time, in a sense.

PROFESSOR SAID: Yes, I think this point was made earlier, but it is very important. This is also part of the tradition of looking at the Orient as essentially a classical civilization which got lost long ago. Everything to be found in Arab society appears degenerate somehow, a degraded version of the great classical past. In a curious way, this attitude is reinforced by the belief of many Arabs that their great days of glory are in the past. It is a strange kind of feedback effect, and it is very influential, and regrettable.

PROFESSOR HUNTINGTON: Professor Stewart, I would like to go back to the question you posed earlier concerning knowledge and attitudes towards knowledge and the use of knowledge. One distinctive element in American culture is in its extraordinary emphasis upon spreading knowledge and information, upon exposés, upon publicity. Much of this activity is undoubtedly ceremonial, as Professor Nader suggested, but it is something that distinguishes American culture, even among Western cultures. One does not find in Great Britain this emphasis upon opening up doors, muckraking, exposure, and so forth. In this connection, the media play a much more important role in American culture than in most other Western cultures, and, I would suspect, than in Arab cultures as well.

PROFESSOR STEWART: I am glad you picked up on that point because I too feel different cultures sometimes stress different systems and different functions, as Dr. Safwan was saying. The Japanese, for instance, have a class of words that give nothing but a taste or flavor of the language and have no other meaning. It is language used for an expressive function rather than for the communication of hard information. There are differences among cultures of this kind, as well as political differences and differences in the exchange of information or knowledge.

PROFESSOR SAID: You are making a distinction between information, which you regard as something useful, and other things that are not directly useful but which might also be information. Even when something is said ceremonially in Japanese, it still conveys information. It is a different kind of information, but why should information always be useful?

PROFESSOR STEWART: Whether information is an essential exchange of hard facts and data, as we would think, or a direct communication to the individual himself depends upon one's value system.

PROFESSOR SAID: Hard facts are matters of judgment—just say, "That is a hard fact," and it becomes one. It may be a little more complicated than that, perhaps, but in generalizing about cultures it is frequently decided arbitrarily that something is information and something else is not. Arabs are said to spend a great deal of time being "emotional," as if being emotional is not quite as useful or important as conveying hard facts. As many novelists have pointed out, imparting hard facts may be a bad thing after all. There may be too many hard facts around and not enough emotions.

PROFESSOR STEWART: Different values might be placed on expressive or emotional communication and communication that tends to be more "pedestrian," which is used for exchanging facts and figures of different kinds.

DR. SAFWAN: Does America have anything like the French Ministry of Information?

PROFESSOR STEWART: I think we have many of those.

DR. SAFWAN: Information is never wholly disinterested as far as a government policy of information may be concerned. Could we say, for example, that there is an Egyptian *citizen* in the sense the term has evolved in the West from its Greek origin? Is there a citizen in Egypt in this sense? There are those who govern and those who are governed, but citizens? I would not dream of trying to answer these questions myself.

PROFESSOR HUNTINGTON: I wish you would engage in some dreaming and answer them for us. They are fascinating questions.

PROFESSOR STEWART: It is often said that in Arab societies people have seen the brilliance of revelation which gives a religious tone to the society and to some of its laws as well. In American society, however, the values of Christianity have become secularized and have lost much of the magnetism of the original revelation. Does this line of thought lead to communication, or is it a block?

PROFESSOR SAID: One of the major presidential candidates certainly does not seem to think that revelation belongs to time past.

PROFESSOR STEWART: He is trying to bring it back.

PROFESSOR SAID: Yes, right. No culture necessarily has a monopoly on revelation. The religious coloration of Arab society has been overstated (I should use the phrase *Arab society* with quotation marks around it because I am not sure which Arab society we are talking about). The same religious coloration can be found in other societies, so the real questions are at what level the religious faith is practiced, whether it influences all aspects of life in society or just some of them, and where, how, and at what times it is practiced.

PROFESSOR HUNTINGTON: If, indeed, Arab society is religiously colored, I would think that would make it more, rather than less, like

American society. Religion and religious values and beliefs play a very large role in our culture. Just a little while ago there was a poll of how religious the different peoples of the world were, and, if I remember correctly, Americans ranked next to the top. In terms of belief in God and the formal aspects of religion, Americans always rate very high. A religious character has been very much a part of the American heritage since the origins of the nation, and, despite modernization and secularization, it is still very much with us.

PROFESSOR STEWART: Can we distinguish between a religion that is merely professed and one that governs our daily actions, and then compare American and Arabic societies?

PROFESSOR NADER: This goes back to what you were saying earlier, Professor Said, about seeing the Middle East through classicist glasses. Some fifteen years ago, I went to the Middle East to see if Islamic law, or religious law, was in fact operating in the villages, or had it, being an urban religion, never really penetrated into the villages. In the villages, when we started talking about everyday conflicts and disputes and how they resolve them, lo and behold, I discovered there is no Islamic law operating at all.

The procedures were very pragmatic. The neighborhood councils operated in a way we are trying to invent in certain parts of the United States today. It was an arbitration procedure, sometimes mediated rather than arbitrated, and it was very pragmatic, very secular. I had absolutely no trouble in this village being invited into the mosque. I was a woman, but that did not make any difference, and all of the stereotypes caved in, one after the other. Islamic women, who are often portrayed as being very compressed and repressed and depressed, were much freer in these villages than middle class women I know in Berkeley. They come and go and do pretty much as they want. They often have the power of their lineage to back their position. There is probably less wife beating in this little village in southern Lebanon than there is in Berkeley, California, according to a recent study of wife beating in upper, middle, and lower income groups in Berkeley.

These stereotypes are just that. Instead of trying to explain many things that may not exist, people who want to study the Middle East should find out what is there, what is happening in the area, rather than taking a stereotype and saying, "I wonder why they are so religious?" We do not even know whether they are or not.

PROFESSOR SAID: The study of the Middle East in the West generally, and in this country specifically, has been focused on large, monolithic Platonic concepts such as "Islam," or "the Arabs," as if they had some unchanging existence of their own. As a result, people who profess to know the Middle East engage in an operation like this. They take an immediate political event, or a web of political events—what is taking place in Egypt, for example, or in Syria—and for an ultimate understanding of it, they take a couple of passages from the Koran or from some twelfth-century jurist, and say, "If you really want to understand what is going on, you have to go back to these lines, which are really the secret to it." In looking at the Arab world, this practice is not only tolerated but encouraged, it seems to me.

The equivalent of such folly is to say, "If you really want to understand what is taking place in the Congress on the energy bill, you have to read the New Testament very carefully, and then everything will be clear to you." You may laugh, but this is regularly done in articles by distinguished scholars who say what is going on in the Middle East is really all about Islam.

DR. SAFWAN: What was said about the Middle East village indicates that customs are in the process of changing, but it does not prove that dogma changes. The hold of dogma on the spirit is another matter.

PROFESSOR STEWART: Dr. Safwan, in discussing Arabs and Arab societies, we have made the point a number of times that there may be quite a difference among different segments of it. Would you care to comment on the notion of Arab identity?

DR. SAFWAN: It is simply maddening to hear the insistence in many countries—not only in America or in an Arab country—that the main purpose of education is to affirm that nation's identity or to stress its contribution to civilization. This is a part of an ongoing process of segregation. The main purpose of education should be to create a sense of cultural relativity, which must start in every country, everywhere, and very early in the school program. Something like a history of architecture, for example, should be taught, so a child can know at the age of seven or eight that there is a Moroccan house, an Egyptian house, an Arabic house, a Roman house, an American suburban house. There must be a whole policy of education oriented toward creating a sense of cultural relativity.

PROFESSOR STEWART: We are concerned about the problem of communication across cultures, in this case Arab and American. If one were to explore the other's culture for the purpose of enriching one's own, what would Arabs recommend to Americans and what would Americans recommend to Arabs?

PROFESSOR HUNTINGTON: We have identified one major recommendation—to try to dissolve the stereotypes and illusions each culture has of the other. We have had a good deal of discussion here about American stereotypes of Arabs, but what are the Arab stereotypes of Americans and American society? How close are they to reality and how are they changing? The point has been made that stereotypes can be easily managed and can change frequently. I suspect that many Arab stereotypes of Americans have been at least as unfavorable as American stereotypes of Arabs, and I would hope that there are institutions at work in the Arab world to change those, too.

PROFESSOR SAID: We have been rather unfair, or at least uneven, in this discussion by focusing on American or Western stereotypes of Arabs and we have not really talked about the other thing. So far as I know, there is no formal institution in the Arab world devoted to the study of the United States. I know of none to be found in any university. There are no departments of American studies, as there are departments of Middle East studies in this country. As for Arab stereotypes of Americans, they may not be as pernicious as American stereotypes of Arabs—or perhaps they are—but they are certainly funnier.

PROFESSOR HUNTINGTON: Americans may be funnier people.

PROFESSOR SAID: Yes, perhaps that is the reason. That means that the stereotypes are more correct. Considering the intimacy and urgency of relationships between the Arab world and the United States, there is an extraordinary lack of Arab purpose in trying to find out more about the United States in any systematic way. There are people who write impressions, travel diaries, and things of that sort, but there are no collective and formalized efforts to be found. Conversely, the means of finding out more about Arabic culture here are very humble, given the politicized and rather nasty atmosphere, which we have pretended is just not there. The solution is to read more. One has to be more involved with literature.

PROFESSOR NADER: I would say that we ought to specify what we can learn from each other—and this is a plea for specificity. If we asked an Arab "What could you teach an American?" he might say "hospitality." Then the southern American would say, "What do you mean? Have you forgotten about southern hospitality?" If we ask an American "What could you teach the Arabs?" he might say "efficiency." Then we look at how the nomads utilize the most forlorn desert areas of the world and think, "Can we really teach the nomads how to utilize that area more efficiently?"

In the area of law, the Arabs can teach us something about situationalism and how to decide cases on a less than zero-sum-game basis, and more on a give-a-little, get-a-little basis. Arabs have something to teach us about cuisine, about art, about expression. We could also turn it around and say the United States might teach the Middle East something about freedom of political speech. The Middle East might trade us some of their shame, and we could give them some of our guilt culture. That would certainly relieve a lot of American working women, I must say.

What are the kinds of things we might cooperate on? Let's take a look at solar technology. They have lots of sun, and some money, and we have a lot of know-how. That would be a good way to get both cultures working together.

PROFESSOR STEWART: Our panelists have been trying to explore some of the aspects of intercultural communication. It is our custom as Americans to consider cultural differences as impediments to communication, but I sense from what our panelists have said that perhaps we should discard that idea. We can perceive culture differences as human resources and learn to use them and enrich our lives thereby. The panelists are now open to questions from the audience.

PETER BECHTOLD, Foreign Service Institute: I listened with great interest and with growing disbelief to some of the comments of the panelists. On one hand we were told that specialists are trying to interpret contemporary events by quoting medieval manuscripts and the Koran. I have spent more than fifteen years in close contact with specialists on Arab affairs, both in government and in academia, and in no more than 1 percent of the cases was that true. In fact, there is a growing familiarity, awareness, and understanding on the part of American audiences toward Arab culture. This brings me to another point. The panelists try to suggest that the stereotypes are bad stereotypes, and perhaps they are. But it has been my experience, and I think that of most of us here, that the effective action of an American in the Arab world depends to a very great degree on the extent to which he does not act like an American. Cultural differences can be bridged, but it would be wrong to underestimate them in terms of speech, in terms of daily behavior, in terms of businesslike conduct versus sociability, et cetera. As a result of the growing awareness of Americans and the growing number of centers of Middle Eastern studies, cultural communication has improved tremendously. I do not see the problems that have been mentioned here.

PROFESSOR NADER: There is certainly a difference between what is written about the Middle East and practical experience with the Middle East, and you are talking about practical experience. In a way, practical experience is quite a bit ahead of academic analyses of the Middle East, but it is from the written material that people without firsthand experience learn about the Middle East. In this country, most people's experience with the Middle East is secondhand experience.

PATRICK VISCUSO, Georgetown University: I am very puzzled by your views on Islam, Dr. Nader. Are you saying that Islam now plays a negligible role in Arab culture and its relations to other cultures, and, if so, is this due to westernization?

PROFESSOR NADER: No, I am not saying that Islam plays a negligible role. I am saying that it is something that needs to be studied. I asked one question, and I spent a summer trying to answer it. The question was, Has Islamic law penetrated into Islamic villages? I studied a Shi'ite Moslem village, a Sunnite village, and then a mixed Christian-Shi'ite village. In settling disputes, all of the villages do some things in common that have nothing to do with their religions. It was a very specific area.

MR. VISCUSO: I assume this was in Lebanon. There is a difference, you realize, between Lebanon and Saudi Arabia, for instance.

PROFESSOR NADER: Absolutely. That is the point.

KAMAL BOULLATA, artist, Washington, D.C.: No culture exists in a vacuum. Dr. Said mentioned that there is miscommunication, perhaps, between America and the Arab world because of the very highly politicized atmosphere. Why was this very important point of politicization never developed by the panel? Individualism in America is a result of a political system. Despotism in the Arab world is a result of political systems. Could anybody respond, please?

PROFESSOR HUNTINGTON: There are two different issues involved in what this gentleman has suggested. One is the differences in political systems between Arab societies and the United States, which nobody on the panel mentioned, perhaps because it is so obvious.

There is the second issue of the nature of Arab-American relations and the extent to which they are politicized, as they clearly are. There is the suggestion made by the questioner that because these relations are heavily politicized, this leads to a miscommunication or a misperception, or great difficulties of perception. That may be true in some respects, but I do not think it necessarily has to be the case. It is quite possible for American political leaders and politicians to deal effectively with Arab political leaders and politicians. One has only to look at Edward Sheehan's descriptions of the negotiations our secretary of state had with Arabs and Israelis to see that his biggest communication problems were in communicating with the Israelis, not the Arabs, at least by Sheehan's account. Politicization is going to exist and it need not be viewed as abnormal or bad in relations between people.

PROFESSOR SAID: When I raised the question at the outset, I did not mean to suggest that politicization was necessarily bad, but that, in intercultural relations, it had a narrowing effect and made the relationships between cultures rather less than broad. Political pressures have made relationships between cultures very specialized and have tended to focus attention on a few matters and to misconstrue certain realities—not only political but also cultural realities. When the atmosphere is politicized and narrowed, certain things are selected for attention and others are not.

The Arabs basically represent two things to America. On the one hand, they are oil producers, and, on the other, they are anti-Israeli. Nearly everything that stands for Arab culture can be placed, more or less, under one of those two headings, and that fact tends to focus the issue a great deal.

There is also a third element—the relationship between the United States and the Arab world is an unequal one. It is unequal because of tradition, because of power, and to a certain extent because of history. The Arab world until very recently was part of the colonial world, and this obviously colors its relationships with the United States. The United States has taken too little account—culturally, politically, or otherwise—of the fact that the Arab world is in a state of extremely turbulent change, a change directly related to its colonial and imperial past.

DONALD TANNENBAUM, Gettysburg College: I heard a remark

about trying to understand the United States Congress by understanding the Bible. My personal point of view is that it might not be a bad approach. I also think it would be well to investigate the villages of the United States to understand what Congress is about. This suggests that there are several levels of culture, perhaps, in very simple terms a micro level and a macro level, with many interlevels between. Would any of the panelists care to state a preference for beginning at one level rather than another in approaching the problem of communication between cultures? Should we communicate macro-cultural concepts or micro-cultural concepts if both are not possible simultaneously?

PROFESSOR NADER: The American Friends Service Committee thinks that there ought to be more communication at the micro level, so they have set up programs whereby young people can go and live in small communities around the world. In the Middle East, the United States has operated largely on the macro level, with the exception of a few things like the Peace Corps.

In regard to American villages, I would like to see Middle Easterners study this country just as we study other countries. There are very few studies of American culture by foreigners. That is one reason why Tocqueville is studied and quoted so often. No Middle Eastern or Arab anthropologist has ever made a study of an American village, city, or town, or Congress, or anything else. Anthropologically, we probably have the most unstudied culture in the world. When it is studied, we will begin to get an interchange of information at the micro level, and I think that is important.

PHILIP N. MARCUS, National Endowment for the Humanities: I would like to ask Mr. Safwan a question to follow up on the discussion about identity. I would like to ask it by referring to two examples. Could an Egyptian psychoanalyst provide treatment for a Syrian? Could an American psychoanalyst provide treatment for an Arab?

DR. SAFWAN: My own experience has been in France, with patients coming from every social class, workers as well as the bourgeoisie. I practiced in Egypt for some few years and had a clientele mainly of university people, but I also treated some with moderate education. I even had some women with no education at all.

The only differences that I found were differences in customs, in manners, or in beliefs. Differences in cultural beliefs and habits may fortify some rationalization or may make their undoing more difficult, but as far as the final issues are concerned—the ultimate bases of neurosis, for example, or positional neuroses or hysteria—they are absolutely the same in every culture. To give a brief answer, the differences I encountered in my practice may influence the modulation of the work but not the sense of it.

PROFESSOR NADER: Are you saying that cultural relativity does not apply to analysis?

DR. SAFWAN: I would circumscribe its effect in that it modulates the work differently. In this context, I would like to hear a definition of *self*. I know it is the current notion in psychiatry and cultural anthropology, but I have never heard an acceptable definition of it.

MUHAMMAD ABDUL RAUF, the Islamic Center in Washington: It seems that the experience of Dr. Nader in some of the Moslem villages and with some Moslem women has led to a suggestion of the alienation of Islamic law. We seem to have certain stereotypes about Islamic law itself and about the Islamic spirit, but I believe that the liberty enjoyed by Moslem women and their pragmatic way of handling daily affairs agree with the spirit of Islamic law and the teaching of Islam itself. That is just an observation, not a question.

FREDERIC CADORA, Ohio State University: My question is related to the one preceding the last. Can an Arab psychoanalyst analyze an American, and can an American psychoanalyst analyze an Arab? Can the differences or the problems highlight differences in their cultural problems?

DR. SAFWAN: Can you make an analysis in a foreign language? I myself made analyses with French-speaking persons, even though some of them were American, because they spoke French perfectly. Knowing French myself, there was absolutely no difficulty. In Egypt, an analysis can be undertaken only with a thorough knowledge of the language of the patient.

PROFESSOR SAID: One matter we have not touched at all is the development since World War II, and particularly in the last decade, of a common language between American, or Western, intellectuals and Arab intellectuals. Intercultural communication, which we have been discussing on the popular level, has also become much more possible on another level, the level of literacy, partly because of the media, partly because communication is mechanically much more simple and direct, and partly because of certain common educational experiences.

190

Most Arab intellectuals today are educated if not in the West, then in a sense by the West. There is a common vocabulary in which the concepts of psychoanalysis, for example, or the notions of political economy and Marxism can be assumed to be understood, albeit in different ways, among Arabs and Americans. That is something we have not discussed but it should be emphasized.

PROFESSOR STEWART: There may be—exaggerating a bit—a kind of universal intellectual culture, which has nothing to do with "culture" culture.

PROFESSOR SAID: Right, or with universalizing that tends to diminish the differences between cultures.

EMILE A. NAKHLEH, Mt. St. Mary's College: Arab-American intellectuals, particularly academics, face a special problem in their attempt to correct some of the stereotypes concerning Arab political society. This problem is particularly acute when questions of individual freedom and liberty are raised. Most Arab-American academics believe that individual freedom and individual liberty are absent in Arab political societies and that totalitarianism is the hallmark of most Arab regimes. I have faced this problem, and I would like Dr. Said to comment on this dilemma in which most of us find ourselves.

PROFESSOR SAID: It is certainly true that Arab-Americans put near the top of their list the question of political freedom and freedom of speech, which they find lacking in their countries of origin or in the Middle East generally. This has not prevented them from making their opinions known. I do not want to sound as if we are patting ourselves on the back, but we have raised the issue, and the issue is an important one for us. As you say, the issue does present problems, because an Arab-American in America is obviously very conscious not only of his Arab identity but also of his existence in a political culture that is largely hostile to him. He is rather torn by a national loyalty to do something about the Arab position on the one hand, and, on the other, he must be honest enough to see that the freedom of the individual is considerably curtailed in Arab society and does not seem to be improving much.

MOHAMMAD HAKKI, Embassy of Egypt, Washington, D.C.: The question should not be whether an American can analyze an Arab or whether an Arab can analyze an American, but rather could Dr. Kissinger, for instance, be psychoanalyzed by an Arab doctor and allow that fact to be published? In other words, are we overcoming the basic bias?

DR. SAFWAN: If he is neurotic, and if he asks us for it, yes, we can analyze him. In answering the other question, I thought the idea of an Arab or an American analyst ill-expressed. It would be better to say an Arabic-speaking analyst or an English-speaking analyst.

MR. HAKKI: My question is, Are we overcoming the basic institutionalized bias? Not long ago there was a long article in the *New York Times Sunday Magazine* about the Arabists in the State Department, as if they were suspect, as if they were somehow anti-Semitic. Are we approaching the time in America when it is no longer suspect to be an Arabist or when being a specialist in Arab affairs is not somehow held against a person in the media or in the publishing world or in other institutions?

PROFESSOR SAID: There is an essay by the famous man of letters—perhaps the most famous one of this century—Edmund Wilson, in a book he wrote in the fifties, *Red, Black, Blond, and Olive,* which deals with his visits in Haiti, the Soviet Union, and Israel. In that book, he says that it is more or less natural for any American, by virtue of his cultural background and training, to hold Arabs and Arab civilizations in contempt. This contempt is a powerful strain, it seems to me, and it has become exacerbated by the political atmosphere. One could use the word *Arab* or *Arabist* as an insult, or as a kind of political designation that is quite suspect. It is equivalent, for example, to *anti-Semitic,* or *fascist.* We are a long way from escaping from that, and I am not sure that the Arabs are entirely blameless in this respect. The anti-Arab feeling is still very much there.

PROFESSOR HUNTINGTON: This is a general problem in relations between Americans and other countries, and not something peculiar to Arab-American relations. The people in the United States who have special relationships or special interests with particular foreign countries are often viewed with suspicion. Almost everybody in the United States concerned in any way with foreign affairs has some sort of special relationship, even in a professional sense. The specialists in Latin America are often viewed by others as overrepresenting the interests of Latin America in American society and culture. We also have people with ethnic ties, obviously, to other parts of the world, though we have fewer with ties to the Arab world than to other regions. In most cases, the ethnic and the professional groups try to influence American policy according to their special interests, and they often succeed.

PROFESSOR NADER: When there are stereotypes about other cultures, such as Mexican culture, for example, or Chicano culture in this country, there are also enough counter examples so that people say, "But some of my best friends are Chicanos, and they are educated." The Arab-American population, however, is very tiny, and so people learn about Arab culture secondhand, for the most part. Also, there is an interest group in this country that is doing a negative P.R. job on the Middle East, and there is nothing to counter it. That is why the Arab-American case is different from the Chicano case or even from the Japanese Americans, who tend to be clustered in one place.

PROFESSOR SAID: I think the case of the Arab in this culture differs from any other foreign or non-American culture group. Prominent Americans take positions on questions relating to South Africa or Chile or other foreign political issues, but none of those Americans takes a similar position in favor of the Arabs. That is a very dramatic and important distinction. A favorable position may be taken on most issues, generally speaking, but not in regard to the Arab world. It would be hard for any of us here to identify an Arab partisan.

PROFESSOR HUNTINGTON: Oh, come on, the chairman of the Senate Foreign Relations Committee for ten or twelve years was prominently identified as an Arab partisan, and with good reason. There is nothing wrong with that.

K. I. SEMAAN, State University of New York at Binghamton: In Malta last year I witnessed firsthand intercultural communication between some of my American students and Libyan students. Without going into any descriptions, since I recorded them and am in the process of formulating my own conclusions, I want to address a question to the panel. Can government policy bring about intercultural communication on the personal level?

DR. SAFWAN: Through education, maybe. The only change I see will come through education policy.

PROFESSOR NADER: Again, China is an example of a dramatic change in the relations not only between governments but also between

193

people on a personal level. Now scientists have personal exchanges, and that is the beginning of further communication.

MR. SEMAAN: I should like to add that some of my American students did strike up good friendships with Libyan students. The Americans were shocked to find the Libyans the exact opposite of what they had expected, based on their government's descriptions of the leader of the Libyan government and on what they had read in the newspapers and elsewhere.

PROFESSOR HUNTINGTON: There have been many U.S. policies and programs designed precisely to encourage communications at the personal level—including the Fulbright programs and the Peace Corps and a variety of others. I do not know how successful they have been, but personal communication has been uppermost, I would think, in the minds of American officials.

PETER S. TANOUS, Peter S. Tanous Co., Inc.: As an American businessman I travel quite a bit in the Middle East. One area that you all have neglected is a micro approach on cultural communications. In my trips to the Middle East, for example, I am absolutely amazed at the number of people I meet who have been educated in the United States and who continue to make trips to the United States. They bring the American culture back to their individual countries.

PROFESSOR NADER: That is much more common than the reverse. There are Americans who were educated at the American University in Beirut and Cairo, but the tourism in the area does not even begin to balance Arab tourism here, so I think you are probably right. There are lots of micro communication patterns opened up by these people but it goes one way mainly.

DAVID DAVIES, American Friends of the Middle East: I taught for three years in Saudi Arabia and I would like to tell a little story to answer Professor Stewart's question, "Do cultural differences cause breakdown in communication?" I was driving with one of my students, and I asked him, "Where are you from?"—four very simple English words. I knew he knew them because I had taught them to him. He named a little village about 500 kilometers away from Riyadh, and I said, "Oh, when did you come to Riyadh?" He looked at me in a very puzzled way, and I said, "If you are from that village, when did you come to Riyadh?" He said, "Oh, I have always lived here in Riyadh."

And I said, "But you are from there." He said, "Oh, my grandfather was from there." So the answer first is, yes, cultural differences can create a barrier to communication. But, in following up and discovering that it was his tribal affiliation that brought on his answer, I learned a lot about his culture. The answer then is, yes, cultural differences can be a great source of information and a great thing to build on for mutual instruction.

PROFESSOR STEWART: Thank you. I do think there has been a tendency on the part of the panel to pass over differences, and I have sensed in the audience an effort to go back to them. Do we have any other questions?

MICHAEL D. SHAFER, Department of State, Bureau of Education and Cultural Affairs: I am intrigued by the way this entire discussion has gone around the question of Islam. One thing that defines American culture is that it, like Europe, lives on the assumption that this is the world that has followed Eden. We live in a fallen world, and I suspect that is one of the reasons we feel so uncomfortable with one of our presidential candidates' statements about being born again.

It seems to me that the Moslem-Arab world is built on exactly the opposite premise—that this is, to borrow an expression from a Christian, the city of God, the world of God. Within the Arab world itself, one of the most important intellectual discussions at present is the reconciliation of the incredible tradition of Islam with the culture brought in by 200 years of European colonization. Would anybody care to comment on the possibilities for conflict and misunderstanding between the United States, as a representative of the European culture, and the Arab-Islamic culture, which is so close to God in some ways?

PROFESSOR SAID: That is a very complicated and subtle question. Earlier, I brought up the question of Islam and how it is used to interpret the Middle East. What I had in mind simply was a tendency among authorities in the field, whose training suggests a rather special relationship with Islam based on classical Islam. The tendency of such commentators is to treat Islam reductively, as if to say Islam is simply this, a very simple thing. And they imply that a very complex phenomenon can be understood by reducing it to a very simple thing, which is Islam.

It is certainly true that there is a widespread and fascinating debate taking place in many places in the Middle East about the relationship between Islam and modernity. But the fact is that these changes are taking place, and they can not be easily reduced to a simple either/or

195

question of whether one should reject Islam or accept it. It is not that simple because human societies do not work that way.

Without wishing to pose as an authority on the subject, I think it is dangerous to be too simplistic and say that, since they are Islamic, *this* is what they are and *that* attitude has prevailed.

PROFESSOR NADER: We need to know more about Islamic behavior. There is a lot written about Islamic thought, but there is a lot less written about the behavior associated with that thought.

THOMAS G. ROULETTE, consulting psychologist: In the decade or so that I have worked at the American-Arab interface, I have perceived a prime dilemma in the Arab world over how to get both feet into the twentieth century and gain all of its technology without giving up Arab and Islamic cultural traditions, and this seems to be quite a problem. I wonder if some of our cultural experts could comment on whether they see this as a problem and how they would bet on the resolution of this dilemma.

PROFESSOR HUNTINGTON: As the person on this panel who has the least knowledge of and least involvement with Arab culture, I am perhaps least qualified to answer that question. I can say, however, that other cultures have wrestled with the same problem and, in many cases, have come up with successful answers to it. Japan has modernized with spectacular success, and yet it has been able to preserve many of the traditional Japanese ways of thought and of doing things.

Other cultures, including the Chinese, are in the process of modernization and yet seem to be able to establish a compromise between modern values and ways of behavior on the one hand and those of their traditional culture on the other.

PROFESSOR NADER: This is a ubiquitous problem—how to have your cake and eat it too. The problem is more serious and more difficult to solve everywhere in the world today for one simple reason—increasing centralization. As long as the strength of multinational corporations increases, they will peddle not only items but also systems, and when systems are being peddled, it is not possible to pick and choose only what is wanted. Either the whole basket of fruit must be accepted or none at all. This is the problem being faced not only by the Middle East but worldwide. It is not the same problem that was faced a hundred years ago. It is of a different magnitude, and it has to do with the increasing centralization of economic interests in the world.

PROFESSOR SAID: Is that the particular problem of the Middle East, of the Arab cultures?

PROFESSOR NADER: Yes, that is right.

PROFESSOR SAID: That was what the question seemed to have expressed, but that may not necessarily be the case. It is a problem, but there may be other more pressing problems, which cannot be dealt with under the title of modernization.

MR. ROULETTE: I am not certain that modernization actually is a problem, but it is perceived and discussed in the Middle East as a problem.

PROFESSOR NADER: The problem often is that importing the technology creates the problem. The Arabs gave Stanford Research Institute a half-million-dollar contract and said, "Tell us how Americans take care of their old people so we can take care of our older people." But the Arabs had never had a problem with aging or with taking care of old people until they gave this contract to SRI. Now the Saudi Arabians are going to have old-age homes, probably scattered throughout the desert in oases and other delightful places.

PROFESSOR STEWART: Time flows on and eventually engulfs us all. Before we run out of time, let me thank the panelists for their contributions, and the audience for its penetrating questions and comments. Thank you. [Applause.]

APPENDIXES

THE INTELLECTUAL LIFE IN CONTEMPORARY EGYPT

Zaki Naguib Mahmoud

The last 150 years could be considered a period of Egyptian cultural rebirth, a period comparable to the sixteenth century in Europe. In both cases there was a creative revival of the classics. Each, of course, had its own classical literature to revive. In both cases, a new scientific outlook was born. Humanism was the central theme in both. Yet there was an essential difference between our renaissance in its first stages and Europe's renaissance in the sixteenth century. Whereas in Europe the cultural product was original, the product in nineteenth century Egypt was imitation. The models to be imitated were two. These were the newly imported culture from European sources on the one hand, and the ancient Arabic classics on the other.

The one and a half centuries of rebirth may be roughly divided into four stages. Each of the first three stages culminated in a political revolution, and we are now living in the fourth.

Early Phases of the Renaissance

With the French expedition led by Napoleon Bonaparte in 1798, Egypt began a new era—the renaissance of modern Arabic culture. After three centuries of dark ages, during which the country was under Ottoman rule, Egypt was again in direct contact with Europe. The year of the Turkish invasion of Egypt (1517) was the termination of a culturally productive period that had begun with the establishment of al-Azhar University in the tenth century. With the arrival of Napoleon, the gates that had blocked the passage of cultural streams were gradually opened.

During the first half of the nineteenth century, two cultural lines ran in parallel: one was translation, mainly from the Italian and French; the other was republication of Arabic classics. A school of languages was founded about 1835 to carry out the translation, and it still exists under the same name. Side by side with the translation movement, scholars busied themselves with the revival of selected Arabic classics.

A government printing press was established for both kinds of publications. The enlightenment resulting from that cultural activity gradually spread, until urgent demands of the people for reforms led to the Urabi Revolution of 1882.

It was then that the British stepped in. With their military occupation, the second stage of our cultural development began. If the role of the intellectuals during the first stage had been to rid the country of the Ottoman dark ages, their role during the second was to liberate the country from the British occupier.

From that time onward, a third cultural line was added to the lines of translation from Europe and republication of Arabic classics. The additional line was that of original work. Original work began, but it remained limited for some time. Translation continued to be vital, but now it came mainly from the English and French.

From the British occupation to 1919, the date of the national revolution against the British, the idea of political liberty was the dominant theme in Egyptian literature.

Apart from straightforward political exhortations, which hardly concern us in this context, the theme of political freedom took various forms in the intellectual life during the late years of the nineteenth century and the first decade of the twentieth. Eminent in the field were Muhammad Abdu, Kassim Amin, and Lutfi al-Sayyid, as well as the great poets Shawqi and Hafiz.

Muhammad Abdu was the leader who, in my opinion, set the program for all intellectuals to follow up to the present day. The program was simply to interpret the traditional culture in such a way as to leave no discrepancy between this culture and the contemporary mind.

By way of direct application of this program, Kassim Amin wrote his epoch-making book *The Emancipation of Women* (1899) and its sequel *The Women* (1900), in which he dealt with the criticisms raised by the earlier book. In both, he attempted to show that the teachings of Islam did not stand in the way of women's freedom.

The emotionalism of patriotism in the first years of the century was counterbalanced by the logical reasoning of Lutfi al-Sayyid. He was the man who, during World War I, retired from public life to translate Aristotle into Arabic, and who, a few years later, became the first rector of the State University of Cairo in 1925.

With the work of the two great poets of that period, Shawqi and Hafiz, the intellectual rebirth took quite a different turn. The importance of the Arabic language to the Arabs—ancient as well as modern, Egyptians or otherwise—can hardly be fully apprehended by other people. There had always been a close relationship between the standard of the language as shown in the prevalent literature and the rise or fall of the political state of affairs. And poetry reflected the status of both language and politics.

After the deterioration of the Arabic language, which was an inescapable correlative of political and social disintegration under Ottoman rule, those two poets, Shawqi and Hafiz, participated in the restoration of the country through the revival of its language in their poetry. They wove a new fabric of language in which the present and the past were not at loggerheads. In their poetry, innovation was not the antithesis of tradition, but, rather, a rediscovery of it. Such a combination of the old and the new in harmony is still the guiding principle in all our cultural production. It is indeed a belief throughout the Arab world today that the Arab renaissance can be achieved on a sound basis only if our distinctive national character is combined with the cultural characteristics of the age in which we live.

The Middle Years

The second decade of the century, during which World War I broke out, witnessed the birth of the Arabic novel in the sense of building plot and drawing character. Of course, classical Arabic literature had been rich with tales. But with the appearance of *Zaynab* (1914), a modern novel by M. H. Haykal, this literary genre was born and it grew rapidly in the following years, reaching a very high standard.

Haykal's novel, which was anonymously published in its first edition, portrayed the life of a young woman in the countryside, where she was helpless and unable to express her emotions freely. The novel was a loud call for independent individuality, something which most Egyptians lacked under foreign rulers. In fact, this was the general call in the literature of the second decade, heralding the 1919 revolution. The call was most marked in poetry. The poetry of the time, particularly that of the most distinguished poet and writer, Abbas al-Aqqad, came as a declaration of human rights, rights which were the essence of the fervently sought renaissance and political independence. The basic theme was that no human being would ever achieve the high goal of freedom and independence without possessing the essential prerequisite: human dignity and self-respect. If the prevailing spirit of those years could be identified in one single poem, "A Biography of Satan" by al-Aqqad might be the one.

In the period between the two world wars (1918-1939) our intellectual life was in one of its most productive phases prior to real rebirth. The movement had two principles: the search for a multidimensional freedom, and the establishment of a rationalistic basis for the new life.

In the opening year of the twenties, al-Aqqad, with his colleague al-Mazini, published a literary manifesto declaring a new era in Arabic poetry. Traditionally, the Arabic poet had been concerned with social content and linguistic form. The poet rarely expressed his individuality. Now the new school came to emphasize the poet himself. This was a remarkable step toward the independent personality of the citizen.

When al-Aqqad and his school protested against traditional poetry in their attempt to save the individual citizen, there appeared in the early thirties another protesting group, working on quite a different basis but aiming at the same purpose. Whereas the former group had been rather intellectual, the latter were thoroughly sentimental.

At the end of the twenties, drama was introduced, almost for the first time, into our literature. Although the novel had appeared some years earlier, it was only by the turn of the thirties that the literary form of this genre ripened. Tawfiq al-Hakim appeared in full maturity both as a novelist and as a dramatist. In his novel *The Return of the Soul,* he expressed his view that Egypt's genius should be reborn, that Western culture would be of little use if it were not grafted onto the metaphysical core of our perennial self. *The People of the Cave* was his first great drama. In it he stated a major theme which has never disappeared from his writings. This theme is to contrast eternal verities with temporal incidents, showing that the latter are only partial truths. Since eternal verities are nonempirical, intuition or revelation should be considered the fundamental source of knowledge. Reliance on perception and logical reasoning alone was taken to be the greatest failing of modern Western thought.

During the twenties, Ahmad Shawqi, then poet laureate, originated the poetic drama. His themes were mainly drawn from our history. And in the thirties, al-Aqqad and al-Mazini, already mentioned as poets and critics, contributed intellectual novels to literary fiction. Haykal's novel *Zaynab* in 1914 portrayed the life of an illiterate village woman. In the thirties these two novelists came to deal with the new lives of women who became urbane and sophisticated.

Along with pure literature in the enlightened period of the twenties and thirties, there ran a stream of rationalism, covering many areas of thought. In 1925 the State University of Cairo was established. Scientific research methods soon spread and transformed the whole educational system. In 1926 Taha Hussein published his book *Pre-Islamic Literature.* The significance of that important publication lay in its Cartesian method. Literary dogma was exposed to doubt. What had been taboo was subjected to scientific inquiry.

In those years, too, the Darwinian theory of evolution was discussed and analyzed. *The Origin of Species* was fully translated into Arabic, and the theory was expounded in many books and magazine articles.

The prevalent attitude of thinkers and men of letters during that period of enlightenment was as follows: If the West has usurped our land and underestimated our culture, one way to be able to meet it on its own ground is to equip ourselves with Western science and the scientific method. Consequently, one of the most important features of that period was the translation of Western thought into Arabic, from the works of the ancient Greeks to those of modern European thinkers. English and French were the dominant sources. American culture was introduced later, in the forties.

After World War II ended in 1945, the stream of culture in Egypt took a new turn. The question which had been imminent before was now disclosed. The question was, Who are we? And the answer, which had been hesitant and uncertain, was now clear and decided. During the twenties and thirties, writers did not agree about whether Egyptians should relate themselves culturally to the ancient Egyptians or to the ancient Arabs. But now thinkers and men of letters were unanimous about the cultural identity with the Arab world. The Pharaohs were too ancient to be a part of the continuous stream between the past and the present. Besides, Egypt's present language is Arabic and its religion is Islam. What stronger ties could there be than the ties of language and religion?

After the war the question of who we are soon became the strongest force in literary production. Leading writers turned for inspiration to the rich legacy of the Arabs, together with the sources of Islam. Many of the ancient Arab and Muslim heroes were written about and commented on, with a view to setting up the ideal paradigm to be followed in creating the new national spirit.

In the interwar period there had been sharp differences in opinion about the language to be used in writing, and the kind of alphabet to be employed. Some advocated the use of the classical, grammatical language, while others wanted everyday vernacular to be the literary medium. Again, some insisted on using the Arabic alphabet, reading from right to left, while others thought that the Latin way was preferable. But all such differences disappeared in the postwar phase. It was the correct classical language that was to be used, as well as the Arabic alphabet.

In those postwar years, the field of philosophical thinking underwent a change. The idea had been current that ancient Arab philosophers were copiers of their Greek predecessors. They were now shown to be original in many ways.

Generally speaking, however, after World War II Egypt experienced seven years of anxiety and unrest. The older writers resorted to the revival of historical heroes, and the younger ones busied themselves with socialism, which seemed the only solution to the country's sad condition. But in those days this was done at the risk of jail and persecution.

Recent Trends

In 1952 a Socialist revolution occurred, under the leadership of the army. A radical change was brought about in the whole intellectual life. The various elements of unrest and frustration, which had been dispersed in our literary and political world, converged in one trend. Poetry, the novel, drama, the essay, music, and art all came to express the intense desire for social justice, together with an independent and genuine culture. Servile imitation was no longer to be allowed. This, of course, was not to exclude opening the gates to all sorts of mental and literary output. Indeed, the cultural life in Egypt was now clearly trinitarian. To the translation of works from Europe and republication of the Arabic classics was now added a third side completing the triangle. This added element was the deeper concern with the production of works that were creative and original.

In poetry, instead of the tentativeness and hesitancy of the enlightenment of the twenties and thirties, steps toward ridding ourselves of the classical form were now self-confident and explicit. No longer did our poets want to be mere followers. The change this time was in both form and content. Chief among the innovators was Salah Abd al-Sabur. His themes, in one way or another, all related to human dignity and Socialist values.

The same trends that appeared in poetry were also evident in the field of drama. Some dramatists kept the traditional form and content that had been used in the twenties and thirties. Aziz Abaza wrote poetic drama just as Ahmad Shawqi had written it in the late twenties. The form was strictly classical, and the content was drawn from Arab history in general, or from Egyptian history in particular. Tawfiq al-Hakim, our greatest playwright, whose work extends from the early twenties up to the present day, is an example of a continuous line of literary development. He has never ceased experimenting with the dramatic form. Sometimes it is purely classical, then it is a combination of the novel and drama, and then it is a kind of new absurd (irrational) literature.

But side by side with these rather classical dramatists, there were many dramatists who made it a principle to innovate in both form and content. Why should a play be given on a stage? Why should the language stick to the grammatically correct way? These revolutionary writers are mostly leftists in their politics.

As to the novel, the shift from the interwar period to the present was a shift from an analysis of ideas to an analysis of social behavior. If the former novelists stressed the theme, the latter stressed the plot and the sequence of events. But there is a political difference between the two phases. Whereas earlier the individual was the center of interest, the center in the latter phase was the set of relations among a group of individuals. Eminent in the former period were Haykal, al-Hakim, Taymour, al-Mazini and al-Aqqad. In the latter period, the lead has been in the hands of Mahfuz, Yusuf Idris, al-Siba'i, and Abd-al-Quddus.

Such divergence can also be seen in the field of literary criticism. At least three schools are evident. Taha Hussein led the way with a sociological view. To him and his followers, a literary critic should look for the social elements behind the poem, the novel, or drama. To them, literature should hold a mirror up to society.

Another group of critics, distinguished among whom was al-Aqqad, wanted literature to hold the mirror not so much to society as to the inner world of the creative author. A third group directed their attention to the ideology implicit in the literary work to be criticized. The difference in the political point of view has been behind the difference in the theories of literary criticism.

Another aspect of the intellectual life is philosophy proper. Professors of philosophy represent almost all the philosophies of our age. Sometimes the conflicting views transcend the academic world, reaching newspapers and magazines. This happens when a relationship is detected between a certain type of philosophy and current politics. Dialectical materialism is first in popularity among common readers; existentialism is second, pragmatism third, and scientific empiricism, represented by the present speaker, comes last and least.

But there is a strange paradox in our philosophical activity. While these lines of thought divide the highbrow club of intellectuals, a sweeping wave of nonphilosophical belief in religious tradition covers the whole population of the country. Oddly enough, it often happens that an individual speaks in favor of, say, dialectical materialism, and simultaneously in favor of traditional religious beliefs—without noticing the contradiction. But by and large, the people of Egypt do not hesitate to give priority to Islamic thought, and whatever idea is found to be contradictory is at once rejected. Many publications at present concern religious thought. Most people consider the revival of Islam the only safe path for national rebirth.

To sum up our intellectual life today, one might say that the unanimous aim of all mental activity is to create a modern identity by means of two roads. One road is the revival of cultural tradition. The other is the importation of recent culture. Divergence comes when we begin to ask: How much of each? And how are the two roads to meet?

THE CULTURAL SITUATION OF THE AMERICAN WRITER

John Updike

The American writer, in many respects, is conspicuously fortunate. He is the citizen of a wealthy, literate country where "the freedom of speech, or of the press," as the Constitution puts it, has been a vigorously defended right for two centuries of national existence. This freedom, by various recent judgments of the Supreme Court, has been extended to protect pornography of the rankest sort, and to permit the most slanderous abuse of poltical figures, and to make it extremely difficult for any citizen successfully to sue for libel. The British libel laws, for instance, are significantly stricter.

In the matter of political expression: though American writers have gone to jail for participation in demonstrations—Norman Mailer, for instance, in 1967—and though a publisher, Ralph Ginzburg, served many months in a federal penitentiary for mailing out a publication called *Eros*—and though journals proclaiming either sexual or political revolution undoubtedly suffer some harassment by local police and courts; for all this, no American writer, to my knowledge, has ever gone to jail for anything he has written. Whatever the inhibitions and limitations cultural circumstances set upon him, governmental censorship is not one of them, and for this he should be grateful.

He can also be grateful that he was born into the English language, that docile and spacious hybrid of the Germanic and Latin stocks, a language with a synonym for everything, and a grammatical flexibility that permits every kind of music to be struck from it, from Hemingway's studied flatness to the baroque orotundities of Milton and Sir Thomas Browne; the language of Shakespeare and Saul Bellow and R. K. Narayan and Chinua Achebe and Patrick White and Nadine Gordimer and Vladimir Nabokov. English is, with the immense insular exception of Mandarin Chinese, the world's largest language, spoken by a third of a billion people, and the second language of many millions more.

The American writer, then, is blessed with a vast potential audience, even beyond the 200 million of his countrymen. Further, the United States as a world power, and, as the foremost demonstration of the strengths and perils of capitalism, inspires curiosity throughout the world; as long ago as the thirties the French seized upon our detective novels and our southern regionalists—Faulkner foremost—as portraitists of an exotic reality, the American way of life. Today, even a writer of chronicles as unspectacular as my own finds himself translated into upwards of twenty languages, including Estonian, Hebrew, and Japanese. In contrast, the Danish, or Dutch, or Turkish writer needs great genius to escape the parish of his native language and reach an international audience.

Domestically, the American writer shares in the affluence of his society. A single best-seller, prudently managed, can guarantee him financial security for life. A huge population of students is compelled to purchase and annotate works of "contemporary literature." A multitudinous publishing industry stands ready each spring and fall to toss a brightly packaged batch of new volumes into the whirlwind of the bookstores; the economics of printing, indeed, demand steady use of the presses. And though most books fall upon stony ground and bear meager fruit, few investments pay such handsome dividends as the ream of paper upon which even a moderate best-seller is composed.

For journalists and short story writers, the magazine market is not what it was; television has bitten deeply into the advertising revenue, and many giants have fallen—*Life, Look, The Saturday Evening Post,* whereby Faulkner and Fitzgerald once gained admittance to the homes of what is now called Middle America. Yet, on the other hand, once-underground publications like the *Village Voice* and *Rolling Stone* rise to a certain prosperity, and in the newly polemical atmosphere of the sixties journalism acquired fresh gusto and heightened pretensions to artistic importance. Nor, in cataloguing the assets of the American writer, should we omit homage to the mighty subject at his back: America itself, with its geographical range from metropolis to wilderness, its panorama of mingled races and nationalities, its extremes of idyll and inferno, its crushed promises, its superb constructions, its violence, its despair, its innocence, its openness to new combinations, its appetite for new adventures.

From such a list of assets, one might expect the contemporary American writer to be exultant in the challenge and rewards that Destiny has thrown his way. Such an expectation, my impression is, will be disappointed. On the contrary, the profession of writer in the United States has been sharply devalued in the last thirty years, and has suffered loss both in the dignity assigned to it by nonwriters, and in the sense of purpose that shapes a profession from within.

Contemporary fiction, at a glance, is ironical, tenuous, and fragmentary, where it is not defiantly pedantic and cumbersome. The various assets I have listed have, it will be noticed, very little to do with the production of art. They are negative advantages at best; no doubt it *is* irksome to be a man of genius writing in a minor language, within a small, ignored nation. But it need not be a hopeless disadvantage, and the opposite condition may generate a bombast of unearned importance. A relatively cohesive and tangible audience is to be preferred to a nebulous, though immense, one; and the curve of national power by no means carries with it a curve of artistic excellence.

If any law at all can be proposed, it is that art flourishes *before* a national potency has been fulfilled: Elizabethan poetry has more patriotic energy than Victorian, the Americans of the 1850s wrote with a confidence impossible to the Americans of the 1950s. Not now could Herman Melville write, "The world is as young today as when it was created; and this Vermont morning dew is as wet to my feet, as Eden's dew to Adam's."

Or consider freedom of speech. Censorship is to some degree flattering. Most art has been produced by subjects of autocratic regimes; in all eras there have been things that, by convention or law, one did not say; and these restrictions have elicited from writers the ingenuities of correlative symbolism, euphemism, and telling omission. Would, for instance, the sexual explicitness of D. H. Lawrence heighten the erotic power of *Anna Karenina,* or a blunt indictment of the Austro-Hungarian bureaucracy enhance *The Castle?* Doubtfully. What is not said has been absorbed, as unexpended energy, into what is said; the maneuver is immemorially artistic.

The vocabulary of gesture and innuendo that society invents to circumvent its taboos is precious to art; one thinks of the moment when Hester Prynne, in Hawthorne's *The Scarlet Letter,* takes off her cap and lets down her hair in the forest: "And down it fell upon her shoulders, dark and rich, with at once a shadow and a light in its abundance, and imparting the charm of softness to her features." This could not be more vivid, nor could female sexuality be more empathetically crystallized than under the single kiss which Isabel Archer receives at the end of Henry James' *Portrait of a Lady*: "His kiss was like white lightning, a flash that spread, and spread again, and stayed; and it was extraordinary as if, while he took it, she felt each thing in his hard manhood that had least pleased her, each aggressive fact of his face, his figure, his presence, justified of its intense identity and made one with this act of possession."

American fiction, for all its present explicitness, has yet to create women as moving as the women of these reticent gentlemen, Hawthorne and James. Freud has assured us that we live for sex acts, and sex acts alone; now that they can be portrayed in fiction, the conversations and transactions that used to compose the fabric of fiction pale into foreplay. Given the right to excite the reader sexually, is a writer being less than man by doing anything else? As to political censorship: may not its complete absence be taken by a writer as a sign of indifference from his society, as a child who is never disciplined concludes that his parents do not love him? Certainly Marxist critics, both within and without America, when challenged on the matter of free expression, do not hesitate to reverse the comparison in their favor, by saying that we of the capitalist countries can say whatever we want because nobody is listening, and words count for nothing amid the iron workings of capitalism.

During a month, spent many years ago, in the Soviet Union, almost exclusively in the company of literary personnel, I did, through the haze of translation, gather some impressions of the situation of the Soviet writer. It is one I do not envy; but a comparison with the American situation is not entirely in its disfavor. Once admitted to the ranks of the talented, a Soviet writer enters the employ of the state; the phrase "people's artist" is not an empty one. Lenin was very specific about literature serving the ongoing revolution of the workers and the peasants.

Through the government monopoly of publishing, and through a pervasive instrument called The Writers Union, a hundred disciplinary devices can be exerted upon the writer—compulsory editorial changes, size of book edition, public rebuke by other writers in the literary publications, periods of nonpublication. The mechanism is by no means monolithic or unanimous; personalities and jealousies play a part, there is a generational gap, literary politics are as intricate as in New York, with a dimension of added seriousness, since there is no alternative establishment, and disfavor means silence. The line between party enforcers and legitimate creative writers is not absolute; the critics and translators that form the muscle of the system are literate and at least as concerned with abstract literary excellence as the average editor in a Manhattan publishing house. The refusal to publish Pasternak's *Doctor Zhivago,* for instance, was described to me as for Pasternak's own good, *Zhivago* was so pitiably beneath the excellence of his revered poetry.

The Soviet writer is not only a servant of communism, he is the inheritor of a noble literary tradition, and the caretaker of a language that Russians love to speak and hear. The excitement of a Russian poetry recital has no equivalent in the West; the poet is bringing not only poetry to his predominantly young audience, he is bringing hope. The Soviet writer is cherished, cherished by the public for the gift of truth he wishes to bring them, and cherished jealously by the State. He lives nearer the top of the social scale than his Western counterpart. The government provides *dachas* by the Black Sea and other pleasant spots where he can retreat and nourish his gifts; busy-work is provided for the uninspired; the Writers Union, my impression was, takes care of its own, and only writers outside the system need fear poverty. Money is not, I think, of much concern to the Soviet writer. The only luxuries he can buy, indeed, are the art works of so-called underground artists. To an American, this indifference toward financial security is striking and appears to make possible a reckless generosity and a fervor in personal relationships that is refreshing.

I present this picture in a spirit of anthropological dispassion, not to condone the stifling, farcical repressiveness that murdered Mandelshtam and Isaac Babel, sent Sinyavsky and Daniel to jail, and condemned Pasternak and Solzhenitsyn for the crime of winning the Nobel Prize. But the American writer also must find his way in a world that can be cruel.

The American writer struggles to survive as a small entrepreneur in the world's largest jungle of private enterprise. True, his overhead is small, and he only risks his own time; but the cost of living presses hard upon those old havens of private income, and part-time sinecure, that used to shelter the writer while he accumulated his artistic capital. The inexpensive sections of the cities, such as the Greenwich Village of the 1920s, have become either fashionable, and therefore expensive, neighborhoods, or dangerous ghettoes of drug-motivated crime. The increasingly suburbanized countryside no more breeds poet-farmers like Robert Frost. But for a few exceptions like Wallace Stevens and William Carlos Williams, Americans have not reconciled professional careers with literary careers, perhaps because the professions in America, unsoftened by any tradition of leisurely noblesse oblige, are too strenuous and consuming. The suave Latin tradition, of the writer as diplomat, is foreign to us. Journalism, the path to greatness trod by Stephen Crane and Hemingway, remains as a diminished possibility; but much color and flair have left the newspapers, as they consolidate and dwindle, and magazines, too, caught between rising printing costs and the advertiser's defection to television, present a less engaging, playful, and spacious scene than they once did.

Only the colleges and the universities still offer a substantial number of young men and women employment that would permit, with diligence, the development of a literary skill. The drawback here is the academization of American literature, the isolation of writers from all of America but the hothouse of the student young, and the dismal, inevitable delusion that writing exists to be studied—grist for a mill, wheat ground to flour in the churning of adolescent dissertations.

What, now, of the few hundred—and, out of that great nation, perhaps one hundred is nearer right—what of those few who achieve the name of writer? The scramble grows worse: the writer is the possessor of a craft that must constantly be relearned, there is no sure formula, no acquired inventory, wherein he can rest. If he is an American writer, he has probably squandered his youthful memories by the age of thirty; perhaps an adventure or two has given him matter for another decade of composition; what then? At his age, his fellow Americans are settling in to the sure accruements to which their experience and degrees entitle them; the writer alone remains, what was exhilarating at twenty and is frightening at forty, a gambler. And let us say he is one of the dozen or two dozen who are beyond financial insecurity; he is rich. Royalties tumble in upon him from his classics; the glamorous men of the media press luncheon invitations and rustling dollars upon him. But is he rich enough? Many sons of manufacturers, just by condescending to be born, are ten times richer. Can the writer, in a land that consumes wealth as rapidly as it bestows it, rest easy with his portion?

I can think of two right now—both serious writers, internationally esteemed—whose gifts are seriously compromised, in my judgment, by their need for money, in one case to support a luxurious life style, in the other to appease a more mystical avarice. Their demands drive them from publisher to publisher, from deal to deal, and make of each book, while it should be most delicately cradled in their heads, already a "property"—hideous, indicative term. Human slaves were defined in American law as property, and many of the brutalities Americans have visited upon others, upon their land, and upon themselves are traceable to this shift of reducing to property things that cannot be owned, and should not be bartered.

The writer's greed for money, however, is perhaps less damaging than his greed for greatness. The United States is a nation propelled by the hope of the lucky strike, the invention or the discovery of the financial coup that may at bottom correspond to Puritan "election." We yearn for Mammon's blessing. One thinks of Mark Twain, who lost a fortune trying to make one, by financing a mechanical typesetter, and who ended as a pet, in white suit, of Wall Street tycoons. Twain, at least, kept his writing and his financeering in separate rooms, the one rather frantically feeding the other. But what of twentieth-century figures like Thomas Wolfe, who sought to, as it were, *buy* greatness with sheer volume of words, and who confused energy of composition with energy of language—a huge man, he battered out ten thousand words a day on a typewriter on the top of an icebox, never mind that the words were repetitive, inflated, commonplace. And what of Norman Mailer, whose new attempt to write fiction is, we are told, entitled brazenly "The Great

American Novel"—a title already used by Philip Roth. In the middle of the last century when gold was found in a mountain in the Western Kansas Territory, covered wagons set forth inscribed PIKE'S PEAK OR BUST. THE GREAT AMERICAN NOVEL OR BUST is inscribed on the side of many battered literary wagons.

Only an American writer would think of greatness as an objective—comprehensiveness, or truthfulness, yes, but greatness must come of itself. The great works have a self-forgetfulness that permitted greatness rather than demanded it. *Ulysses* and *The Magic Mountain* both began as short stories; *Remembrance of Things Past* unfolded from a more modest and stylized intention. Too much, the American emphasis on accomplishment makes of life itself a tasteless, colorless, meaningless scaffolding for certain external feats; in the case of the writer, the great book is emphasized instead of the career, the book is felt as something the writer achieves in spite of himself, against the grain of his life, instead of as the fruit of a continuing inward attitude and refinement. A sort of punchy bravado prevails, as among cowboys down on their luck; Hemingway discussed in detail his imaginary boxing matches with Stendhal and Maupassant, and ended as a victim of his athletic metaphor. More modernly, the fiction of J. D. Salinger, Kurt Vonnegut, and Donald Barthelme abounds with gallows humor, with assurances as to the immense difficulty, nay, downright impossibility, of doing what they are doing.

Let us briskly assume, in summation, that the seeming advantages of the American writer are, many of them, in fact disadvantages to the real business of the writer, which is to communicate, with a responsive audience, images and ideas developed to a degree of fullness and order comparable to that of reality itself. What, you may ask, of the situation I have so far sketched, is peculiarly American, and how much are the difficulties generally modern or even universal to artistic endeavor? Certainly personal distractions were experienced by Aeschylus, and Michelangelo and Mozart were often disaccommodated by the patronage of their times.

The special American experience has been the rapid taming and exploitation of an immense virgin territory discovered by Europeans at the historical moment when the Middle Ages were yielding to the centuries of technology, capitalism, and industrialism. The scope of available riches made a new sort of individualism possible. In distinction from Latin America, the United States was settled by Protestants, and its expansion has continued, right up to the moon shots, in the ethos of Protestantism. The communal theocracy of the Puritan settlements and the solidarity of the pioneers in the face of danger are makeshift fabrics

215

compared with the ecclesiastical and feudal interdependences of the Old World; by rejecting the mediating institutions of Catholicism, Luther and Calvin freed men to be independent, competitive, and lonely; and so Americans are.

By giving to the individual conscience full responsibility for relations with God, Protestantism, in its Puritan shading, conjured up a new virtue: that of *sincerity*. The abhorrence of the phony and the half-felt lies behind Pound's and Hemingway's radical renovations of English usage and prosody. The same passion for sincerity, however, tends to bind the writer to confessional honesty and to an intensity which cannot be consistently willed. Hence the American writer's erratic lapses from common sense, his frequent stridency and self-indulgence, his uncertain sense of proportion, his inability to make artistic capital out of mature experiences and social perceptions. Among American novelists, Henry James is all but unique, in continuing and extending his mastery through middle age, and in ending strong; and of course he emigrated to England, and became an English citizen at the end.

Perhaps a mention of the English writer's cultural situation is in order here. His possible rewards, since the era of George Bernard Shaw and H. G. Wells, are smaller than his American counterpart's, and since D. H. Lawrence and Virginia Woolf no novelist has seemed possessed of the highest type of ambition. Yet the English writer suffers fewer delusions than his more romantic counterpart in the United States, and occupies a securer place in society. No living Englishman of letters is more respected than V. S. Pritchett, or more various and subtle in his writing; he has described his career—I quote from memory—as standing by his stall in Grub Street every day. There you have it; the English writer has a craft to practice steadily, and a name—however comic and humble—for the place where he practices it. In contrast, the main street of American publishing, Madison Avenue, is a byword for a different literary industry—the advertising industry. The English writer stands in the long tradition of the Anglo-Saxon bard and the medieval allegorist; he has a sense of himself as a component of a social order, a craftsman. Such a sense permits him hackwork and a sometimes unfeeling facility; but it permits him to write, to let his natural voice out, to infuse his curious product with something of a man's normal, unforced wisdom. In the absence of an assumed and generally recognized craftsman's role—which implies a craftsman's modesty and dependable public for the product—the American writer tends to take upon himself the role of priest; but a priest, in these agnostic times, of no god save himself.

The American surge of agricultural settlement and industrial development created small space for the artist. Sermons and brothels were what the new land cried for. The wilderness, as it was destroyed, became in memory a paradise, and the ousted Indians its heroes. As soon as American literature found, in mid-nineteenth century, its mature voice, it scorned the enveloping creed of boosterism and expansion. "What's the railroad to me?" Thoreau asked in a poem:

> What's the railroad to me?
> I never go to see
> Where it ends.
> It fills a few hollows,
> And makes banks for the swallows,
> It sets the sand a-blowing,
> And the blackberries a growing.

Thoreau's famous retreat to Walden Pond epitomizes a national type, the writer as hermit, as dreamer of counter-realities. Poe and Hawthorne come to mind, and Emily Dickinson, whose shy life and exquisitely willful quatrains give us the closest we have to a literary saint. The alternative, perhaps, to the dreamer, is the celebrant—the Whitmanesque embrace of American energy, of the splendid monism of the universe as expressed in American democracy. Yet the celebrant's posture, as later manifested in Carl Sandburg and Thomas Wolfe and Jack Kerouac, abandons tension, tension with the notions of selection and order that, whatever their position in a philosophical theory of art, seem to me essential to interesting reading.

We read to confront reality as mediated to us by another human mind. Though Melville spoke of American writers as "ironic points of light," our literature contains oddly little light, of the sort that intelligently and compassionately illumines the mundane world. The American writer, surprising to say, is rather typically baffled and disgusted by what would seem his prime subject, the daily life of his society; instead he flees to the woods, to abroad, to the psychiatrist's couch, to opium under one name or another, and seeks to shock, dazzle, taunt, or *save* his audience—anything, almost, but engage it in conversation.

Let me end with a few personal impressions.

I grew up, and formulated my ambition to be a "creative artist" of some sort, in a world where the radio and the cinema were the mass media. Both bathed the American consciousness in emanations from worlds distinctly artificial; even the radio personalities that used their own names, like Jack Benny and Fred Allen, presented themselves as residents of a fictional environment. The motion pictures, though they featured stars of independent celebrity and rather unchanged presence, did so within the frame of a fictional "story" that had artistic integrity,

217

as well as a morality so absolute that the turns of its plot could be predicted from the moral make-up of its characters. These films and radio shows were made things, fictions; and novels, fictions in book form, were the chief staple of the book industry; the best sellers were primarily fiction, and the writers of fiction were the heroes of the literary world.

Now, so-called nonfiction dominates, and the dominant mass medium is television, and the characteristic form of television is not the play but the event—the sports event, the panel discussion, the talk show, the quiz show. These things are not *made*; under conditions of high control they *happen*. The language of "happening" and "confrontation" is common currency, and the notion of art as an item, however exquisite, of manufacture is replaced by a sense of art as a detachable moment of the continuous dynamic medley and flow of forces that make up our immensely interconnected and self-conscious society. Looking back, one can see the 1950s as a turning point, when Abstract Expressionism proclaimed that painting was paint, paint in the process of the adventure of painting, and when Norman Mailer, unable to write the novel his artistic superego demanded he write, instead published a large book of fragments and self-interviews called *Advertisements for Myself*. In some insidious way, for those of us with aspirations to be "serious" writers, even the coolest third-person novel has become an advertisement for the author. Authors are expected by their publishers to become television personalities if they can; Woodward and Bernstein, having reported the Watergate affair, are now themselves the heroes of a movie.

Nor does the tide of cultural reemphasis fail to reach the writing desk and the most intimate recesses of the creative process. When I sit down to draw a character, or set a scene, or devise a plot in the manner of my mighty precedessors in the art of fiction, strange forces drag at my pen. The itch to parody—sure sign of decadence and impending revolution—takes over; plot seems absurd, character "traits" dissolve or manifest themselves as mechanical, artlessness becomes a new art, and as such newly dubious. The act of writing has become incorrigibly visible. However determinedly one weaves a veil of invention, one's own person seeps through, like some overripe cheese pushing through the cheesecloth. Madison Avenue tells us that the way to sell books is to put the author's photo on the front of the jacket, not the back inside flap. Well, perhaps we are reverting to some ancient bardic tradition: the harpist in the center of the mead-hall. Yet something vital goes out of fiction when the author cannot achieve self-forgetfulness. An ancient magic, perhaps, comes into play with the donning of a mask. The American author, at the moment, has taken off his mask, revealing a rather vacant and embarrassed face.

218

The American writer, like America, is uncertain as to what is expected of him. Less, surely, than formerly. This may be to the good; like the nation of which he is a citizen he has had to shed some illusions of inevitable importance and righteousness. Once, demanding so much of himself, he burned out into early silence, and, others demanding so little of him, he drank or despaired himself to death. Now, in the scathingly cleared air of post-Vietnam, post-Watergate, and post-bicentennial America, he may take a more pragmatic grip on his opportunities and his hazards. His native pessimism dances with an equally native optimism, that finds a perpetual freshness in things. ". . . this Vermont morning dew is as wet to my feet, as Eden's dew to Adam's." Melville went on, "The trillionth part has not yet been said; and all that has been said but multiplies the avenues to what remains to be said."

Who knows what remains to be said? Homer left little more to say about war, and Madame de Lafayette left little to say about love. Yet something in us—and by "us" I mean readers, not writers—asks that our condition be described to us over and over, for from year to year our condition is never the same, and the world's condition is not only never the same but always unprecedented. A conference such as this is a new thing, a new combination, and something, it may prove, to write about.

If I try to envision the future, two images come to me, both in rainbow colors. In the one, all the flat patches of red and yellow and purple and green that used to represent nations on maps of the world are rising up and are seen to be colored transparencies, that shuffle in and out, to make our global blue. The second rainbow that comes to my mind's eye is the iridescence that streams, in force-analytical photographs, from the tip of a projectile as it hurtles forward against resistance. Whichever way the arrow of the future is heading, its tip is here, or near here; after two hundred years this presumption continues to be part of the cultural situation of the American writer.

219

ARAB DIPLOMACY:
FAILURES AND SUCCESSES

Boutros Boutros-Ghali

There can be no proper understanding of Arab diplomacy in general, and of international organizations in particular, without an appreciation of certain historical factors which have played an important role in the shaping of Arab diplomacy in the past and which still affect its approach to the problems of today. The principal and most preoccupying factor in the diplomatic activity of the Arab world since its partition and military occupation after World War 1 has been the attempt to secure the restoration of its independence. There was not a single Arab diplomacy but many Arab diplomacies, working at cross-purposes. The separation between Arabs in Asia and Arabs in Africa became almost absolute.

Between the two world wars, the only diplomatic expression of a rapprochement was the conclusion of a Treaty of Friendship and Perpetual Peace signed in 1936 between Ibn Saud of Saudi Arabia and the King of Egypt. In 1937, four years after the independence of Iraq, Egypt elevated its consulate at Baghdad into a legation, but it is abundantly clear that there was no true Arab diplomacy right up to the beginning of World War II. There was no unified Arab diplomacy but rather a spectrum of various Arab diplomatic attitudes and methods.

The Palestine problem put an end to this lack of coordination among the different Arab diplomacies. The Palestine conference in London (1939) was the first formal international recognition of the gestation of an Arab diplomacy. The delegations of Egypt, Iraq, Saudi Arabia, and Transjordan drew up a common program in preliminary discussions at Cairo. They also tried to mediate between the two rival Palestine factions. If the London conference was a failure for the British, the Arabs refusing to sit with the Zionists, it marked, nevertheless, the first expression of a common Arab diplomacy.

In September 1944, after nearly two years of consultations, an Arab conference met in Alexandria, presided over by Nahhas Pasha, prime minister of Egypt. It was attended by delegates from Iraq, Jordan (then Transjordan), Lebanon, Saudi Arabia, Syria, and Yemen. The

Protocol of Alexandria, which formulated the aims and a proposed constitution of an Arab League, was drawn up. Six months later, the Pact of the Arab League, based on this protocol, was signed in Cairo. This offered the Arab states an institutional framework for a common Arab diplomacy. Before dealing with the aims and principles as well as the successes and failures of this Arab diplomacy, I should offer a definition of the term *Arab diplomacy*.

Diplomacy, according to Sir Ernest Satow, is "the application of intelligence and tact to the conduct of official relations between the governments of independent states . . . or more briefly still, the conduct of business between states by peaceful means." [1] Even using this definition, Arab diplomacy remains difficult to explain because the word *Arab* has always been the subject of controversy. How should the word *Arab* be understood?

The matter was discussed during the meetings which preceded the drafting of the Pact of the Arab League in 1944. It was understood that the word *Arab* should be interpreted as implying a concept of civilization, that is, a common culture, a common language, and a common aspiration to create an Arab nation.

One mistake that is often made is to confuse *Arab* with *Muslim*. Arabs are not necessarily Muslim, and reciprocally not all Muslims are Arab. There are Christian Arabs in Lebanon, Syria, Palestine, Egypt, and Sudan. On the other hand, the Iranians, Indonesians, Nigerians, and Senegalese are Muslims but not Arabs. Only Arab states can join the Arab League. Muslim states which are not Arab cannot become part of the Arab League.

A second mistake is to consider that the Arab state or Arab diplomacy is based on a racist concept. This confusion is related to the Arab anti-Zionist policy, which is sometimes wrongly considered anti-Semitic.

Indeed, to the extent that they can be counted, so-called pure Arabs number no more than 10 million and the remaining 100 million are simply Arabized or Arabic-speaking. Berbers, Copts, Nubians, and Somalians comprise a mosaic of ethnic groups sometimes called "the Arab melting pot." Arabism is based on the concept of an open society and Arabization is a dynamic, continuous process. Somalia, an African country that has embraced Islam, has adopted Arabic as the official language and become an Arab country. It was admitted to the Arab League. The same Arabization will probably take place with the Comoro Islands, which obtained independence in 1976. It intends to join the Arab League.

---

[1] Ernest Satow, *A Guide to Diplomatic Practice*, 4th ed. (London: Longmans, Green and Co., 1957), p. 1.

In conclusion, Arab diplomacy is the common diplomacy of all the Arab states committed to settling inter-Arab problems in an Arab framework and presenting a common front towards the foreign world. Keeping in mind this elementary definition of Arab diplomacy, let us examine its failures and successes over the last thirty years.

The Failures of Arab Diplomacy

The failures of Arab diplomacy are reflected in four fields of activity: (1) the failure to have joint diplomatic representation; (2) the failure to project a positive image of the Arabs; (3) the failure to control the treaties signed by the Arab states; and (4) the failure to settle inter-Arab disputes in an Arab framework.

Joint Diplomatic Representation. The Pact of the Arab League does not mention the problem of joint diplomatic representation of the Arab states. There are no provisions concerning representation by the Arab League of all the Arab states, or even of a certain number of states with any given government. There is no mention of common diplomatic representation of several member states in any foreign country.

This problem soon arose as a result of the increase in new nations. Young Arab states entering the international arena faced practical difficulties in bilateral and parliamentary diplomacy.

The Council of the Arab League studied this problem and, in November 1946, adopted a resolution recommending that Arab states coordinate their diplomatic representation abroad. The resolution called upon those states that as yet had no diplomatic representation in a given country to entrust the protection of their interests to another Arab state already diplomatically represented there.[2]

This recommendation for joint Arab diplomatic representation was judicious since all the member states of the League were represented in certain great capitals, such as Paris, London, and Washington, but had only fragmentary representation in African, Asian, and South American countries.

The task of establishing this delicate coordination was entrusted to the Political Commission of the Arab League, which noted the unequal representation of Arab states throughout the world. It has been unable to solve this problem. A resolution adopted by the League's council in March 1953 noted these difficulties and called upon the

---

[2] Resolution 96/5.

Political Commission to pursue its efforts further.[3] The council later reexamined the matter, but no progress was made.[4]

Later the Arab League approached the problem of common diplomacy from a different angle. In a sense, it created its own diplomatic representation, in the form of information offices opened in New York, Bonn, Geneva, Paris, Rome, London, New Delhi, Tokyo, Buenos Aires, Rio de Janeiro, and other cities. One of the functions of the director of each office is to coordinate the action of Arab diplomats accredited there, generally by holding meetings of the heads of diplomatic missions of Arab states. In addition, these meetings usually admit the representatives of nationalist movements recognized by all the Arab states (National Liberation Front and Provisional Government of the Republic of Algeria in 1959-1962 and the Palestine Liberation Organization since 1966). But these meetings ultimately remain rather limited, since they deal only with relations between the country in question and all Arab nations. These matters include joint diplomatic protests, joint communiques, joint exhibitions, invitations to local personalities to visit several Arab countries, and so forth.

It is, of course, difficult to create a common Arab diplomacy through common diplomatic representation if the policies of the different Arab states are working at cross-purposes. With the exception of the Commonwealth during the first half of the twentieth century, there has been no instance of joint diplomacy which has actually functioned. Since diplomacy remains the most spectacular prerogative of the newly rich but underdeveloped states, it is not difficult to understand why Arab states have failed to establish joint diplomatic representation.

Projection of the Arab Image. Although African diplomacy in the 1960s succeeded in reinforcing the position and image of Africa in the world, Arab diplomacy has clearly failed to promote a positive Arab image. How can we explain this in view of the fact that Arab and African countries belong to the same community and are confronted with the same diplomatic problems?

The principal explanation may be found in the attitude of the world community toward Arabism and Africanism. While Arabism was never really accepted, either on its own merits or as a program of diplomatic action, Africanism was accepted by the world community.

There is an explanation for the difference in world attitudes toward the two concepts. Arab diplomacy was created when the prin-

---

[3] Resolution 516/18.
[4] See Resolution 673/2, Resolution 842/22, and Resolution 1347/27.

ciple of decolonization was considered seditious and incompatible with the aims and early ideals of the United Nations. On the other hand, Africanism and African diplomacy developed when the policy of decolonization not only was accepted but also legitimized and encouraged, in conformity with the later philosophy of the United Nations. For Western public opinion, Arabism and Arab diplomacy were stained with the original sin of sedition, and they continued to be regarded in this light, regardless of the changing attitudes toward decolonization. Another hypothesis is that the Arab world represents the traditional enemy of Christendom and the West, an attitude inherited from the Crusaders, which has not disappeared with the passing of the centuries.

This anti-Arab and anti-Muslim attitude has culminated in the sympathy of the West for the Israeli state. The struggle of Arab diplomacy against Zionism is not acceptable to certain segments of Western opinion, which is as pro-Zionist as it is sometimes unavowedly anti-Semitic.

Arab anti-Zionist diplomacy is considered incompatible with the aims and principles of the United Nations. Israel was first officially created by the UN and then admitted to its membership. On the other hand, the struggle of African diplomacy against apartheid is viewed in a different light. The campaign against racial discrimination in Africa has become an international article of faith.

Finally, the new wealth of certain Arab countries, resulting from the new prices of oil, has created greed and envy among the family of nations. The picture of the so-called ugly Arab, squandering money in Western capitals, has been added to that of the Palestinian desperado, throwing bombs in order to make his voice audible above the hubbub of international indifference.

Control of the Treaties Signed by the Arab States. Any confederal system, or any treaty organization, calls for control over treaties between member states and foreign powers.

The Arab League in fact did not call for such control. The Pact of Arab Collective Defense of 1950 clearly stipulated that the "contracting parties bind themselves not to sign an international agreement which constitutes a derogation of the present treaty and not to adopt, in their dealings with other powers, an attitude which is inconsistent with the aims of the present treaty." [5]

The problem of consistency between the League's system and the treaties and alliances of the member states arose in full force at the

---

[5] Article 10 of the Treaty of Collective Defense and Economic Cooperation.

225

time of the signing of the Baghdad Pact in 1955. From the standpoint of most Arab states, this new alliance was inconsistent with the Arab League. Iraq, like all other member states, had agreed from the start not to enter into any alliance which would be likely to compromise the unity of the Arab front. This unity was seriously shaken by the adherence of an Arab state to a non-Arab alliance, especially one so closely connected to the Atlantic pact. Iraq insisted, however, that the new alliance met all the conditions of compatibility. This controversy has now lost all practical interest, since Iraq has withdrawn from the Baghdad Pact.

Yet a decade later Egypt signed a treaty of alliance with the Soviet Union, and Iraq concluded a similar treaty a few months later. This new policy adopted by two Arab states was to cause a serious political and ideological conflict within the Arab world. The pro-Eastern bloc and pro-Atlantic bloc opposed each other violently, endangering a common Arab policy with respect to the inter-Arab system and the outside world.

With the exception of the period between 1945 and 1955, the general principle qualifying the right of Arab states to contract international obligations and not allowing any Arab state to pursue a foreign policy prejudicial to the common Arab diplomacy was never accepted. Without such a guideline it is very difficult to have any Arab diplomacy at all.

The Peaceful Settlement of Inter-Arab Disputes. In 1945, the ideology which prevailed in the Arab world was the rule of law. The ruling elites were impregnated with Western constitutionalism and believed that inter-Arab conflicts could be settled by an international judge or an arbitrator. One need only read the minutes of the preparatory meetings that preceded the drafting of the pact of the Arab League to realize the emphasis certain delegates placed on the principle of compulsory arbitration. Because of the opposition of some states, however, a compromise was needed. It stated that the pact of the Arab League can be amended to establish an Arab court of arbitration. The creation of this Arab court has been the subject of numerous discussions and even more numerous resolutions, but it has not yet materialized. Inter-Arab disputes have been settled only by diplomatic negotiations.

Arab countries are suspicious of international law, which they know only through its colonial aspect. It was invariably concerned with legitimizing European acquisitions and privileges. Arab mistrust of Western-oriented international law has been transposed to the regional level. The Arab nations still have not developed a regional international law that can help them solve disputes. Hence a common Arab diplomacy is all the more important because it is more in line with Arab inclinations and traditions.

Article 52 of the United Nations Charter provides that members shall make every effort to achieve peaceful settlement of local disputes through regional organizations before referring them to the Security Council. The Arab League and the Arab states have repeatedly expressed the belief that Arab conflicts should be settled in an Arab context, but the Arab states have rarely observed this principle. They have always gone simultaneously to the Arab League and to the Security Council, effectively bypassing the inter-Arab system. Examples are the dispute between Egypt and the Sudan in February 1958, the conflict between Lebanon and the United Arab Republic in August 1958, and the conflict between Kuwait and Iraq in June-September 1967. Furthermore, in the conflict between Algeria and Morocco (October 1963), the two Arab states turned to the Organization of African Unity, a newly constituted regional organization, when the League should normally have been the framework within which to settle the conflict.

How should one understand the inadequacy of Arab diplomacy and the Arab League in settling the Lebanese civil war? Or the last conflict between Morocco and Mauritania on one side and Algeria on the other? How can one explain the lack of confidence of the Arab states with respect to their own diplomacy or their own organization as an instrument for the peaceful settlement of their disputes?

Some have claimed that this phenomenon had its origin in the archaic and obsolete nature of Arab diplomacy, which is related to the underdevelopment of the Arab world. Some believe it had its origin in the weak machinery set up by the League to deal with conflicts. If there were a court of arbitration, or at least a conciliation committee, then Arab states would be less hesitant.

Others believe that this crisis of Arab diplomacy has nothing to do with the system set up by the League. In their view, it originates in the profound contradictions inherent in the Arab world, which lead Arab states to prefer mediation by a non-Arab third party (be it a state or an international organization) rather than by an Arab one. Consequently, setting up an Arab court of arbitration or any other body to settle disputes would not solve the problem.

Still another body of opinion attributes the inadequacy of Arab diplomacy in settling Arab conflicts to the preponderant role played by Egypt during the Nasserite period. Most Arab states that have pre-

227

ferred the mediation of the United Nations or a foreign country to the Arab League Council or a third Arab state were in conflict with either Egypt or an Egyptian ally. A similar phenomenon can be seen in Pan-American practice: states in conflict with the United States or with a state that has close ties to Washington turn to the United Nations rather than to the Organization of American States, where the preponderance of the United States is beyond dispute. On the other hand, the fact that no African state has preponderance in the Organization of African Unity is the main factor in its success in settling inter-African disputes.

If the preponderant role of Nasser between 1957 and 1967 explains the failure of Arab diplomacy in settling inter-Arab disputes, how can we explain the failure of Arab diplomacy during the Sadat period, that is, after 1970? This question is all the more difficult to answer if we bear in mind the main characteristics of President Sadat's policy toward the Arab world, namely, nonintervention in internal affairs and a conciliatory stance toward inter-Arab disputes.

Another explanation is that inter-Arab disputes have been contaminated by the cold war. Arab diplomacy may settle a local inter-Arab dispute (for example, the conflict between Egypt and the Sudan in February 1958, the conflict between Kuwait and Iraq in June-September 1967, and the conflict between Egypt and Syria after the dissolution of the United Arab Republic in 1961), but it cannot settle a conflict involving the superpowers directly or indirectly (for example, the conflict between Lebanon and the United Arab Republic in August 1958 and the civil war in Lebanon in 1976). But Arab diplomacy has failed frequently to solve even purely local inter-Arab disputes.

In conclusion, whatever the case may be, it must be admitted that Arab diplomacy, within the framework of the Arab League and outside it, has almost always failed in a field of vital importance, that of the settlement of disputes between Arab states.

The Successes of Arab Diplomacy

The successes of Arab diplomacy are reflected in four fields of activity: (1) the decolonization of the Arab world, (2) the coordination of Arab policies within international organizations, (3) the development of nonalignment, and (4) the Arab-African dialogue.

The Decolonization of the Arab World. After World War II, the Arab world had not yet become fully aware of the scope or nature of the colonial phenomenon. Decolonization was conceived as formal political independence within the framework of economic and cultural interdependence with the former metropolitan countries. Militarily occupied and economically enslaved, the Arab states could not afford to antagonize the colonial powers openly. In the aftermath of World War II, these powers seemed to be in a position to maintain their domination over Africa and Asia indefinitely. Furthermore, Arab diplomacy seemed less preoccupied by neocolonialism than were the diplomacies of other African or Asian countries.

Two explanations may be put forward to account for this difference in attitude. First, the Arab cultural heritage offers a better defense against foreign cultural assimilation and linguistic domination. Second, Zionist colonialism was, from the start, the immediate preoccupation of the Arab struggle against colonialism. Arab diplomacy went so far as to give this struggle priority over the achievement of the decolonization of the other Arab states.

The Arab fight for the decolonization of Palestine has been marked by a series of spectacular defeats, with the Zionist state expanding its territorial possessions or strengthening its domination on each occasion. The decolonization of the other Arab states, however, has been very successful, largely because of actions undertaken by Arab diplomacy.

Thanks to this common Arab diplomacy, France's conflict with Lebanon and Syria in June 1945 was, from the start, given an international dimension.[6] The result of this first Arab intervention was significant, particularly since it coincided with the San Francisco Conference, which drafted the Charter of the United Nations. For the first time, successful Arab diplomacy was demonstrated to international public opinion. Arab diplomacy was decisive in preventing the partition of Libya.[7] When Libya was finally declared independent on December 24, 1951, and was admitted as the eighth member of the Arab League on March 28, 1953, it appeared that Arab diplomacy had achieved an objective most experts had considered impossible eight years before. Arab diplomacy helped in reinforcing Egypt's position in the face of the British, who intended to remain at the Suez Canal indefinitely.[8] It was Arab diplomacy that linked the issue of the Middle East defense with the solution of the Anglo-Egyptian dispute. Commenting on the Anglo-Egyptian Agreement of 1954, U.S. Secretary of

---

[6] See Resolutions 1/1, 1/2, and 24/3 adopted by the Council of the Arab League.
[7] Resolutions 41/3, 54/4, 62/4, 210/7, 239/10, 331/13, 405/15 adopted by the Council of the Arab League.
[8] See Resolutions 23/5-148/6, 184/7, 390/15, 570/18, 597/20, 803/22 adopted by the Council of the Arab League.

State John Foster Dulles declared to the press that this agreement eliminated a problem that had affected not only the relations between the United Kingdom and Egypt but also those of the Western nations as a whole with the Arab states.[9]

Arab diplomacy contributed to the formation of the Maghreb Bureau in Cairo, where the North African states were represented by the liberation movements in exile. The bureau gave an international dimension to the liberation claims of Morocco, Tunisia, and later Algeria.[10] Arab diplomacy was important in bringing an end to the disputes between the various factions within South Yemen on the eve of its independence.[11] Finally, Arab diplomacy's role was vital in bringing to independence the principalities of the Persian Gulf, Bahrain, Qatar, the United Arab Emirates, and Oman.

It could be argued that the decolonization of the Arab world would have taken place regardless of Arab solidarity and regardless of the Arab League's action. But the Arab League and Arab diplomacy offered a framework for the claims of dependent Arab states and for the collective intervention by independent Arab states, which could not be condemned as a form of Arab neocolonialism toward other Arab states. Collective Arab diplomacy, conducted by a regional international organization and supported by the system and the ideology of this organization, gave legitimacy to Arab action in the face of the colonialist view that all liberation movements were seditious. Arab diplomacy has contributed to making decolonization a doctrine and a principle of international law; had this been its only contribution, it would have been a very significant one indeed.

The Coordination of Arab Policies within International Organizations.
The formation of the Arab group in the United Nations preceded, in

---

[9] *U.S. Dept. of State Bulletin,* vol. 21, no. 789 (Aug. 9, 1954), p. 198; also the declaration of Anthony Eden in the House of Commons, published in Weekly Hansard, House of Commons *Parliamentary Debates,* no. 299 (July 23-30, 1954), pp. 496-497.

[10] Common Arab diplomacy approached the problem of the Maghreb states for the first time in the Resolution 63/4 passed on June 11, 1946, by the Council of the Arab League. The speech made by the King of Morocco on April 9, 1947, in Tangier, in which he referred to the Arab League, and the arrival in May 1947, at Port Said of Abdel Karim, the instigator of the Riff War (1921-1926), were incidents which were to force Arab diplomacy into adopting a more militant policy concerning the liberation of the Maghreb countries. This diplomacy is reflected in Resolutions 611/VII, 612/VII passed by the United Nations General Assembly at the initiative of the Arab states. This effort was extended to Algeria, whose case was submitted to the Security Council for the first time on January 5, 1955 (United Nations Doc. S/3341).

[11] See Resolutions 2295/47, 2357/47, and 2373/48.

a sense, the creation of the world organization, since the Arab League was created before the United Nations. The founding members of the League took part in the San Francisco Conference as a closely associated group, and defended the Arab position on several issues.

The Arab group, which showed great homogeneity and cohesion, and the Arab-Asian group came together when the Indonesian case was brought before the United Nations General Assembly in 1947.[12] The success of the action of the Arab-Asian group on the Indonesian question clearly indicated to the members of this group the importance of this coalition in the parliamentary diplomacy.

In 1952, this group began a transformation and became the Afro-Asian group. Under the leadership of Arab diplomacy, it initiated the fight to decolonize Africa and Asia.[13]

As the institutional framework of collective Arab diplomacy, the Arab League adopted on January 21, 1954, a detailed program of action to reinforce the close ties between the Arab states and the states of the Asian-African bloc:

(1) The Arab states should strengthen their diplomatic representation with the states of the Asian bloc.

(2) They should exchange political delegations with a view to consolidating the ties of friendship and cooperation in the political domain as well as consolidating cultural and economic relations.

(3) The secretariat general (of the Arab League) should study all means necessary for consolidating relations between the states of the Arab League and the Asian-African bloc, including the convening of periodic meetings at high level. . . .[14]

As a direct consequence of this new trend in Arab diplomacy, the Arab League participated in the Bandung Conference in April 1955. It did not participate officially, since the secretary general of the League was present as a member of the Egyptian delegation. Similarly, the mufti of Jerusalem was present as a member of the Yemenite delegation, and the delegates of Algeria, Morocco, and Tunisia were members of the delegation of Iraq. These details show how Arab diplomacy was operating at the practical or pragmatic level. The Arab

---

[12] United Nations Documents A/A.C.31/L.50. See also *Egypt and the United Nations: Report of a study group set up by the Egyptian Society of International Law* (New York: Manhattan Publishing Co., 1957), pp. 74-75.

[13] Samaan Boutros Faragallah, *Le groupe Afro-Asiatique dans le cadre des Nations Unies* (Geneva: Droz, 1963); and Boutros Boutros-Ghali, *Le Mouvement Afro-Asiatique* (Paris: Presses Universitaires de France, 1969).

[14] Resolution 605/20 adopted by the Council of the Arab League.

League even tried to become, in a sense, an *ad hoc* secretariat of the Afro-Asian movement. However, the nature and the structure of the Arab League did not allow it to undertake a policy of this sort: it possessed neither the administrative machinery, nor the political power, nor the financial means necessary to coordinate the policy of forty Afro-Asian states, themselves dominated, for all practical purposes, by foreign powers. Moreover, the Afro-Asian states would never have countenanced the possibility of being directed by Arab diplomacy, even at the secretarial and administrative levels.

In spite of these difficulties, Arab diplomacy supported all the non-Arab African countries in their fight against foreign domination, in the condemnation of racial discrimination in South Africa, and in the entire course of struggle on behalf of decolonization.

The Arab states adopted a global policy to reinforce a new solidarity in the countries of the Third World in Asia, Africa, and Latin America. Such an activity was not devoid of risks. In becoming so involved, the Arab states overburdened their young diplomacies and became entangled with problems they were not equipped to solve. They also risked diluting their actions and further compromising the Arab image and Arab credibility. Yet, Arab diplomatic activism compensated for the intrinsic weaknesses of Arab states in particular and the Third World states in general, and it transformed international organizations into a forum for underdeveloped countries. It offered new possibilities for a dialogue in which underdeveloped countries could engage the developed world from a position of strength. Partly because of Arab diplomacy, the developing countries have undergone a qualitative change from being the objects of international law and politics to becoming the subjects of a dynamic new relationship with the world of the industrialized rich.

The Development of Nonalignment. The controversy between Iraq and the other Arab states over the formation of the Baghdad Pact in 1955 is interesting from a historical point of view inasmuch as it was the starting point of a nonalignment policy adopted by the Arab states. This new foreign policy was to cause a serious political and ideological conflict within the Arab world: aligned and nonaligned Arab states violently opposed each other, endangering common Arab diplomacy with respect to the outside world. The revolution of July 14, 1958, in Baghdad sanctioned the victory of the nonaligned Arab states. Arab neutralism grew steadily to become the most important element of Arab diplomacy.

At the preliminary meetings for the first summit of the nonaligned nations held in Cairo (June 5-12, 1961), seven Arab states were represented: Iraq, Saudi Arabia, Sudan, the United Arab Republic (Egypt and Syria), Morocco, Yemen, and the Provisional Government of Algeria. The conference adopted five criteria which became the guidelines of the policy of nonalignment: (1) an independent policy founded on peaceful coexistence and nonalignment; (2) support for national movements of liberation; (3) nonadherence to any collective military alliance involving conflicts between the great powers; (4) no conclusion of any bilateral alliance with a great power; and (5) no acceptance of military bases belonging to one of the great powers.

By the first conference of the nonaligned countries, in Belgrade in 1961, the number of Arab states had increased from seven to nine, with the participation of Lebanon and Tunisia. With the exception of Libya, Jordan, and Kuwait, all the Arab states were present. At the second conference of nonaligned states, in Cairo in 1964, all the Arab states were present and the secretary general of the Arab League was also present as an observer. At the third conference, in Lusaka in 1970, the fourth conference, in Algiers in 1973, and the fifth conference, in Colombo in 1976, almost all the Arab states were present and played an active role. It thus appears that Arab states have a new common denominator for their foreign policy and for common diplomacy, that is, nonalignment.

Arab diplomacy played an important role in the development of nonalignment, though certain Arab countries have occasionally violated that principle by concluding bilateral treaties with the Soviet Union (for example, Egypt from May 27, 1971, to March 14, 1976, and Iraq through the present). Such violations do not diminish the basic contribution of Arab diplomacy to the formation of this policy. The policy is essentially Afro-Asian, or, in other words, Arab, since Arabism is, in the final analysis, a micro Afro-Asianism.

Although Arab diplomacy has been incapable of settling inter-Arab disputes and of projecting a positive image of the Arabs, it has on the other hand contributed greatly to the creation and the development of the Afro-Asian ideology and the development of the policy of nonalignment.

The Arab-African Dialogue. During the October War against Israel, the Arab oil producers announced a dramatic increase in the price of oil and a ban on the shipment of Arab oil to the allies of Israel. This decision was the first major success scored by Arab diplomacy in thirty years. This success was also a victory for the developing countries of the world in general, and for the producers of other raw materials,

233

in particular. However, the increased price of oil placed a special burden on the developing countries of Africa and Asia, which suffered more than the industrial countries.

At this point Arab diplomacy showed imagination and generosity for the first time. The Arab countries decided to recycle part of their oil funds on behalf of the developing countries of Africa. The purpose of this action was threefold:

(1) To oppose the widening of the gap between the haves and have-nots of the Third World.

(2) To reinforce the new solidarity between Africa and the Arab world. It must not be forgotten that 70 percent of the Arab community and 75 percent of the Arab lands are in Africa. Africanism offers a defense for Arabism, a source of solidarity, and a new opportunity for the Arab world, situated as it is between Europe and Black Africa.

(3) To create a new bloc of producers of raw materials in the Third World and accelerate the collapse of the dominance of the industrial countries over the developing countries.

This program was facilitated by the fact that almost all African countries severed their diplomatic relations with Israel before and during the October War. It was also facilitated by the resolution passed by the Organization of African Unity equating Zionism in Israel with apartheid in South Africa, by the agreement among the Arab oil producers to ban Arab oil exports to white-ruled South Africa, and by the agreement to set up technical and financial aid for all Africa. But in this unprecedented solidarity between the two groups of developing countries there were seeds of disagreement.

African criticism of the Arabs can be summed up as follows. First, the Arabs are investing most of their money in Europe and America—that is, rechanneling capital to areas where it is least needed. Second, the present world economic crisis stems from profound inequalities in economic and social progress between different nations; by investing in the industrial world, the Arab countries are now the main contributors to this disequilibrium. And, finally, Arab oil investments in Africa have been restricted to the Arab Bank for Africa, the Special Arab Fund for Africa, the Arab-African Bank, the Islamic Development Bank, and the Arab Technical Assistance Fund for Africa. In total, this represents only a drop in an ocean.

On the other hand, Arab criticism of the Africans can be summed up as follows: First, the Arab states are, without exception, developing countries and therefore, by definition, they need money to develop their own economies. Second, in terms of technical know-how, both the Arab states and the African states are in the process of development; neither is competent to undertake common projects—a very important obstacle to the Afro-Arab dialogue. Furthermore, the former colonial powers and the superpowers are opposed to such a dialogue unless it should take place within the framework of their economic institutions. Finally, African criticism takes into consideration neither bilateral aid from Arab states to the developing countries of Africa nor the multilateral aid from Arab states through international agencies.

In conclusion, whatever the criticisms of the two partners with regard to the dialogue and whatever the difficulties in the development of the Arab-African economic and political cooperation, the very start of such cooperation is a success for Arab diplomacy and a positive contribution to the new economic order.[15]

Some might object that this paper makes no mention of the Arab-European dialogue, which was first promoted by Arab diplomacy. Since no positive results can yet be ascertained, one might be forgiven for wondering whether this subject can properly be discussed under the rubric of success or failure. In view of the necessity of suspending judgment, for the time being at least, a prudent discretion should be observed.

Conclusion

For more than thirty years, Arab diplomacy has been an avant garde diplomacy, a pilot institution for Asia, for Africa, and for the Third World as a whole. It was the first diplomacy to oppose the colonial powers and the two superpowers systematically and collectively, and it was the first to make political, economic, and cultural decolonization its supreme objective. It was also the first to place the anticolonial struggle at the level of a doctrine of regional and international law.

Within the framework of the United Nations and other specialized international agencies, Arab diplomacy has contributed to the creation of the Afro-Asian group. This group gave the poor nations and the underdeveloped countries their first institutional voice speaking to the rich industrialized world.

However, chronic crises in the Arab world still result from the

---

[15] See the mimeographed papers presented at the Afro-Arab Symposium on Liberation and Development (Khartoum, January 7-11, 1976) sponsored by the League of Arab States and the Sudanese Government and particularly the paper of Chedly Ayari entitled: *Mécanismes et Institutions de la co-opération Arabo-Africaine. Le rôle de la B.A.D.E.A.*

clumsiness and inefficiency of the Arab League, the lack of coordination among the various Arab diplomacies, the incessant disputes among the Arab countries, and the incapacity of Arab diplomacy to settle such disputes. The creation of the Zionist state remains another cause of these problems. This dynamic and domineering state has augmented and accentuated the international contradictions in the Arab world by adding to them a cold-war dimension. It has also created a situation with which Arab diplomacy seems incapable of dealing.

Arab diplomacy can help towards the integration and, later, the federation of the Arab world. Only a common Arab diplomacy can save the Arab world from its reduction to a state of neocolonial vassalage or its division into zones of influence.

One of the saddest episodes in modern history is that one of the richest and most promising regions of the world, with one of the oldest and most authentic civilizations known to man, is becoming the permanent field for local wars and internal strife because of the lack of imagination, the lack of generosity, and the lack of diplomacy shown by its elite.